Life as **Jamie** Knows It

Jamie Bérubé, senior portrait, State College Area High School yearbook, 2011.
Photo: Helen Richardson, courtesy of the Bérubé family

Life as Jamie Knows It

An Exceptional Child Grows Up

□ □ □ □ □

Michael **Bérubé**

BEACON PRESS
BOSTON

Beacon Press
Boston, Massachusetts
www.beacon.org

Beacon Press books
are published under the auspices of
the Unitarian Universalist Association of Congregations.

19 18 17 16   8 7 6 5 4 3 2 1

This book is printed on acid-free paper that meets the uncoated paper
ANSI/NISO specifications for permanence as revised in 1992.

Text design and composition by Kim Arney

Library of Congress Cataloging-in-Publication Data

Names: Bérubé, Michael, author.
Title: Life as Jamie knows it : an exceptional child grows up / Michael Bérubé.
Description: Boston : Beacon Press, 2016. | Includes bibliographical references.
Identifiers: LCCN 2016007675 (print) | LCCN 2016029597 (ebook) |
ISBN 9780807019313 (hardback) | ISBN 9780807019320 (ebook)
Subjects: LCSH: Bérubé, Michael | Bérubé, Jamie. | Parents of
children with disabilities—United States—Biography. | Children with
mental disabilities—United States—Biography. | People with mental
disabilities—United States—Biography. | Down syndrome—United
States—Case studies. | BISAC: BIOGRAPHY & AUTOBIOGRAPHY /
Personal Memoirs. | SOCIAL SCIENCE / People with Disabilities.
Classification: LCC HQ759.913 .B469 2016 (print) |
LCC HQ759.913 (ebook) |
DDC 649/.151092 [B] —dc23
LC record available at https://lccn.loc.gov/2016007675

It took a couple of villages to raise Jamie. He is lucky to have a wonderful extended family and family friends; on Janet's side especially, he has spent innumerable days of delight with awesome aunts, uncles, and cousins, and my own birth family has always loved him dearly. But in the villages of Champaign, Illinois, and State College, Pennsylvania, we could not have raised Jamie without the help of the physical, occupational, and speech therapists of his youth, his medical professionals, and his dozens of teachers and paraprofessionals—not to mention his legions of paid companions (formerly known as "babysitters"), all of whom he remembers fondly and vividly. To all of them, to his Special Olympics coaches and volunteers, and to his current employers and assistants and associates in the grown-up world of work, this book is dedicated.

Contents

□ □ □ □ □

Reintroducing Jamie Bérubé

□ □ □ □ □

My little Jamie loves lists. That was how I opened *Life as We Know It* twenty
years ago, writing my first draft when Jamie was only three and a half
years old. Well, my Jamie is no longer little. But he still loves lists; he
is, I think, the most astonishing and assiduous maker of lists I have
ever met. When he has to entertain himself—when he is waiting for
breakfast or sitting through one of his parents' lectures or just keeping
himself occupied while he watches one of his dozens of wrestling videos—he takes out a legal pad and writes down (a) various Beatles songs
along with the year of their release or (b) various opponents of the wres-
tler known as the Undertaker or (c) cities from one of his world atlases,
cities from the Middle East or Central Asia or Indonesia or South America or Wisconsin, or (d) all sixty-seven Pennsylvania counties in alphabetical order, from Adams to York. He makes all his lists from memory,
with the exception of the cities lists, which he copies out of the atlas.

We have hundreds of these legal pads in our house, and we are always buying more.

I am not sure exactly when little Jamie stopped being little. In his
tween years he was still a waif—short, skinny, and easy to carry if carrying was needed. I have a video of him from late 2002, when he was
eleven, and his voice is impossibly high and squeaky. Then again, that
was true also of preadolescent Nick, and I wondered, as I went through
our old family videos to convert them to DVDs, *Was there a time when
my children huffed helium?* Down syndrome is associated with shortness
of stature, and my wife, Janet, once predicted that Jamie would grow

no taller than 5 feet 2 inches. I said 5 feet 6 inches. I won the Jamie height-prediction pool: Jamie is now 5 feet 7 inches, and somewhere in his teen years he developed wide, powerful shoulders and a strong upper body. He is a Special Olympics swimmer and loves work tasks that involve physical exertion. Buying him dress shirts is a challenge: he has an eighteen-inch neck, almost like a football lineman's, and a short torso. But we think that, all in all, he is a reasonably attractive young man.

In French, he would be (and I sometimes call him) *un gentil et sympathique jeune homme.* (*Aussi, entre nous, il est adorable.*) He is bright, gregarious, even ebullient in social gatherings, and his lists are the product of his amazing cataloguing memory and his insatiable intellectual curiosity about the world—its people, its creatures, its nations, its languages, and (perhaps most of all) its culinary traditions. If it were possible for Jamie to travel everywhere on the inhabited globe, he would do it, and he would try to ingratiate himself with his hosts, just as he does when he greets the owner of our local Indian restaurant by bowing, hands clasped, and saying, "Namaskar." (The owner, Sohan Dadra, is delighted by this.)

In the years after the publication of *Life as We Know It,* I was warned—repeatedly and emphatically—that it's all very well and good to write about a child with an intellectual disability when your child is young and cute. Children with intellectual disabilities go over best, evidently, when they are young and cute, long before anybody has to worry about things like their adolescent friendships (or lack thereof) and their burgeoning sexuality and their thoughts about mortality and their prospects for employment. Adults with intellectual disabilities are another thing entirely: any number of people—though I have not made a list of their names—who coo solicitously over a toddler with Down syndrome might find themselves recoiling, either from awkwardness or from outright revulsion, from the adult with Down syndrome who sits down next to them on the bus.

So let me establish this much at the very outset: my little Jamie is no longer little. But he has remained cute for twenty years—except that his "cuteness," as he has grown, has taken forms no one could have imagined when he was little. Sometimes it is a matter of realizing that our Jamie can be witty and observant, even incisively so; sometimes it is a matter of understanding how dramatically his own self-understanding has deepened as he has grown.

I think of the fresh spring day in 2002 when Jamie informed me that we could not walk to school (he was in fourth grade) because the ground was strewn with berries "and we would have polka-dot feet." Or I think of the moment in early 2005 when we emerged from the local gym, having done our racquetball-and-swimming routine for the weekend, and Jamie, seeing me put his gym card in my wallet, declared, "Michael! That's *my* card! I can have a wallet. I'm a teenager. I'm allowed." (Ever since then he has called me "Michael," though we occasionally call each other "sir." And ever since then, he has had a wallet. I took him at once to Target, where we bought a wallet and placed his gym card and his school ID in it. The next morning he walked to the bus stop with his right hand placed firmly on his back pocket, with his mind on his wallet and his wallet on his mind.) Or I think of our trip to Boulder, Colorado, in 2008, where I was to speak at the Coleman Institute for Cognitive Disabilities, and I showed Jamie the design of the Denver International Airport, with its famous peaked canopy roof, white fabric stretched over the skeleton of the main terminal. "Some people say it looks like the snowy mountains of Colorado," I told Jamie, "some people say it looks like tents or Native American tepees. And some people say it looks like the meringue on a lemon meringue pie. You know, the pie with the white fluffy stuff on top?"

"Mm hm." Jamie nodded, adding something unintelligible.

"I'm sorry, sweetie, what did you say?"

He repeated the unintelligible word unintelligibly. This happens now and again; his speech tends to be unclear, and he sometimes isn't sure he has the right word, as when he told me to shave with a rooster when he meant "shave with a razor" (he was four) or when he complained, in the course of a long walk, that we would be like the Ramones (he was sixteen, and Nick and I never found out just what he meant). To make matters worse, he speaks too quickly, most likely because he has a father who speaks too quickly. Fortunately, he has seemingly endless reserves of patience when people ask him to repeat himself, and I know of only a

handful of instances in which he became frustrated with his auditors—
as when he finally explained to his family, after repeatedly asking for
soosee, that "it comes from Japan." *Ah*, we said, *sushi. . . .* And yet, one
morning Janet overheard him talking to some of his stuffed animals,
saying, "Jamie Bérubé. No, Jamie Bérubé. Jamie Bérubé. J-A-M-I-E." It
was then that Janet proposed the theory that Jamie loved his dog Lucy
in part because she was the only creature in his world that never asked
him to repeat himself.

This time, it took him three or four tries before I understood that he
was saying "Sidney." "Sidney who?" I asked.

Finally he got a wee bit weary with me. "Not Sidney who," he replied.
"Sydney in Australia."

Oh, holy mother of Moloch. *Sydney in Australia.* I started to tear
up behind the wheel. Here was my teenage son with Down syndrome,
likening the architectural design of the Denver International Airport
to the white-shell roofs of the Sydney Opera House. I did not see *that*
one coming.

But my favorite story from Jamie's teen years involves a watershed
moment, which happened at the very end of a business trip to Blaine,
Washington, on the Canadian border. Jamie has always loved everything
about traveling—the packing, the driving, the airport (he will ask about
connections and gates months in advance of any connections or gates),
the rental car, the hotel, and the pool (for there must be a pool). So even
though we had to drive three hours to Pittsburgh in pouring rain, fly to
Seattle, then drive another three hours to Blaine, he loved all of it. We got
in at 1 a.m.—1 a.m. Pacific time, that is; 4 a.m. to us.

During my presentation, Jamie sat quietly at the back of a large room
for ninety minutes and played his *Harry Potter and the Prisoner of Az-
kaban* CD-ROM game on my laptop with headphones while I did my
bit. Afterward, we visited the Vancouver Aquarium, the Capilano Sus-
pension Bridge, and the Grouse Mountain Skyride; then it was back
to Seattle for a midnight flight to Pittsburgh and the drive back to our
home in the unimaginatively named town of State College. Jamie was
cool with getting ready for bed at the airport, even though this initially
made no sense to him. He asked only for a glass of chocolate milk before

he had to brush his teeth, and when I explained to him that most of the shops and stores in the Seattle-Tacoma airport were closed, he said, "We should ask," and promptly stopped a person at random: "Do you know where there is chocolate milk?" I explained to Jamie that this somewhat nice man—he merely half-smiled at the question—did not work at the airport. We found a Starbucks shortly thereafter, and Jamie decided to wait on a bench near security while I got some water for me and some chocolate milk for him. I was being served just as they began to close up shop, at 10 p.m. I knew it would cause Jamie some distress to see his father being trapped in Starbucks behind a metal grate, so I looked back, and sure enough, there he was, on his bench with his hands to his cheeks and his mouth open in the "Home Alone" position. I gave him the thumbs-up to let him know I could get out again, and came back in a minute or two with his freshly mixed chocolate milk.

And yet, back then, Jamie could be a bit of a challenge as a traveling companion. He had learned much in the course of the previous year, when I started taking him with me as I traveled for work, partly to give Janet a break from single-parent child care and partly to get Jamie to become more adept as a traveler. He began our trip from Baltimore to Houston by nearly stepping off a curb at BWI into the path of an oncoming shuttle bus. (The "nearly" part was me grabbing him by the shoulders.) He could also still get into a little harmless mischief here and there. On our way up to Vancouver, he announced that we were running out of film. I assured him that he was quite wrong about this, because I was sure that there were twelve exposures left on the disposable camera I had gotten for him. But when we sat down to lunch al fresco at a little restaurant across from the Capilano Bridge, I watched Jamie drinking his soda and said, "You look so cool like that. Hold on and I'll take your picture," whereupon I discovered that there was, in fact, no film left in the camera.

"We're running out," Jamie said, just as he had noted an hour or two earlier.

"Ah, I see," I replied. "You mean that when we got into Canada and I left you in the car while I went to get Canadian dollars, you took all the pictures in the camera? And then you told me we were running out of film?"

"Yes," Jamie said, with a wry smile. "Are you gonna sigh?"

Are you gonna sigh? So he was entirely aware of the fact that he had been a mischievous ignatz.

"No," I sighed, "we'll just get another camera, you mischievous ignatz."

But Jamie was relishing this. "Say, 'Oh, what am I gonna do with you,'" he demanded. This is a line from the film version of *Curious George*, and fourteen-year-old Jamie found it appropriate at such moments.

"Yes, Jamie, that was a very Curious George thing to do, to use up all the film and take all the pictures in the car. What am I gonna do with you?" He grinned and rubbed his hands together.

As we finished lunch, I told him we both had to go to the men's room before we went to the bridge. But Jamie didn't want me to go with him. He insisted, instead, that he would go into the restaurant alone and find the bathroom *all by himself*. I approved, reminding him to ask a server if he couldn't find it right away; I told him I would wait for the check. He came back in a few minutes, hands washed and everything, all set to go. But the check still hadn't arrived, even though we were now one of only two parties in the place. "Let's go," Jamie insisted.

"We're still waiting for the check," I replied.

"Why?" he asked.

"I don't know why," I said. Finally, our server arrived, and I had the credit card ready for her, and soon we were all paid up. I told Jamie to wait at the table while I went to the men's room. When I returned, Jamie was waiting very patiently . . . but he had a funny expression on his face, almost a half-smirk. My spider sense told me to check the check, and guess what? On the $23.51 bill, Jamie had written, just under my "$30.00," the figure "$90.51." I gave him a narrow-eyed, sidelong look.

"Say, 'I wish you wouldn't,'" Jamie said. Again, the deliberate, self-aware rascality.

"I wish you wouldn't," I dutifully replied. "You cannot leave ninety dollars on this check. It is too much money." Jamie grinned again. "No, really," I said. "Don't do that, please. It will make our server very confused, and besides, thirty dollars is really enough." Jamie understands tipping. He just wasn't clear on the details—and over the next ten years, this turned into a serious consideration once Jamie got his own bank card (which he keeps in his wallet, of course!) and began taking himself out to solo lunches in downtown State College.

When we dropped off the rental car, I informed Jamie that I would change out of my shorts and into jeans after I got him into his pajamas. He objected: "Michael," he advised me, "you should not be nude and naked in public." This admonition—which he and I use to this day, whenever disrobing is called for—involved a hard-won realization for Jamie, who, a few years earlier, had been dismayed to find that the difference between "public" and "private" could hinge on the difference, and the few inches of distance, between the "private" space of the boys' locker room and the "public" space of the adjacent hallway.

"No, sweetie," I assured him. "We'll change in the men's room at the airport, and you'll brush your teeth. Do you want to wear long pants on the plane?"

"No," he said after some deliberation. "I'm OK in shorts."

Then when we learned that our plane would be an hour late, I told Jamie that we would have to wait until after midnight before we could board. We set up shop on a little couch-like structure right by our gate, and Jamie played his Harry Potter games on the laptop. At eleven I asked him if he wanted to stretch out with his pillow on the couch-like structure. "Are you sleepy?"

"Um, a little bit," he said, "not that sleepy."

"You're not that sleepy? I am *very* sleepy," I admitted.

"You sleep," Jamie suggested. "I will play Harry Potter right here."

I was stunned. The kid who couldn't be left alone in the car for five minutes without using up all the film in the disposable camera was offering to keep watch over me? "Oh, thank you, Jamie," I said. "That is very sweet of you. But I don't want to fall asleep and miss our plane." I did not think there was any chance of his wandering off—not at the age of fourteen. A few years earlier, I would have had serious cause for concern. But still, sleeping on the job is sleeping on the job. What if someone tried to mess with him? What if someone lured him away with promises of chocolate milk? What if he got engrossed in his game and didn't notice the arrival of the plane? He was not a seasoned traveler, not then.

"Michael! You will not miss the plane!" Jamie exclaimed, almost indignant. "I will tell you when it comes."

I looked at him with genuine surprise. "You will tell me when the plane comes?"

"Uh-huh," he said. "Now you sleep right here."

In taking Jamie on these trips of mine, I was trying to enhance his independence, paradoxical though that may sound, encouraging him to feel more at home in the world and capable of doing things like finding restaurant bathrooms by himself. But this seemed a bit much: he would keep an eye out for our plane while his weary father slept? On the other hand, what could possibly happen? I would be right next to him, and I certainly wouldn't sleep so heavily as to be unable to snap to attention if a passing lunatic accosted him in some way. And I would just close my eyes for a second. . . . But . . . how would he know when the plane arrived . . . or if it was the right plane. . . . ?

Twenty minutes later, Jamie jostled my elbow. "Wake up, Michael," he said gently. "Our plane is here." And sure enough, the passengers had just begun to disembark. Jamie had been watching carefully the whole time, even while dodging dementors and imps and skeleton men in the dungeons of Hogwarts. This was his watershed moment, and mine: I did not have to monitor him or keep a watchful eye over his use of the camera or worry about his finding the men's room. I was grateful—and deeply reassured. Because, as I told him on the way home (as part of my ongoing project to give him a good range of good descriptions of himself—*diligent, observant, patient*), he is very *conscientious*. And *responsible*. And from that day forward, more and more *independent*. And capable, for the first time, of taking care of me.

□   □   □

Jamie did not wander off in the Seattle-Tacoma Airport that night. I was right, may all the relevant deities be thanked, that he had learned to stay put. But over the course of his childhood, Janet and I managed to lose Jamie three times—and I think Janet will find it eminently fair and just if I say that one time was her fault, one time was my fault, and one time was our fault. You have to understand: I grew up in a family in which no story of mishap or travail can be properly concluded until someone has been blamed.

The first time was in Filene's Basement in Chicago in the summer of 1996. I was shopping for a sports coat, and Janet and ten-year-old Nick were doing something else. But as I was trying on jackets and doing the triple-mirror thing, Janet came up to me in a panic and told me that Jamie was gone. He was only four, and not very verbal, so we had no confidence that he would respond to calls of "Jamie!" But we found him, after ten frantic minutes. For reasons we will never understand, he had crawled into a cabinet below an array of dress shirts.

The second time was in the IMPE (Intramural-Phys Ed) building of the University of Illinois at Urbana-Champaign in 2000, after Jamie and I had done some weekend swimming. As we were leaving the building, I realized that I had left something in the locker room. Perhaps—no, almost definitely—I should have brought Jamie back to the locker room with me, but I thought that he would understand the sentence "Stay right here and don't go anywhere until I come back" (and yes, I do know that there is an entire scene of *Monty Python and the Holy Grail* devoted to the misunderstanding of a sentence such as this one). I was not gone long. Three minutes? Maybe four? But it was long enough for Jamie to wander off, doh dee doh dee doh, my little duck. The IMPE building is huge, with endless rabbit warrens of squash and racquetball courts, a pool, a cardio room, a weight room . . . and I ran down corridor after corridor, calling, "Jamie! Jamie!" to no avail. Finally I found him near the building's entrance, in the corner of a cavernous room housing three or four basketball courts, watching a pickup game with intense interest.

"Jamie!" I cried. "I have been looking all over for you!"

"I'm right here," he replied, puzzled and yet somehow unfazed.

The third time was in the Nittany Mall in State College in early 2004, as Janet and I were doing some post-holiday shopping. We were looking at some deeply discounted 2004 calendars in a temporary kiosk festooned with pictures of kittens and dolphins, and suddenly . . . where was he?

We scoured the promenade of the mall. This was 2004, and malls— even the Nittany Mall, struggling as it was—had not yet become the vast empty structures, evacuated by the irresistible forces of the Internet, that they are today. Swarms of people swarmed among us, and none of them was Jamie. After we had made one full circuit, we began to break down. Janet was starting to cry. We were beginning to imagine why anyone would abduct our son, and we couldn't imagine anything but horrors.

Just as we were wondering whether to call the police, we spotted him: there he was, walking from kiosk to kiosk, nonchalantly checking out the merchandise, doh dee doh dee doh, our little duck. We ran to him, gathered him into our arms, relieved beyond measure that he had come to no harm. I imagined him thinking to himself, *I'm right here.* That was certainly the attitude he had three years later, when we "lost" him for all of a minute—but it could have been a fateful minute. We were on the shore of Rangeley Lake in northwestern Maine, a little beach in the center of the town of Rangeley. There was a playground, some tennis courts, a strip of sand trucked in from somewhere, and a dock. Janet and I, together with her sister Barbara and Barbara's partner, Steve, were chatting on the sand, and Jamie was playing in the shallow water. I was keeping an eye on him; there were dozens of kids in the water, and Jamie was diving with his goggles, emerging for a few seconds and then diving in again.

Suddenly I realized that he had not come back up. Alarmed, I ran onto the dock to get the best possible view of everything, but even from that vantage point I could not see him. Once again I had that moment of sheer panic, of thinking the worst. The lifeguard noticed my distress and came over to join me; just then, Jamie popped up on the other side of the dock, away from the designated swimming area. Doh dee doh dee doh, just paddling away . . .

"Jamie!" I yelled. "Come up here!" I extended my arm.

The lifeguard spoke to me sternly. "He's not allowed to be over there. Or to swim under the dock."

"I'm well aware of that," I replied evenly. To Jamie, I said, as I hauled him up out of the water, "You cannot swim under the dock. It is too dangerous! You might hit your head!"

"I did!" he said merrily. "Three times!"

□   □   □

In the summer of 2011, Jamie, Janet, and I were hanging out in the New York apartment we have shared with another couple from Pennsylvania State University, where I teach; we spend weekends there whenever our schedules (and our friends' schedules) permit. We got a call from Jamie's cousin Trevor, who lives on the Upper West Side; Trevor proposed to visit us and hang out with Jamie for the day. And he told us that he'd take the subway by himself and walk from 59th Street and Lexington to our place, on 62nd and 1st Avenue. When Jamie heard that, he turned to me in astonishment, saying, "Trevor will take the subway by himself—*and he has disability!*"

Trevor was born in the waning days of 1994, three months premature. He spent weeks in the NICU (neonatal intensive care unit), as did his twin brother, Dash, who was tragically mis-medicated during his stay and is now on the severe-and-profound end of the scale of human variation. (Trevor and Dash make a brief appearance, as neonates, in *Life as We Know It.*) Trevor has some mild cerebral palsy and probably resides somewhere on the autism spectrum; he sometimes has an odd affect because he has trouble with social cues, but he has blossomed into a bright, sweet, and deeply reflective young man who can (and will!) converse at great length about his job at a law firm, the history of racism in America, and the vicissitudes of the New York Mets and Rangers. To Jamie, he has been a good cousin and a good friend; for Jamie, he had become *a kid with disability who can get around by himself*—on the New York subways, on intercity buses, and on commuter trains.

That day, a light bulb went on for Jamie. It was visible at the time, I believe, incandescent, and it appeared roughly eight or nine inches above his head, but we didn't get official notice of his epiphany until a few days later, when we all went to a picnic in Central Park for families of kids with Down syndrome. The picnic was held in Heckscher Playground in the southwest corner of the park, and I spent much of my time following Jamie around the various structures, making sure to keep him in my line of sight at all times. Rachel Adams, who teaches at Columbia University and has a young son with Down syndrome (Henry, then three, about whom she has written movingly in *Raising Henry*), told me that it was a little depressing watching me hover around Jamie, because it suggested to her that she would be doing the same thing with Henry fifteen or twenty years from now. I told Rachel that for as long as I have visited New York with Jamie, ever since we came to Penn State in 2001, I have been terrified by the thought that he would dart into a subway train just as the doors closed. "Oh, yes, I have that subway-darting fear about both my kids," Rachel replied.

"As well you should," I said, "but with Jamie I stopped having that fear only when he became capable of understanding that if such a thing ever happened, he should simply get off at the next stop and wait for me."

With impeccable timing, Jamie took a break from playing and cavorting and eating just then. He approached me and Janet and asked, "Can I live independently?" Janet was puzzled at first, since the question did sound a bit abstract and general, but I knew (or thought I knew) exactly what he meant. "Are you asking about taking the subway by yourself?" I said.

"Yes!" Jamie replied. "I can visit my cousin. . . ." And he held it just like that, with an ellipsis rather than a period or a question mark: you know, I could always go visit my cousin. . . .

I thought for a moment—wait, no, that's not true. I thought for maybe one-third of a moment. "No, I'm sorry, Jamie," I said, "you cannot take the subway by yourself."

Deep breath.

People who know New York will know that the trip from the southwest corner of Central Park to 102nd and West End is a very simple one: you get on the 1 train at Columbus Circle and you get off at 103rd Street. No transfers. At the age of twenty, Jamie was certainly capable of managing that much; thanks partly to his own remarkable internal-GPS intelligence and partly to my decade-long program of trying to make him more familiar with New York, Jamie is now capable of saying, "To go to Madison Square Garden we need to take the N, R, or Q and change at Times Square for the 1, 2, or 3." (Yes! Exactly right!) However, some transfers are exceptionally difficult to navigate; New York's subways are made up of three different systems (the IRT, BMT, and IND), and connections among them can be baffling.

And as I told Jamie a couple of days later (when he asked me again why I didn't allow him to travel by himself), the complexity of the subway system is only one problem. "I know you would pay attention to the signs," I said. "I know you would go uptown instead of downtown, and I know you would get off the 1 train at 103rd Street." Jamie nodded emphatically. "But Jamie . . . you have no idea how to get from the station to 102nd and West End Avenue. You would not know whether to turn right or left off Broadway, because you don't know yet that West End is just west of Broadway, and you wouldn't know where 'west' was when you came up the subway stairs."

"True," Jamie admitted soberly, lips pursed.

"And so," I continued, "that is why I didn't let you travel by yourself to Trevor's apartment. You still have to learn about the streets in Manhattan and how to get around after you get out of the subway."

So there is the navigating-the-surface-streets problem, and then there is the psychopath problem. As fate would have it, Jamie made his request the same week that eight-year-old Leiby Kletzky was abducted and murdered in a quiet Hasidic neighborhood in Brooklyn while walking home from his summer day camp. He had asked his parents about . . . well, about living independently, and they had agreed, doing a practice run with him beforehand. But on his first trip home by himself, he got lost, and asked a man named Levi Aron for help. Levi Aron did not help.

Jamie says hello to strangers all the time. At the American Studies Association conference in San Antonio in 2010, he made a habit of telling everyone in the elevator—on every single elevator ride—that his father was the director of the Institute for the Arts and Humanities at Penn State. "You have to stop doing that," I told him. "Why?" he asked slyly, with an expression I remembered from Vancouver. "Because there are people here who really do go around introducing themselves to people that way, that's why." Not that I would expect Jamie to care about such things. "You can just say hello and leave it at that. Please."

So instead of letting him take the subway by himself, Janet and I decided to take a baby-steps approach to Jamie's attempts to navigate New York (where he can walk to nearby stores and markets, which he cannot do in State College): we would give him five bucks and let him go down to the fruit stand below our apartment, the Space Market, to buy Orangina or beef jerky or bagels and chocolate milk. Janet gave him strict instructions: No talking to strangers. Get your change. Come right back home.

And yes, the first time he went to the Space Market by himself, I waited thirty seconds and then tailed him. As he paid for his merchandise and turned to leave the store, I ducked behind the oranges. He did not see me.

Today, Jamie is totally comfortable with buying himself stuff from the Space Market, and his parents are too. And now that his father has finally figured out how to manage his Supplemental Security Income (SSI) payments (from the branch of Social Security that provides for adults with disabilities) and has gotten him a fully functioning debit card, Jamie is able to buy himself stuff whenever he wants to. So eventually, Jamie asked if he could go to the Food Emporium by himself, three long blocks away at 59th Street, under the Queensboro Bridge.

I told him he could go to the Food Emporium if I followed one block behind him—just to keep an eye on him, not to interfere. We eventually put this plan into action in 2013, but before we could implement it in 2012, events overtook us.

The weekend of July 14–15, 2012, was complicated. Janet was attending a friend's funeral, and I was attending (of all things) a reunion of my sixth-grade class from PS 32 in Queens. (I had never attended a reunion of anything before.) And Jamie? Jamie was with Trevor. On Thursday night, July 12, they texted us a lovely picture of themselves in the bleachers at Yankee Stadium. "How nice," I thought. "Bud [Trevor's father, Janet's brother] took the boys to a game and took a picture of them in the stands." But I was wrong. Bud did not take the boys to Yankee Stadium. They took *themselves* to Yankee Stadium, and took a selfie in the stands. When they got back from the game, around 11 p.m., they took themselves out for sushi. Then, on Saturday, as the Lyon clan made its way to the funeral according to a plan only slightly less complex than the invasion of Normandy, I learned that part of that plan involved Jamie and Trevor taking the subway by themselves from Trevor's apartment to Grand Central Station, thence to New Haven via MetroNorth.

The adventure took a bit longer than I would have liked; I didn't get confirmation of their arrival in Connecticut until seven or eight that evening. But it was historic. At the end of the weekend, I drew up a tally: Jamie and Trevor got themselves to Yankee Stadium, they took themselves out for a late-night dinner, and then they proceeded to navigate two transportation systems in the sprawling NYC metro area with style and grace and savoir faire.

And just like that, Jamie began to live a little more independently— thanks, in part, to his savvy cousin *with disability.*

□   □   □

There are more recent chapters of Jamie's adventures: in 2014 I bought Amtrak tickets for Jamie and Trevor to go from New York's Penn Station to Boston's South Station, where they would be picked up by their aunt and uncle, Barbara and Steve. That experiment went reasonably well, though they got lost for ten or fifteen minutes on their return to Penn Station, which is a rat maze. When I finally found them on the second level (though Trevor had told me they were still on the platform), Jamie said plaintively, "We've been going around in circles!" I had been quite anxious about the retrieval-from-Penn-Station part of the journey, and as I learned later, Trevor's sensitive antennae had picked up on my anxiety, rendering him (what else?) anxious. And then there was the fact that they couldn't get proper seats for the trip to Boston because they didn't move quickly or aggressively enough (the Amtrak boarding process is ridiculous, which also caused me some anxiety) and had to make the trip in the dining car. Though they did not really mind that.

And when Jamie returned home after this ambitious Cousins' Weekend, he wrote a thank-you note to Barbara and Steve, with minimal help from Janet:

> Dear Barbara and Steve,
>
> I had a wonderful time with you in Boston and Maine. Thank you so much for the weekend. I really liked staying your house. Playing games on the beach, swimming, jumping on Steve, eating delicious

seafood, roosting hot dogs, play wiffleball. It was all great. Thanks
so much.

Love

Jamie

But Jamie's travels are only one aspect of his journey through this life. They are an important aspect, to be sure, deepening Jamie's experience of the world and giving him a dossier of stories to tell. And part of the narrative of this book will involve the story of how Jamie gradually learned to tell his own stories. But *Life as Jamie Knows It* will also follow in the tracks of its predecessor, a book that was not so much a memoir as an all-terrain vehicle covering matters of history, philosophy, and social policy. In the following pages, Jamie and I will tell you about his experiences at school, his evolving relationship with his brother, his demeanor in sickness and in health, and his career as a Special Olympics athlete. And we'll tangle with bioethicists, politicians, philosophers, and a wide array of people we believe to be mistaken about some very important questions, such as whether life is worth living with a significant disability and whether it would be better for all the world if we could cure Down syndrome. (Quick preview: Yes. No.) But we will not tell you that Jamie is a sweet angel/cherub whose plucky triumphs over disability inspire us all. We will not tell you that special-needs children are gifts sent to special parents. And we will definitely not tell you that God never gives someone more than he or she can handle, because, as a matter of fact, God does that all the time—whether through malice or incompetence I cannot say.

Yet it is undeniable that my life (and Janet's, and Nick's) is far richer than it would be if we did not have Jamie, far richer than we could have imagined before Jamie was born. This is one of the major themes of the book, should you be looking for major themes: we did not know what to expect from Jamie, and we have had to adjust our expectations time and time again. Even the very phrase "life expectancy" makes me cringe now: on the day Jamie was born, my knowledge about people with Down syndrome was so outdated and inadequate that I believed he would have a life expectancy of twenty-one. (That is not a thought I can bear today.) This phenomenon—our process of learning that our expectations for Jamie, and for people with Down syndrome, are subject to constant revision—is very possibly the most important, the most consequential thing we can tell about our own journey, because of course prospective parents who undergo prenatal testing and receive a positive diagnosis for Down syndrome make their decisions to continue or to terminate the pregnancy on the basis of their expectations about what their child will or will not be able to do, their expectations about the quality of life they and their child can enjoy.

In *Life as We Know It*, I admitted that before Jamie was born, I did not think I was capable of feeding a neonate with a nasal gavage tube. Political scientist Jean Bethke Elshtain, reviewing the book for a Christian journal, told her readers that, in other words (other words that she was quite confident in attributing to me), had I known that Jamie would have required that level of care in his first year, I would have chosen abortion. This, folks, is as bad as misreadings get, and whether Elshtain misread that part of the book through malice or incompetence I cannot say.

Here's the relevant passage from my book:

> If you had told me in August 1991—or, for that matter, after an am-
> niocentesis in April 1991—that I'd have to feed my infant by dip-
> ping a small plastic tube in K-Y jelly and slipping it into his nose
> and down his pharynx into his teeny tummy, I'd have told you that
> I wasn't capable of caring for such a child. But by mid-October, I
> felt as if I had grown new limbs and new areas of the brain to direct
> them. Weirdest of all, I was able to accept nasal feedings as part of
> a routine, using nothing more than the flimsy emotional apparatus
> I was born with.

The point—and I suppose I should have made it crystal clear the first time around—is that because we had Jamie, I learned to do stuff I didn't know I was capable of doing. (The rest of the paragraph explains that this was also true of my relationship to Nick, and indeed it might as well be The Lesson All Reasonably Competent Parents Learn.) I was trying to tell prospective parents, or people with young children with Down syndrome, that *you never know*. It might just be OK after all—even if you find yourself doing some difficult things on the way to OK. This time around, I will try to tell prospective parents—and bioethicists, politicians, philosophers, and a wide array of people—that it is critically important that you never know. This is why it is so crucial (however arduous it may be) to try to see the world with what Buddhists call "beginner's mind." In *The Case Against Perfection*, Michael Sandel quotes theologian Arthur F. May's phrase "openness to the unbidden," suggesting, in the course of his argument against genetic engineering for "designer babies," that such openness is the very essence of parenting. Or, as John Lennon put it in his one song about being a father, life is what happens to you while you're busy making other plans. *That* is life as we know it, and life as Jamie has known it.

As Jamie has grown and matured, becoming more independent and self-aware, he has developed his own sense of public and private. Accordingly, the ethics of writing and speaking about him have gotten more complicated as he has become increasingly capable of representing himself. For me, the terrain first shifted—as did my expectations of Jamie, once again—as we were packing up to go to the Canadian Down Syndrome Society convention in Waterloo, Ontario, in 2005. I was one of the featured speakers, and I was planning to talk about Jamie's transition to adolescence; that transition included something he was eagerly looking forward to—being part of the thirteen-to-seventeen group at the conference, with scheduled activities ranging from martial arts to encounters with reptiles. I asked Jamie if it would be OK for me to talk about an encounter he'd recently had at the town pool, which marked the first time I had seen him experience self-doubt. Jamie replied that the story was private—and it has remained so ever since. (Though I am allowed to talk *about* the story without telling it, as a way of explaining the kind of things we will and won't say in public.) Though Jamie is, in his way, a public figure, his private affairs are his private affairs. So, for instance, when we talked about what would and would not go into this book, Jamie insisted that we divulge no details about the girls on whom he has had crushes since adolescence. We decided that we would say only this: like billions of other people, Jamie would like a life partner, a companion, who loves him and wants to spend her life with him.

When Jamie was still little, it meant everything to us to meet parents with older kids, parents who could give us some details on *it might be OK after all* and (or but) *you never know*. Now that Janet and I are in the position of parents-with-older-kids, we try to return the favor: *your mileage may vary, but our journey has been more complex and wonderful than we could have dreamed*. We take deep joy from narratives like that of the man who was initially so distraught by the idea of having a child with Down syndrome that he could not talk to us about it—and has since found (you never know!) that his child is charming, beautiful, and the light of his life. We are honest about the challenges involved in raising children with disabilities, and we respect the decisions of prospective parents who, for whatever reasons, come to the conclusion that this journey is not for them. But I hope that even though some of Jamie's story must be private, he and I can do a public service by describing his life. We know that his story can only do so much, even for other parents of children with disabilities. Jamie's life has little in common, other than being surrounded by a loving family, with that of his fifteen-year-old uncle Johnny, my half-brother, the child of my father and his second wife. Johnny is a sweet, slightly built, nonverbal child with autism and requires far more vigilant care than Jamie does—including a personal aide paid for by a Medicaid waiver. Even in my extended family, it is impossible to generalize about disability. Over the years, Janet and I have learned that some parents need help with the child who keeps throwing the car keys down the toilet; some parents need help with the nondisabled sibling who feels burdened; some parents need help with feelings of failure; some parents need help with feelings of denial. Sometimes the children are far apart in age, sometimes less than a year apart; sometimes the child with a disability is the oldest, watching his or her siblings grow up more quickly; sometimes the youngest, getting more developmentally remote from siblings each year; sometimes there's more than one child with a disability, or more than one disability. . . . And sometimes I think the only advice that's equally applicable to all of us is the advice that we should seek advice.

But I remember something Jamie taught me in the spring of 1997. It was his last season at First United Methodist day care before he started

His Brother's Keeper

□   □   □   □   □

I will never forget the first thing Nick said about Jamie in public, even though I wasn't there to hear it. It was the spring of 1992. Janet and baby Jamie had gone to Nick's kindergarten for lunch one day. It was one of those events in which a kindergarten class decorates their room like a pirate ship and the kids don pirate clothing, talk pirate talk, and serve lunch to visitors. Arrrrhh, me mateys, sure ye know the drill. At one point another mother asked Janet, cradling Jamie in the crook of her elbow, how old her baby was. Janet told her (he was five or six months, thereabouts) and added, matter-of-factly, "He has Down syndrome."

"Oh my God," the other mother exclaimed, too startled to stop herself from expressing her horror aloud.

Just then, Nick the Pirate Waiter was walking by. Overhearing the woman, Nick replied, nonchalantly, "He's perfectly all *right*."

I say that Nick delivered this wonderful line nonchalantly, but then again, I wasn't there, was I? I am going by Janet's account. And even if Nick said this in the most deadpan manner possible for a six-year-old, it would still constitute a biting criticism of the woman's remark.

Nick certainly thought so two years later, when he read the first draft of the essay that would become the version of "Life as We Know It" that was published in *Harper's* magazine in late 1994. At eight, Nick was capable of reading that essay and offering advice about it, and I believed I owed him the opportunity to comment, since he certainly seemed old enough to understand the implications of being represented in his father's writing.

As it turned out, he had an exceptionally fine sense of the implications of being represented in his father's writing. He asked me to take out my account of that exchange. I did; it does not appear in the essay or the book. But first, I asked him why.

"Because it makes me sound like I think I know it all," he replied. He elaborated, in words I don't remember, about the possibility that he might come off as having been rude to an adult.

I told him that I would respect his wishes, but, I added, "Just for the record, just between you and me, you said *exactly* the right thing. That was *exactly* what that woman needed to hear. And I'm very proud of you for saying it."

Nick nodded solemnly.

And now that the statute of limitations has expired on Nick's scrupulous, eight-year-old's sense of propriety, I can start my narrative of Nick and Jamie with the story I wanted to tell twenty years ago.

He's perfectly all right. In 1992, there were many ways in which Jamie was not perfectly all right: he required substantial care, from the gavage tube to the apnea monitor. For many months, he required supplemental oxygen at night, wearing a nasal cannula around his head and an apnea monitor strapped around his chest. He threw up often. He had very low muscle tone, torticollis, and laryngomalacia. He would not walk or talk until he was two. And he was frighteningly susceptible to colds. But Nick was not, I take it, talking about Jamie's health. He was talking about Jamie's being.

That was basically Nick's attitude throughout Jamie's childhood and early teen years: Jamie is perfectly all right. In treating Jamie as perfectly all right, Nick also performed the invaluable service of showing his peers, especially his playmates around the neighborhood, how to incorporate Jamie into games and activities. He modeled inclusion by example without being didactic, and he never had to confront any cruel or clueless behavior on the part of his friends. (Nick confirms this.) He did chafe sometimes, of course, because Jamie was his little brother. "He messed up all my Legos," Nick complained one morning, and with good reason: Jamie had gotten into the playroom before anyone else had risen and had disarranged, without quite destroying, the various Lego villages, scenarios, and entourages Nick had painstakingly assembled. He did not get at the monorail. Yes, by the mid-1990s Lego had an assembly set that allowed you to build a working monorail, batteries not included, which prompted me to lament that when *I* was a child, all we had were 2 x 2 Lego pieces and 4 x 2 Lego pieces and could build nothing more complicated than tiny narrow towers and tiny rudimentary trucks. Now there are Lego Taj Mahals and Petronas Towers and Fallingwater sets on a 1:1 scale, it seems. So we had put the monorail on a table where Jamie couldn't reach it.

Nick seemed upset not only by the prospect of hours of rebuilding but also—and ultimately more importantly—by the realization that he could not get angry at Jamie himself. "But you have to understand," I told him, "Jamie didn't mess up your Lego structures because he's your little brother with Down syndrome. He messed up your Lego structures because he's your little brother. I'm afraid to say it kinda goes with the territory."

Around that time, Nick also admitted being vexed by the fact that Jamie would claim some of Nick's Matchbox cars as his own, telling me he always let Jamie play with them but just wanted Jamie to understand that they were *his*, not Jamie's. I read this as one part annoyance at Jamie's aggressive (and quite mistaken) claim to Nick's cars and one part annoyance that Jamie didn't understand or acknowledge Nick's generosity. But I laughed anyway and then quickly explained to a suddenly more-vexed Nick that I was not laughing at him: "There is a story," I told him, "of a soldier in Vietnam escorting President Johnson across an airfield, and telling him, 'That's your helicopter, Mr. President,' and LBJ replying, 'Son, they're *all* my helicopters.' When Jamie gets possessive, you can just say that—'Son, they're *all* my cars.'"

"Jamie won't get that joke, Dad," Nick said with a sidelong look.

"No, he won't," I said. "But you will."

Nick never behaved as if being Jamie's sibling was a hardship or a disappointment. Nor did he tout the fact that he had a sibling with a disability, in the sense that he did not see himself, or carry himself, as especially noble or virtuous. He simply—though there is nothing simple about it—met Jamie where he was, and was full of love and encouragement.

There is no question that Jamie's arrival required that Janet and I spend less time and attention on Nick. But as with the battles over Matchboxes and Legos, that would happen with any little brother. To his eternal credit, Nick adapted to the arrival of a sibling far more graciously than I did when my sister Jean was born. By 1965 I had had my house, and my parents and great aunt, to myself for three and a half years, and when Jeannie joined us I decided it would be a Fun Thing to play games like "hide the baby's pacifier." By contrast, Nick was five and a half when Jamie was born and had gotten tired of being the only child. Fortunately, caring for Jamie—after that first harrowing year—did not prevent us from taking Nick to soccer (he named his team the Werewolves, to the horror of some other parents but to the delight of their kids) and tae kwon do (in which he eventually earned a black belt). Because these were local sports, not games in organized leagues that involved travel, I was able to attend most of Nick's soccer games and tae kwon do practices, and to videotape far too many of them.

In 1994 my parents were visiting Champaign, Illinois, where we lived at the time, and as we drove to one of Nick's tae kwon do tests, my father decided to chastise me for letting Nick take these classes. "It's too violent," he said, knowing precisely nothing about a martial art that involved a great deal of skilled movement, light sparring, and the occasional breaking of a board.

"Too violent!" I laughed, grateful that I did not have anything liquid in my mouth at the time. "This from the guy who took up boxing and put his son into hockey."

As my father muttered something illogical or incoherent, I decided to pay back a long-overdue debt. "I've been thinking that when I ferry Nick around town to these things, I'm usually driving maybe eight or ten minutes each way, whereas you drove me all over New York and Long Island and New England for four years. Coney Island, Staten Island, the Bronx, 4 a.m., rush hour, it didn't matter; you took me to hundreds of practices and games and tournaments. So, thank you."

"Don't forget," he replied, "I also picked you up every day after school to take you to public sessions at Skateland in New Hyde Park."

"OK," I parried, "that's enough thanks for now."

But just as Nick was doing so well treating Jamie as he would any little brother, I was trying to treat Nick like any other kid. I didn't think we—or he—needed to compensate for Jamie, and I felt guilty enough as it was that Nick had two busy parents on the tenure track. I used to joke that you could pick out the children of academic couples by the way they (the children) had learned, by the age of six, to eat hors d'oeuvres on napkins at receptions while also holding a plastic tumbler of ginger ale and chatting about their work. But the joke was only funny because it was true. And I know there were times, partly because of Jamie and partly because of academe, when we had less time for Nick than Nick would have liked.

On the other hand, Nick got all kinds of gratification from the fact that Jamie clearly believed his big brother was the coolest person on the planet. The best way to motivate Jamie to acquire a skill or learn a behavior, without question, was to tell him that if he acquired said skill or learned said behavior, he would *be like Nick*. The first experiment in this vein involved a bunk bed. In order to persuade Jamie—who was, and still is, very wary of conditions in which he might fall or lose his balance—to abandon the crib for a big boy's bed at the age of two and a half, we assured him that if he slept in a bunk bed with Nick he would be like Nick. The initial results of the experiment were discouraging: Jamie, who was then a fitful sleeper, rolled right out of the bottom bed and onto the floor the first two nights. We responded by placing a second mattress on the floor (at first he rolled off and kept sleeping) and then a small barrier to the side of the lower bunk. Jamie learned how to stay in a bed for an entire night.

Soon after, something interesting happened: One day I came into the boys' room and saw four-year-old Jamie in the top bunk. I was visibly startled; I had not thought Jamie capable of climbing the ladder, which was metal and a straight vertical, far more forbidding than the slanted wooden models with stairs. Jamie was delighted that I was startled. He knew he had done something surprising—a major accomplishment, given his physical challenges at the time and his fear of falling or losing his balance.

"Jamie!" I exclaimed, mock-alarmed. "You *cannot* climb up into *Nick's bed!*"

"Yes, I can!" he chirped, collapsing into helpless laughter.

I wondered, at the time, if Jamie had any inkling of the wordplay involved in his reply. I am not sure whether he understood that my "cannot" was prescriptive, and that his declaration of fact—oh, but I *can*—was a sly evasion of the real meaning of my exclamation, *do not climb up into Nick's bed*. But it was clear that Jamie was thrilled with his achievement. And with my response, which quickly became part of one of Jamie's favorite routines. He would climb into Nick's bunk, and summon me from my study next door. I would exclaim, mock-alarmed, "Jamie! You *cannot* climb up into *Nick's bed!*" "Yes, I can," he would chirp, laughing gleefully as I ran around the room in mock-flummoxation at this state of affairs, crying, "Yes, you can?" and stopping only when I had hit the pull cord on the ceiling fan. (Don't ask. For some reason Jamie found this hilarious.)

And all this because Jamie wanted to be like Nick. Though I should add that Jamie had no idea how to get back down the ladder.

□   □   □

Because Nick believed that having a sibling with Down syndrome was no big deal, he was great as a big brother—and useless, I feared, as a mentor or guide for other siblings who were struggling with disability-and-family issues. I asked Nick many times if he would sit in on sessions with siblings, compare notes and stories with other siblings, share experiences and maybe even coping tips—to no avail.

Finally, when Nick was fourteen, I asked him to do a favor for a friend, a special-education professor. The class was about disability and family dynamics, and the professor, knowing Nick from a distance, believed very strongly that Nick would be exceptionally helpful for students training to become counselors and aides. With only minimal hesitation, Nick agreed.

I accompanied him to the class. He was paired with another kid with a disabled sibling, a girl about his age, and at one point, his counterpart told the class that her family was always pressuring her to do well in school because she was the only one who would be going to college.

Nick smiled ruefully and said, "Yeah, my family is the same way."

I was sitting at the back of the room, and I believe I did a very good job of stifling my complete astonishment and dismay. I also thought that jumping up to contradict him would be counterproductive on two fronts. After all, I had insisted that he get involved with the sibling thing, so I certainly couldn't edit or censor him, thereby effectively telling him, *Talk about your feelings and experiences with Jamie, but only in ways that I approve of.* And I thought any protest on my part would look, to the class, as if I really were the kind of parent who would pressure his kid to compensate intellectually for his disabled little brother.

So I sat on my hands, bit my cheeks, and waited. When the class was over and I was driving Nick home, I told him that he had done a great job and that his remarks about his life with Jamie would certainly be useful in the future for everyone in the class, the professor included. I also told him how surprised I was to hear him say that he felt parental pressure to do well in school because of Jamie, and that I hoped he knew that I never, ever expected him to try to compensate for having a brother with a developmental disability.

"It's not you," Nick replied. "It's Mom."

"Really?" I squawked, incredulous. "Are you kidding me? When did Mom ever say anything like that to you?"

It turned out that Janet had remarked on one of his subpar seventh-grade report cards, where "subpar" meant "not all A's for a change." And what Janet had actually said—as I recalled to Nick—was that she worried that he was coasting through a school that wasn't challenging him. And it wasn't: he himself complained on a weekly basis that his homework amounted to coloring and connect-the-dots, and I gently reminded him of that. The point was that Janet's comment had nothing to do with Jamie. Nevertheless, Nick somehow heard it as having *something* to do with Jamie, and I have never forgotten the lesson.

Actually, there was more than one lesson. The most obvious one, the one I understood immediately, was that Nick might be more affected by Jamie than he was ordinarily willing to say, and that he might well be feeling the pressure of being the only child who would go to college (with all that implies—moving out of our home, graduating, beginning a career). Another, which unfolded more slowly, was that adolescent

Nick would have a different relationship with Jamie than would pre-teen Nick, and that their relationship would change and evolve as they made their separate ways into adulthood. Still another, which informs the way I think about how Nick will care for Jamie after Janet and I are gone (and the way I talk to Nick about this, as I began to do when Nick was twenty), is that Jamie's influence on adult Nick is indelible and will make itself felt in ways I can neither enumerate nor anticipate. I think this is true for many people with siblings with intellectual disabilities: as one such sibling has told me, you grow up thinking that intellectual disability is just an ordinary part of life—but you also find out very quickly that you understand things other people don't understand. And sometimes that experience sets you on your life path, and the effects are apparent in your life's work. I often think of Jill Bolte Taylor, author of the extraordinary account of her nearly fatal stroke, *My Stroke of Insight*, who became fascinated with how brains work because she wanted to understand her brother's schizophrenia. Timothy Shriver's book *Fully Alive* suggests that his aunt Rosemary Kennedy was always at the heart of her siblings' lives, both before and after the Kennedy family acknowledged her publicly. About his mother, Eunice, who founded Special Olympics, he writes, "She was determined to prove to others a lesson Rosemary had proved to her years before, a lesson that remains shocking in its simplicity and shocking in its continuing and persistent disregard: people with intellectual disabilities are human beings, deserving of love, opportunity, and acceptance just as they are."

Not long before we moved from the University of Illinois to Penn State, in 2001, Nick had introduced his first form of mock-competition with Jamie, which, at the time, was simply a clever way of getting Jamie to stop playing in the playroom and come upstairs for dinner. Janet or I would summon the boys, and Nick would say to Jamie, "I'll be first—*you'll be last.*" This would invariably elicit a "No, Nick! *You* be last!" from Jamie, and the two of them would scamper up the gray-carpeted stairs of our split-level house. Occasionally Jamie would object to something Nick did, as when Nick interrupted his play by intercepting the rubber ball he was throwing off a wall, exclaiming, "Nick! Don't have a Christmas hand!" (This cracked Nick up, and we never did learn what Jamie meant by it.) But for the most part, they were heading into adolescence without any major conflicts or rivalries.

Moving to State College was hard on both of them, particularly on fifteen-year-old Nick, who went from a Derek Jeter-esque farewell tour among his many high school friends to a lonely room in a house in a town in which he knew no one. I was quite sure that Nick would make friends quickly and easily. I was right about that much. But it was a difficult transition nevertheless. We arrived on July 1, 2001, with two months of summer stretching before us. Nick had no readily available way to make friends, no school or summer program to attend, whereas Jamie had a summer day camp I had arranged at Park Forest Middle School. That camp turned out to be a mistake on my part: I should have enrolled Jamie in the YMCA camp, which I did every year thereafter until he aged out (the age limit is twelve, but the Y staff very kindly allowed Jamie to enroll until he was sixteen). The camp for which I had signed up had no staff with experience working with children with disabilities, and Jamie sometimes required individual attention that their staff could not provide. But Nick saved the summer for all of us, volunteering to accompany Jamie to camp and keep watch over him. The camp agreed to this arrangement, and Janet and I, vastly relieved, threw ourselves back into the sixteen-hour-a-day tasks of moving in and redecorating.

Over the next three years our new lives settled into place. Nick made many friends and developed a well-deserved reputation for calligraphy and design skills; Jamie adapted to his new school, Corl Street, and it adapted to him; Janet and I learned the ropes at Penn State. Nick invented a series of increasingly elaborate nicknames for his little brother. Starting from Jamsenbrunner (pronounced *yomsenbrunner*, and taken from the former NHL star Jamie Langenbrunner), the names quickly metamorphosed to Jatemint (pronouncing the J), then to Mint, Minthoven, and Minté Bleu. This delighted Minté Bleu no end. "Call my names," Jamie would say, and Nick would oblige. Jamie had afterschool and summer programs at the Y, and three very happy birthday parties, to which many of his classmates came. Gradually, our house became Teen Lounge, and I used to say (with good reason) that I never knew how many people would be in it when I woke up each morning. Nick had a

charming way of befriending people undergoing difficult domestic dra-
mas, one result of which was that some of his friends preferred hanging
out chez nous. There was no alcohol, no drugs, no funny business. The
worst we endured, as parents, was a 3 a.m. doorbell for pizza delivery
(Nick swore to us that he had told the place not to let the driver ring the
bell) and a bafflingly large number of soda cans covering nearly every
horizontal surface, all of them not-quite-empty. And then it came time
for Nick to leave for college.

We packed up, set a course for St. Louis, and joined the throngs of
families jostling for hampers and backpacks and storage cubes at the
Target in Clayton, Missouri. We booked a lousy hotel. We went to Orientation. Jamie met Nick's roommates—he'd been assigned to a tiny room
along with two other unfortunates—and made much of the paper pine-
apple dangling from one of Nick's roommate's beds. Jamie climbed up
into Nick's bed, because he could. After a few days of this, it was finally
time to leave. Janet burst into tears in the parking lot. Jamie marveled at
all the license plates from all the different states.

We came back to a very empty house—and, more important, to a
house that stayed empty, day after day after day. Teen Lounge had closed
for the season. And Jamie gradually realized that the people he'd known
and welcomed for the past three years had really been Nick's friends
all along. They were unfailingly kind to Jamie; they liked him and engaged him eagerly. But they really were Nick's friends, some of whom
were off to college themselves, and as for Jamie's friends . . . well, as he
moved to middle school he stayed with much of his Corl Street cohort.
But with one exception, those kids didn't invite him over after school or
drop by to hang out. And that one exceptional person's family dropped
us decisively a few weeks later, the day they saw a Kerry/Edwards sign
in our yard.

▫ ▫ ▫

And so began the most difficult transition of Jamie's life. It is hard to
say how much he missed his big brother, because he never said a word
to suggest that he missed his big brother. But it was obvious that Jamie
was bewildered. He understood what it meant that Nick would be going

to college, and he was very proud of Nick. But at the same time, he didn't quite seem to understand why it was that Nick, the brother and companion he'd known all his life, had to be away. Every. Single. Day.

We didn't get a sense of the depth of Jamie's sadness until the following spring. At some point that year, I read a story about a young man with Down syndrome living in the South. It was a follow-up story to something the paper had run a few years earlier; the first profile was a feel-good piece about how this winsome young man with intellectual disabilities was graduating from high school, had plenty of friendly classmates, and was a heartwarming example of the benefits of inclusion. The second profile, which I admired the paper for running, was a considerably more somber account of how isolated and sad this young man had become in the couple of years since graduation. Shortly thereafter, I told Jamie—without mentioning the article—that if he was ever sad or worried or confused, he could always talk to me about how he was feeling. He shook me off: he was not sad! "OK," I replied, content to let Jamie know that he would always be allowed to acknowledge sadness—even though it was something he had never done in his life.

I know the exact date on which Jamie first spoke of his sadness. It was April 22, 2005, Nick's nineteenth birthday, his first birthday away from home. Janet, Jamie, and I went shopping that evening for groceries and things, and we were very anxious to get home by seven because Nick would be calling. So we bundled up our loaves of bread and our seafood salad and our cereal and our trash bags, and we collected all the ingredients for Nick's care package of finals-week cookies—the Toll House chips and the sugar, the milk and the cookie mix—but we didn't make it back in time. Nick's call came while we were still in the supermarket, and Janet picked it up on her cell.

Nick sounded weary but happy. The first year of the architecture program was grueling, but tremendously stimulating. The rumors were true: architecture students did not sleep, and at the end of every semester they worked twenty-eight-hour days. Nick spoke to Jamie with warmth and enthusiasm. He said he couldn't wait to finish his freshman year and come home. He couldn't believe he was turning nineteen. Neither could we.

When we got home and unloaded the groceries, it quickly became clear that Jamie was disappointed. Well beyond disappointed: he was crushed. He sat in the back room, cross-legged, with his head in his hands, and only after a few minutes of my worried prodding did it become clear that he'd believed that Nick was coming home for his birthday. More than that: he thought Nick would be home to greet us when we got back from the store, and that *that* was why we needed to be back by seven.

"Oh, sweetie," I said. "And that's why you were so excited about making him cookies?"

"Yes," Jamie replied, barely audible. "Nick could come home right now."

"Well, no, he can't come home right now," I said, putting my arm around his shoulders. "He is in St. Louis. But he'll be home in just two weeks, and you can see him then."

"Nick could come home *right now*," Jamie insisted. I began to realize that his sadness must have resonated for months. By now, that loneliness had become unbearable.

In those years I would sometimes measure Jamie's maturity by gauging how he handled disappointment. Actually, that's one way I'd measure anyone's maturity. For example: one day I took him for one of our weekend swims at the gym only to find that the pool was closed for cleaning. Jamie simply did not understand this. It was Saturday; the pool should be open. The pool is always open on Saturday. *Maybe the pool is open! Let's try and see!* I let Jamie pull at the locker room door for a few minutes, and I even gave him help when he asked for it, but in the end, I had to say, "Really, Jamie, the pool is closed. Let's do something else today." He did not welcome the suggestion, and it took him hours to snap out of his funk. A year later, when we arrived at the same gym only to find that it was closing early, Jamie turned to me and said, "Oh well! Let's go to the Y." I praised him effusively for this, and, of course, I took him to the Y.

By adolescence, Jamie had acquired words for emotional states like "disappointed" and "frustrated," partly by asking about how characters in stories are feeling. But his emotional state on Nick's birthday went well beyond either.

I reassured Jamie, again, that Nick would be coming home very soon and that Nick would take him out to dinner with all his friends. "I know," Jamie said. "But I'm still sad." I nodded. "I understand, Jamie. You know what? I'm sad too. I miss Nick too."

And then Jamie said something stunning. Dejectedly, he mumbled, "How can I stop being sad?"

"Ah!" I replied. "That's a very good question. Well, usually, people are sad for a while, and then gradually, the sadness goes away, little by little."

This didn't do any good. Jamie waited a few seconds, then said, "But I'm *still sad.*" I was reminded of the time when he was eleven and had a sudden fever; a few minutes after Janet gave him his Tylenol and antibiotics, he stomped up the stairs, complaining that he was *still sick.* As I'll explain in more detail when I get to The Tale of Jamie's Pneumonia, he eventually had a hospital-induced epiphany that illness doesn't fade just like that. Now he'd have to have a Nick-induced epiphany in order to learn the same thing about sadness.

So I decided that this might be a good time to pass along something I'd learned about grief: It washes over you and sweeps everything before it, and there's no resisting it. Eventually it recedes, just like elation or anxiety or anger. But it recedes at its own pace. Buddhists taught me this, perplexing Buddhists with their "this is arising and is known" subject-lessness (which is supposed to wean you from attachment to your own thoughts and feelings, and which I find extremely difficult to inhabit, so identified with my thoughts as I am), and I thought it might be a good idea to try to teach it to Jamie as best I could.

"OK, Jamie," I said. "I'll tell you about how sadness comes and goes. Are you ready?" He brightened up and gave me his full attention. "You know how you like to play in the waves at the beach?" Jamie brightened. "Mm!" he mm'd. "And you know how a wave comes and knocks you down and it's so much fun, and the wave tumbles you up the sand, and then you get up and play in another wave?" By this point Jamie was rubbing his hands together with glee. "Well, sadness is like that, and happiness is like that too. They're like waves that come and knock you down and tumble you around, and then you get up and they're all gone."

Jamie froze. Up to the point at which I'd described playing in the waves, he was thrilled, because playing in the waves is one of his favorite things about being alive. But then I'd taken this weird philosophical "sadness and happiness are like that" turn, and he didn't know what to think about it. Jamie puzzled for a moment, and then said, darkly, "There will be *more waves*."

Shit, I thought. *It didn't take very long for him to figure that out, now, did it*. Here I was trying to tell him that sadness, like all things, will pass, but he'd gone right past that lesson to the obvious corollary, namely, after this sadness passes, there will be more sadness yet to come.

"Well, yeah, sweetie," I said, trying to rally, "but some of those waves will be happy waves, when you . . ."

"How about *no waves*," Jamie countered in a growl, waving his arm dismissively and going back to his slumped, head-in-hands posture.

"You don't want to talk about waves anymore?"

"No." And with that, he turned on the TV and sent me away.

□   □   □

The wave passed, being a wave. Jamie got used to the rhythms of Nick's life as a college student: away for four months, back for two weeks, away for four months, back for three months or so. And we got used to the rhythms of Nick's life as a college student: In his second year, we showed up in St. Louis a day early to beat the other parents to the hampers and backpacks and storage cubes at Target. We booked a better hotel. We executed a move-in to his spacious, six-person suite with brutal efficiency. In his third year, we skipped Target altogether, moving him and his audio equipment and his closest friend (Shachar Shimonovich, aka Shash, one of his first-year roommates and one of Jamie's favorite people) into an off-campus apartment. In his fourth year, I drove Nick solo in our Subaru Outback, stuffed to the last cubic centimeter and garlanded with a bicycle rack, and upon depositing him in St. Louis flew home alone, leaving him with the car we'd promised him for his senior year. And Jamie got used to having his parents all to himself, most of the time. In the summer of 2008, after Nick graduated, Janet was teaching in Ireland, and I had the boys to myself for one last time. They are, as you have probably gathered by now, more alike than different despite Jamie's extra chromosome. Neither of them is very good at keeping track of where they put things. And so, after our first week together, I made an announcement to them both: *From this point on, through the rest of the summer, I will no longer answer any questions that begin with "where."* (Jamie, clever like his brother, now asks me, "Have you seen my iPod?" and "Do you know where my wallet is?"—and when I tell him that it is his job to keep track of his things, he replies, "I did not say 'where.'")

I had one other heart-piercing moment in those four years. (Only one! I got off light!) On one of Nick's visits home over the 2007–08 winter break, Jamie came into my study and plopped himself down on a chair I almost never use. "I don't have anything to do," he said. This was surprising, because the house had once again become Teen Lounge (or Twenty-Year-Old Lounge), and although Nick's friends were really Nick's friends, they continued to like Jamie and engage him eagerly. I assured Jamie that Nick's friends were (in a way) his friends too, and that he could hang out with any of the groups of Nick-friends gathered in conversation in this room or that. At the time, there may have been four or five clumps of three or four, hanging out and catching up over the break.

Jamie nodded. He would go and hang out with Nick's friends.

Ten minutes later he returned to my study, plopped himself back in the chair, and said gloomily but with astonishing self-awareness, "I don't know how to hang out."

I caught my breath. This was even more striking, I thought, than the *There will be more waves* insight of Nick's first year away. I know now that Jamie engages in serious introspection and self-reflection, but he does not often utter sentences that testify to this; the first I can recall, from when he was fifteen, involved his refusal to make a booking for fifteen minutes in a shark tank (in a cage, with scuba gear, accompanied by his father) on the grounds that he had become so fascinated with sharks as a young child primarily "because I was afraid of them." A perfectly good reason! But more important, a perfectly good self-reflection. *I was afraid of the creatures I have studied for years, and this is in fact how I sublimated my fear: by studying them.* Cool. *So please don't ask me to spend fifteen minutes in a cage in a shark tank.* Got it! Message received.

So that night, I turned in my chair and faced him. "You're right, you know," I replied. "You *don't* know how to hang out. Lots of people don't know how—it is really very difficult. You have to listen carefully, and you have to know when it might be your turn to talk, and then you have to say something that contributes to the conversation. It is very tricky, especially when there is more than one person in the conversation and everyone is talking very quickly." Jamie nodded. "So you can hang out with me for now. And we will work on hanging out."

Jamie has done reasonably well when he is given a project like this. The first, when he was ten or eleven, involved my response to his desire, after a Saturday swim, to do about nine more things by the end of the day. Go to lunch and play racquetball and go to the movies and play laser tag and get groceries and play mini-golf and . . . I told him there wasn't enough time to do all those things; he asked why. Since Jamie thinks in terms of checklists, and since at that age he would become frustrated if he did not hit every item on his checklist, I sat him down and had a talk. I imagined myself as a hockey coach telling a player that he has many strengths as a scoring forward but needs to work on his backchecking. I praised Jamie for his facility with math and his great memory and his powers of observation, but told him he really, really needed to work on understanding time. He took this in very thoughtfully, and later that day, Janet and I bought him a digital watch. He has worn a watch ever since, and he is ridiculously, meticulously punctual. If you tell him we will leave the house at 4, he appears at the door at 4:00:00, ready and waiting. He checks the running times of movies. He keeps track of how long it takes to drive to various cities and states from State College. He has never been late for work. So this project has been a pretty spectacular success.

The next big project involved money, another pretty spectacular success story with some rough patches. The first time Jamie took himself out to lunch in downtown State College, at the age of twenty-two, he announced to me proudly that he had gone to Cozy Thai, gotten himself a table for one, ordered the panang curry with chicken, and paid with his debit card. "Wow," I said, thoroughly impressed. "Did you leave a tip?" "Shoot," Jamie replied. Within a few weeks, however, Jamie became adept in such matters, remembering to tip servers and Jimmy John's delivery guys—though upon reviewing his bank statement online I did see a $35 charge for lunch at India Pavilion that reminded me of the mischievous ignatz in Vancouver (at the time, the lunch buffet there was $8).

The learning-how-to-hang-out project is still developing as I write: he has gotten better at being social in small groups, and if he interrupts someone or introduces something irrelevant to the conversation, we gently correct him. Likewise, when he has patiently waited his turn to put in his oar, we tell him it's his turn, and if he refers to things only he knows about, we ask him to explain. He does not understand that not everyone has seen *Galaxy Quest* or the film version of *How the Grinch Stole Christmas*, and that therefore not everyone understands his allusions to or imitations of Alan Rickman or Jim Carrey (though his family does). It is very much a work in progress.

Meanwhile, at college, Nick began dating. And right around the same time, Jamie became noticeably colder around Nick. Nick's visits home, for Jamie, were no longer occasions for hand-rubbing glee; to everyone's dismay, they became weekends or holiday breaks during which Jamie would avoid Nick or refuse overtures to join in games or activities. Janet told Jamie he was hurting Nick's feelings (and he was, though Nick took it remarkably well), but to no effect. So one night, I invited Jamie to accompany me as I walked Lucy the Dog around the neighborhood. He fussed, but I insisted. We had had, by that point, a handful of serious talks on dog walks, and it was clearly time for another. On this one, I told Jamie that I had a theory about why he was no longer being nice to Nick.

"What is it?" he asked, grumpily.

"I think," I said, "that you have decided that you like having your parents all to yourself, and you like being the big kid in the house. I remember how sad you were when Nick left for college, but you've gotten used to it, and now you resent it a little bit when Nick comes back and *he's* the big kid and you're not alone with us."

"That's not it," Jamie snapped back immediately. Oho! So it was something, just not *that*. Interesting. And suddenly I knew what it was.

"Really that's not it?" I asked. "Are you sure?"

"Yes."

"Well, then, is it . . . Rachel?"

"Yes."

Oh, my. "So you are upset that Nick has a girlfriend?"

"Yes." Bless him, he is as honest as the day is long.

"And you do not."

"*Yes.*"

I promised in the introduction that I would not discuss Jamie's crushes out of respect for his privacy, and I won't. But I can say that in his later teen years, he began talking about someday being M-A-R-R-I-E-D (and that's the way he says it, letter by letter). From the age of seventeen, he began asking me when he would have a girlfriend. I always told him that I honestly did not know—that it was a question no parent, nobody could answer. *Que sera, sera.* . . . He pointed out that he was "available" (where did he pick up that term? From the movie *Percy Jackson and the Olympians: The Lightning Thief*, that's where), and I acknowledged that he was indeed available and that many people liked him. One night I told him that I did not have a girlfriend in high school, and he shut me down pronto, saying, "*Not you*"—which I took to mean, sensibly enough, that this was not about me. I tried this tack only once more; the second time, when I tried to speak of my loneliness as a teen, I was met with "But you met Janet," to which I could only think, *touché. I will not go there again.*

Part of the problem—a very large part—is that Jamie wants to have a girlfriend who does not have a disability. He has told me this many times, but the first time he told me I was taken aback. "Uh," I replied (and there may have been more than one "uh"), "well, Jamie, people without disabilities don't usually date or marry people with Down syndrome."

"Why not?" he asked ingenuously.

"Uh" (again), "that's a very good question. OK, let me put it this way. You know that Todd and Hayward were girlfriend and boyfriend."

"Mm-hm," Jamie replied, a bit puzzled.

"Well, fifty or sixty or more years ago, it was very rare to see a black person dating a white person. In some states it was actually against the law for black people and white people to get married."

"That is crazy!" Jamie exclaimed.

"It was definitely crazy. But now it is no big deal, right? You see people of different races and colors getting married all the time. And of course you know boys and boys can be together, like your friends Tim and Ramon, and girls and girls, too. But not very long ago, *that* was against the law, and if a boy was in love with another boy, or a girl with another girl, they had to hide their love from everyone else or they might be arrested and thrown in jail."

"Nutty," Jamie replied.

"Right. But that changed too, and now most people don't think it is weird to see black people with white people or boys with boys or girls with girls. Maybe the day will come when people without Down syndrome date people with Down syndrome. Or people without intellectual disabilities date people with intellectual disabilities. Right now it doesn't happen. But someday it might."

In other variations on this conversation, I have pointed out to Jamie that he cannot drive a car and needs help with grown-up living skills, and that this might be an issue for any potential love interest. But those answers, it seems to me, amount to kicking the can down the road. His inability to drive a car or cook dinner isn't the main issue. The main issue is that the analogy to interracial or same-sex couples doesn't quite hold up when it comes to intellectual disability. There are any number of couples today with one member on the high-functioning end of the autism spectrum, but no examples anywhere, so far as I know, of someone with two twenty-first chromosomes dating someone with three. I feel terrible telling Jamie, in effect, *One of your own kind, stick to your own kind,* but I cannot lie to him about his prospects, no matter how available he might be.

So there was nothing to do with this wave except to let it wash over him, however many years it might take. Rachel was, for her part, charmingly sweet and generous to Jamie, and that probably made things all the harder for him at first. The wave passed, being a wave. But it receded only very gradually, and Nick weathered the turn in Jamie's behavior mostly by telling Jamie that he had become "cheeky." For his part, Jamie did have an on-again, off-again thing with a local girl with Down syndrome, mostly off-again (it is now permanently off), and he grew to embrace Rachel as a member of the family and to warm again to Nick. And yet there is still a remnant of the tensions of that time, and it is noticeable whenever Nick taunts Jamie lightly by telling him it will be his job to clean the gutters. The gutters at our house are about twenty feet off the ground, and no one here is getting on a ladder to go that high. It is beyond preposterous. But the idea gets under Jamie's skin somehow, and though I have told him repeatedly that he should respond in kind, perhaps by telling Nick that his job is to clean the garage or paint the basement (far more plausible tasks!), Jamie always responds straightforwardly and angrily to these provocations. Then again, during the time I was writing the first draft of this chapter, our family was playing a card game with friends one night, and Jamie read his cards aloud and told me to "go sleep in the yard" when I corrected him on some small detail. So there is hope that he will become fluent in trash talk after all. It is part of hanging out.

Thankfully, that period of chilled Nick-Jamie relations is now scar tissue, a slight blemish in an otherwise rich relationship. Janet and I know we got very lucky with these two kids, these *jeunes hommes*. It is not a question of being good parents, though we have tried to be good parents. We know legions of good parents whose kids got tumbled by waves and are struggling to stay afloat. Nick is always solicitous of Jamie's many interests, especially in geography, in which Nick has excelled since he was five. He shares his music (mostly indie rock) with Jamie and makes compilation CDs for him. (As a result, Jamie has puzzled more than one DJ at holiday parties by asking to hear the New Pornographers.) He has Jamie for sleepovers and hangings-out. And he is not merely indulgent but supportive of Jamie's various obsessions, from sharks to Beatles to food. In late adolescence, Jamie got on a kick of asking to eat [some ethnic] food in [some city]. It was a little like Mad Libs: Jamie would fill in the blanks in the most random and curious ways. *Let's eat Cambodian food in Pittsburgh*, he proposed one day, and sure enough, the Google revealed that there is indeed a Cambodian restaurant downtown, the Lemongrass Café, not far from the PNC Park, home of the Pittsburgh Pirates. *Let's eat Ethiopian food in Charlotte. Let's eat Bosnian food in St. Louis.* These are all real examples, and they all led to fabulous dinners;

when Nick got his master's degree in architecture from Washington University in St. Louis, in 2013, Jamie hit upon the Bosnian idea, and he and Nick discovered Grbic, a terrific place where even Janet, the vegetarian, emerged raving about how subtle and tasty everything was. (We also learned that St. Louis has the largest Bosnian population of any city outside Bosnia. Who knew? Perhaps Jamie knew.)

At the same time, Nick does not indulge some of Jamie's more fanciful notions about world cuisine. When he first embarked on his mission to eat the foods of all nations, Jamie became fascinated by the fact that some people do not eat pork and some do not eat beef, some eat naan and some eat couscous, some eat injera and some eat quinoa. For a while, until I asked him to desist, he got into the habit of describing regional preferences in meat by saying, "They do cut up [some animal] in [some country]." (This was especially disconcerting in restaurants, for anyone within earshot.) Most of the time, he is right; they do cut up yak in Nepal, for instance. But on one of Nick's visits home, Jamie tried to tell Nick that "they do cut up badgers in Iran."

"Jamie," Nick said with a raised eyebrow. "They do no such thing."

"They do, Nick."

"Jamie. What kind of country is Iran? What kind of land is in Iran?"

Jamie thought for a moment. "Desert."

"And do badgers live in the desert?"

Jamie thought for a longer moment. He knew he was boxed in. But he rallied: "They could cut up meerkats."

Nick laughed too hard to bother with reminding Jamie that the meerkat is native to southern Africa.

And then came Nick's big moment as a TV star. Jamie was twenty-three; Nick was twenty-eight. Nick had applied to appear on *Jeopardy!* and had passed the online test and in-person audition. Janet and her sister Cynthia accompanied him to Los Angeles to offer moral support; as it happens, *Jeopardy!* tapes five shows in a row on Tuesdays and Wednesdays, and Nick's game, which he won, took place on the final half hour of taping on Wednesday. So he would have to come back the following week, though *Jeopardy!* pays the airfare to Los Angeles for contestants who have to defend their titles.

Jamie and I decided to go with Nick for round two, on the grounds that there would never be another moment for Jamie and me to see him on *Jeopardy!* and that we could not allow Nick to be the only contestant with no family members cheering him on. (He eventually won two games and led throughout the third before losing in Final Jeopardy.) I told Nick afterward that I had never had such hopeless parental anxiety for him as I did watching him in those two games. He had not played Little League baseball or youth hockey, and I never had to fear for his safety in his soccer and tae kwon do careers. But watching him on *Jeopardy!* I was ridiculously nervous. I did not mutter the answers to myself in the stands, because the *Jeopardy!* staff make a point of announcing to the audience at the outset, "We know you all watch the show, and we know you all watch it out loud. *Do not do that here.* There are microphones everywhere, and if we pick up so much as a whisper we will throw the question out, stop, and retape." Jamie was so struck by this announcement that he tried to prevent me from waving back when Nick waved to us before the start of the first contest.

For his third (and, though he could not know it, final) game, Nick had something prepared for the brief, stilted chats between Alex Trebek and the contestants.

TREBEK: Nicholas Bérubé, one thing we've discovered in your two appearances on our program is that you seem to be very well prepared. And . . . you had help.
NICK: I did, yes! My little brother Jamie, who's actually in the audience right now—he's over there [points]—helped me, especially with the painters and composers, 'cause he's got all that stuff completely locked down and I'm a little iffy on it, so we just went through . . . baroque, Impressionist, all that stuff. . . .
TREBEK: Is he going to try out for the program?
NICK: He better, yeah, he better do it.

I was flummoxed, caught totally off guard. It is true that Jamie has a brilliant cataloguing memory for the major artists and composers of Western Civ—so much so that he introduced a graduate student in Penn

State's School of Music to some new material. A few months after Nick's *Jeopardy!* appearance, Mark Minnich, who tutors Jamie in music for an hour every Wednesday (this was Jamie's idea, and I got in touch with music faculty who might know someone who wanted to work with Jamie), asked by e-mail, "Would it be OK for me to mention Jamie in the acknowledgments of my thesis? He gave me the original idea for what I'm writing about (motivic inspirations for Maurice Ravel's *Tzigane*) through his interest in the music of Leoncavallo, whom I'd never heard of before Jamie asked." And ever since he was first introduced to the medieval-Renaissance-baroque-classic-romantic-modern-atonal-contemporary narrative of Western music and the medieval-Renaissance-baroque-neoclassical-romantic-realist-impressionist-postimpressionist-modernist-Cubist-abstract expressionist-postmodernist narrative of Western art, Jamie has gotten all that stuff locked down. It is true that Jamie helped Nick to prepare for *Jeopardy!*, though the moment I remember best involved Rachel reading a clue from a show that aired long ago (the Internet being what it is, of course there is a site that archives all *Jeopardy!* questions since the fall of Troy). It was a $2,000 question, a tough one, in a category dealing with anatomy, and it said something about a tube in your body that stretches from this point in your body to that point in your body. As Nick, Janet, Rachel, and I riffled through our mental files on bodies and tubes, Jamie chimed in, with perfect hanging-out timing, "What is the esophagus?"

So I supposed that if Nick were going to give Jamie a shout-out on national television, it would be for the esophagus rather than for the painters and composers. But in the end, I didn't care what domains of knowledge Nick credited to Jamie.

When Nick gestured, in that exchange with Alex Trebek, saying, "He's over there," the *Jeopardy!* crew was ready with a camera trained right on Jamie. I had seen the cameraman standing over us, of course, and I saw when his bright light came on, and I knew we were being taped; but I never thought Jamie would actually appear on TV, because *Jeopardy!* almost never does audience shots.

You can find that episode somewhere in the vast breadth and depth of the Internet, I guess, but if for the demands of intellectual property

To His Health

□   □   □   □   □

In one way Jamie is the healthiest person in his family: he's the only one of us who doesn't have asthma and animal allergies. He does not often get colds, despite his cold-prone infancy. He does have recurring cysts on the back of his neck, on the right side, that are occasionally large and painful and always cause for parental concern. (We have had him seen by a dermatologist. But we were not sure that we were doing enough, so we took him to a second dermatologist and then to a cosmetic surgeon, who removed some cystic material from his neck.) And he has flat feet, for which we should have gotten him orthotics inserts years before we finally did so, in his early teen years. He takes Levothyroxine (synthroid) for hypothyroidism, and he is diligent about taking his pill every day in the late afternoon. Otherwise, he's perfectly all right.

Most of this chapter will be devoted to the moments at which he was not perfectly all right, and I hope this narrative will be of some use to parents, caretakers, and people in the medical professions. I will close with a pleasant little rant about health care in general. But subtending this narrative is a particularly dicey version of the larger question of this book, namely, *How did Jamie mature through childhood, adolescence, and adulthood?* Every child who makes it to adulthood has navigated his or her way through health issues ranging from mild to severe, and every parent who is doing his or her job watches anxiously over every sick child. And yet Jamie's journey was a bit more harrowing at times of crisis, because he could not give so full an account of himself as could most children his age (and to this day he underreports pain—so far as we can tell, since this question entails very difficult philosophical questions about pain and language) and because for a painfully long time, he could not understand what was happening to him or why he was being treated in this or that way.

Likewise, every child is liable to stick his or her finger in the electrical outlet or wander off into the woods. But Jamie, in this as in so much else, was more vulnerable than most. I think of the evening of the Pizza in the Microwave Incident, late in 2001. I had just gone upstairs to get dressed for a dinner with friends (our bedroom is on the third floor of our house) when I heard ten-year-old Jamie coming up the stairs and calling, "Daddy, Daddy, help!" I remember thinking petulantly, *What can it be now? I have been up here for all of thirty seconds,* before hearing Jamie add, "Kitchen, stove, smoke," which wasn't a proper English sentence but managed to convey the urgency of the situation very efficiently. As I ran downstairs to see precisely what was happening with the kitchen and the stove and the smoke, I realized that Jamie had decided to reheat a slice of pizza for himself without removing the aluminum foil in which it was wrapped. The foil was burned, smoke was everywhere, and the smoke alarm was screeching.

Jamie was horrified, so I assured him that although he had certainly made a mistake by putting aluminum foil in the microwave, he had done *exactly* the right thing by coming to get me. No, I was not upset. No, I was not angry. I have yelled at Jamie in the course of his life, a handful of times, always when he is being obstinate to the point of extreme orneriness. (My favorite example comes from his early childhood, when Janet, exasperated by his dawdling before bedtime, issued the ultimatum "Get ready for bed or else," and he replied, in precisely the same tone of urgency, "Else!") Strangely, yelling never helps. What does help in those situations is saying, "You are making me very aggravated and I am wanting to use my loud voice." But this was not an occasion for a loud voice. This was an occasion for developing a new Microwave Protocol according to which one should take the pizza out of the foil, put it on a plate, and reheat it for twenty-two seconds. Jamie followed this protocol so faithfully that he began to chastise me whenever I microwaved something for him for half a minute or more.

The other moment of danger in Jamie's life was far more serious. I cannot think about it now without a shudder. He was in Penn State's indoor track facility, along with the rest of the Special Olympics track-and-field athletes and some of their parents. Most of the time, Janet and I simply drop him at track practice on Mondays at 6:30 and pick him up again at 7:45, but for the first couple of years I stayed with him during practice and usually did professor work—reading, mostly, or grading papers. But on that one night, before practice started, the indoor track was banked, and the turns were raised, as they would be for an intercollegiate event. Banked curves are not necessary for Special Olympics track practice, so someone decided to flatten the track. Incredibly, Jamie was resting on one of the track's barriers, a metal fence with three rungs. One of his feet was on the lowest rung of the fence, and the other . . . was about to be crushed by whatever hydraulic mechanism raised and lowered the curves of the track. Panicked (and this *was* a time for a loud voice!), I screamed, "Jamie!" and dashed to pull his left leg out of harm's way. My timing was like unto the timing of heroes in science fiction and action movies who disarm the self-destruct device with 00:01 reading on the liquid-crystal display: I yanked his leg just as the track came down on his sneaker. The sneaker was briefly trapped, and was freed only when the track operator raised the track again briefly. Jamie's foot was fine. But if I hadn't been right there, at just that moment? Or if I had been up in the stands, doing professor work? I have to think that the front half of Jamie's left foot would have been crushed, damaged beyond repair.

OK, I have stopped shuddering now. His foot is fine. He is perfectly all right.

The episode highlighted something important for me, quite apart from the obvious *OMG my kid's foot is going to be crushed by a huge machine*. Thanks to the disability rights movement and its academic offshoot, disability studies, we have become accustomed to understanding disability not as a matter of individual bodies and minds but as a matter of forms of social organization. In the standard disability-studies example, wheelchair users may have *impairments* that do not allow them to walk, but they are *disabled* by the social arrangements that do not provide curb cuts, ramps, kneeling buses, or widened doorways and bathroom stalls. The distinction between impairment and disability is critical to any understanding of how and why disability is a social phenomenon, and it is especially pertinent, I think, to people with physical disabilities, many of whom can function reasonably well in the world if they have closed captioning or Braille or ASL interpreters or ramps or curb cuts, kneeling buses, and widened doorways. It is arguably less useful for people with intellectual disabilities or mental illness, who might need more complicated accommodations and/or medication and who might find themselves "disabled" in every conceivable form of social organization.

The "social model" is an absolutely essential corrective to any of the usual "medical" understandings of disability as deficit, debility, or disease. And yet I cannot think of Jamie's brush with serious injury *except* in terms of deficit, of loss. No disability rights advocate or disability-studies scholar would say that it does not matter whether people with disabilities acquire more disabilities. One can say this without re-stigmatizing disability across the board: Jamie is a young man with Down syndrome, and Down syndrome seems to me an ordinary form of intraspecies variation. It is not a "disease" that needs to be eradicated from the species. I do not waste my time (and will not waste yours) thinking about what Jamie would be like if he did not have Down syndrome; if he did not have Down syndrome, he would not be Jamie. We love him for the person he is, and do not worry about the person he might have been if he were an entirely different person. All that said, we would rather that his foot not be crushed by a huge machine. That would entail a disability we would consider to be a significant loss.

◻ ◻ ◻

In his early years, Jamie was so well treated by every medical professional he encountered—from the NICU nurse, Kay, who devised an effective way of bottle-feeding him, to all the occupational and speech therapists he saw in his early childhood—that it never occurred to me that anyone would offer him a lower standard of care because of his disability. So it took me longer than I would like to admit, in retrospect, to figure out what was going on with his dentist. When Jamie was eight and a half,

I asked his dentist why Jamie still had so many baby teeth and why all his teeth were so crooked. I was assured that it was no problem. I was incredulous; how, I wondered, is it *not* a problem that his baby teeth are hanging around so long and preventing his adult teeth from coming in straight? Within the week I got a second opinion from another dentist who, quite sensibly, told me that this was potentially a serious problem and that Jamie should be referred to an orthodontist who would do some tooth extractions. I can only think that the first dentist, whom we never saw again, was thinking *C'mon, the kid has Down syndrome, and you're worried about a little thing like his teeth?* (We have since encountered a similarly deplorable attitude with an ophthalmologist.)

Later that same year, Janet learned that Jamie had developed sleep apnea, a condition for which a tonsillectomy is usually recommended. So Jamie went into surgery for a tonsillectomy and a multiple tooth extraction. We wanted to have these things done before we left Champaign, Illinois, and all the doctors most familiar with him (we would be moving at the end of the month), and we wanted to combine the procedures rather than submit Jamie to general anesthesia twice with his possibly compromised airways. (Children with Down syndrome typically have smaller nasal and throat cavities.) Jamie's tonsils and five of his teeth were to be removed in two simultaneous surgical procedures, involving one surgeon from ear-nose-throat and another surgeon from oral-maxillofacial in a plan that required only eleven months of preparation and a couple of reams of hospital paperwork.

Jamie had very little idea of what would happen to him before he went in for surgery that day—and what pained us most, in the aftermath, was his bewilderment. Months earlier, he'd been subjected to the requisite sleep apnea test, which required him to show up at the hospital for an overnight stay during which he would have an array of electrodes fastened to his skull. Janet accompanied him and assured him that although he would have to wear some "wires," everything would be all right. Jamie responded by asking whether "Lemur," his little stuffed lemur (all his stuffed animals had such names, like "Anteater" and "Buffalo" and "Gibbon"; only later did he get more fanciful and start giving his animals names like Glenn Close, Mister Kooshduck, and TV Woman

Show), could have a wire too; the hospital tech staff went along, dutifully prepping Lemur for his electrode. All this was very cute, as was Jamie's faint but palpable delight, in his post-surgery bed, at having four small stuffed animals stacked on his bed, all of whom would fall over when we pulled Anteater's nose. But in the exhausting weeks that followed his surgery, nothing was cute and nothing was delightful.

Jamie had his surgery on a Tuesday morning, and his doctors determined that it would be best for him to stay overnight. Janet stayed with him. He coughed up some blood that night, but his surgeon came in to look at him and decided that all was well. Janet, now on high alert, didn't sleep again until I arrived early the next morning. Jamie was watched carefully all day, particularly for signs of dehydration, and was released later that afternoon.

We told Jamie that he needed to drink lots of juice and Gatorade. Jamie's throat was raw and five of his teeth were missing; he didn't feel like doing anything but watching TV and drifting in and out of sleep, which was most unlike him. Janet kept up a steady flow of liquids—and warnings, gentle but firm: You have to have fluids, and if you don't drink them through your mouth, we'll have to go back to the hospital for an IV. And you don't want that, so here's your juice, and your pillow, and your lemur, too.

On Friday morning Janet left Jamie in the playroom for a moment, put on some coffee, and then came back to find him bleeding from the mouth. Lucy the Dog, with her preternatural dog-sense and her vigilant love of Jamie, had run into the kitchen to alert Janet that something was wrong: he had popped a bleeder, as they say in the business. But we didn't know that at the time. All we knew was that we needed to get him to the hospital immediately for another dose of general anesthesia and (at the very least) a cauterization of whatever had opened in his throat. Jamie looked at me desperately and pointed to the blood that had soaked his shirt. "Please clean?" he asked in a tremulous voice.

Jamie was treated and released on the same day. Although the morning had been dramatic and heartrending, it gradually became clear that the bleeding was only a minor glitch, that a quick cauterization would in fact do the job. So Jamie was all right physically by Friday night, but psychologically he was shaken. For seventy-two hours he'd been told that if he drank his juice and Gatorade he would get better and wouldn't have to go back to the hospital. He'd done as he was told, but to no avail: he'd gone back to the hospital anyway, to anesthesia and grogginess and a fresh IV in the back of his aching hand. And now he was inconsolable.

The weekend was terrible. Because we would be moving to Penn State in three weeks, Janet had to fly to Pennsylvania to close the deal on our new house. Nick and I had Jamie for four solid days. Jamie doesn't eat sweets and was oblivious to all the nurses and assorted well-wishers who tried to cheer him up with meaningless promises of ice cream and popsicles. His throat was now so sore and scraped that even the tiniest little swallows were excruciating, and I had to force fluids into him every day along with 10cc of Tylenol every four hours and antibiotics every six. To get anything into him I had to immobilize his limbs and his head with one arm while squirting a syringe into his mouth with the other. The pain this caused him—especially when he protested vocally—almost made the Tylenol seem worse than useless. It was like his infancy all over again, except that now he was nearly ten, and fully conscious of everything I was saying to him, and very strong in resistance—though he was weakening measurably every day, and that wasn't a welcome development either. I took him to the movies again and again, hoping he would forget himself and drink some soda along the way; back then, he would routinely drain a large cup before the opening credits finished rolling. We saw *Shrek* four times in five days, and Jamie drank some Sprite and Gatorade each time, much to my relief. Thank you, Shrek.

You know how doctors and nurses ask you to report your pain on a scale of 1 to 10? Well, as child-care stories go, this is maybe a 2. We are talking about tonsils and teeth, not about cancer or seizure disorders. Though Jamie endured serious pain for days and lost eight pounds in one week—one-eighth his body weight at the time—he recovered fully and rapidly. But what made this tonsillectomy (and its aftermath) so disturbing was precisely the realization that Jamie could not have given his "informed consent" to the surgery in any meaningful sense of the term. I am aware that the standard of informed consent is legally irrelevant here: Jamie was a child. And because the law renders it moot as to whether children under eighteen can give their informed consent to their medical treatment, the question of what kinds of medical treatment parents and guardians can choose for—or withhold from—their children is profoundly difficult. I believe the state should not have the power to coerce prospective parents into having children they do not want, but that the state should have the power to compel parents to vaccinate their children against common childhood diseases. (That is because I believe a child is a very different thing from a fetus, an embryo, or a zygote.) And, yet, should parents have the right to forgo life-saving procedures that would save their children but would conflict with their religious beliefs? Or the right to provide their deaf children with cochlear implants? (My answers are an uneasy no and an uneasy yes, and I know others vehemently disagree.) My ethical dilemma about Jamie's medical treatment was far simpler: I agonized that he didn't understand what was going to happen to him, he didn't understand what *was* happening to him, and he didn't understand how long it was going to keep happening. Although I told him that his throat would get better and would not hurt any more, I know there must have been times when he wondered if *this* was how he was going to feel for the rest of his life. At one point I imagined, watching him tongue the space where his teeth had been, that he had begun to fear that he'd lose a couple more teeth every time he fell asleep.

Today Jamie knows this story well, and he now understands what the hell all the fuss was about. But only gradually did we find out what Jamie thought about it. That summer, after we moved, Janet tried to prep him gently for the next phase—namely, braces—and we started shopping around State College for dentists who have experience dealing with kids with special needs. But Janet's attempts to explain things to Jamie, which included the reassuring information that Nick had had braces too, had a perverse effect: she told him that he would probably get braces when he was ten, and so, when he turned ten, on September 16, 2001, he insisted that he was "still nine" or "almost ten." After a few days of this mystifying behavior, I finally got him to tell me why he wasn't ten: "I will be eleven and have no bracelet," he replied. Apparently he had come to the conclusion, literal-minded as he is, that he would be fitted with braces from September 16, 2001, to September 15, 2002, and this was his way of letting us know he didn't care for the idea. Well, as it happened, he didn't get braces when he was ten. His adult teeth came in just fine as a result of the multiple tooth extraction, but we still weren't sure just how aggressive we wanted to be about crooked teeth. Our options ranged from the extreme—a procedure so complex and intervention-laden that I referred to it as skull replacement surgery—to the laissez-faire—let's just chill and see if any problems develop down the road. After a bunch of consultations, including consultations with Jamie, we agreed that braces would be sufficient, and that oral-maxillofacial surgery would be going way overboard.

We asked ourselves whether we were pursuing even this mild course of action for aesthetic reasons. Was it really just a matter of crooked teeth? As you might imagine, there is a spirited debate about such matters in the bioethics community, one version of which can be found in the 2006 Hastings Center report *Surgically Shaping Children: Technology, Ethics and the Pursuit of Normality*. Hard as it is for us to believe, there are people out there who actually approve of elective surgery for their children with Down syndrome, hoping that this will render their facial features more like those of their nondisabled peers. In 2002, Janet wrote a brilliant paper about this; she has never published it, though it would have made a substantial contribution to disability studies. In the course of her research, she discovered a rich and disturbing phenomenon wherein parents feared that their children would look less like them (that is, the parents) than like other children with the same condition, as if their *real* family, and their family resemblances, were their fellow humans with Down syndrome. And she argued that while some surgeries might be medically necessary (for cleft lip and palate, for instance), surgical interventions for children with Down syndrome constituted a pernicious form of "normalization" that is best resisted. That was one of the reasons why we decided against more aggressive measures that involved putting a spanner in Jamie's mouth to widen his palate. We didn't want to reshape him. We simply wanted to minimize his chances of having oral health problems as a teenager.

Much later, we had cause to reflect not only on these decisions but on Nick's dental history as well. By the time Nick graduated from college in 2008, he had developed a strangely prominent jaw, thanks to the fact that the upper half of his mouth had not grown out properly. The oral-maxillofacial surgeon we consulted suggested that this was the result of excessively aggressive orthodontics when Nick was a child, which would mean that we wound up subjecting Nick to surgery at twenty-one—and six weeks of being unable to talk or eat solid food—thanks to the fact that we initially subjected him to braces as a tween. Nick, of course, gave his informed consent to this; he was not entirely "subjected" to it. We learned of other parents and children in the same position, regretting what they had thought was their diligence in seeing to their children's dental health. Nick endured those six weeks patiently, carrying around a dry-erase board and writing us many notes, and he even managed to smile when Jamie told a waiter in a local restaurant, "This is my brother, Nick. He won't eat and he won't talk."

Jamie got his braces about three years after his tonsillectomy. At first they were painful and weird, and his speech was unintelligible for a few days. He needed wax to soften the feeling of having a bunch of metal in his mouth, but he got used to the metal and ditched the wax, and he got used to using one of those tiny between-the-braces brushes. Given that his initial resistance was so strong as to make him abjure his tenth birthday, he was really quite mature about the whole thing, and we praised him heartily and often for being such a great kid about his braces. And I promised him that when they finally came off, he would be allowed to eat . . . a Slim Jim! Every so often Janet and I would take him to the orthodontist to have the braces adjusted, repaired, tweaked, refined, augmented, or replaced, so Jamie understood that this was a process rather than a one-time thing. There was one almost-scary moment when one of his wires popped loose from a molar bracket, so that he had a fine metal wire sticking out on the right side of his mouth. "Michael," he said, calling me into the TV room, "I need help." I asked him to hold very, very still while I cut the wire with, well, you know, wire cutters—something I never thought I would be putting anywhere near my child's mouth. I barely managed to keep the cut wire from falling into his throat. There was also one almost-comic moment when I drove him to school after a braces appointment only to realize that I'd left his backpack at the orthodontist's. "What's the matter, Michael?" he asked when he saw me slap my forehead. "Oh, sweetie, we have to go all the way back to the doctor's and get your bag," I said. "I'm just doing everything wrong today. I feel like Neville Longbottom," invoking the perpetually forgetful Harry Potter character. Jamie put his hand on my shoulder and consoled me: "You are not like Neville Longbottom, Michael. It's OK."

Jamie's orthodontist visits varied widely in intensity and duration. Sometimes he would zip in and out after a routine checkup determined that everything was fine; sometimes he would need new brackets, new wires, or other procedures that involved keeping his mouth open for long periods (and keeping very still) while people poked at his teeth with metal implements and shone the heating lamp on them to dry the glue. Jamie quickly learned to ask for the zip in–zip out kind of visit upon arriving at the doctor's office. "We will just talk and have no tools," he would propose to the lab assistants, who would usually reply by telling him that maybe they would have to use just one or two tools. Janet and I traded off taking Jamie to each appointment, but if one of us endured a thrash visit, then the other one usually had to go to the next two, so as to spread the parental dental-care burden around as evenly as possible.

But at long last Gehenna froze over, pigs learned to fly, and the braces came off eighteen months after they went on . . . whereupon Jamie learned that he would have to wear retainers for another six months or more.

Retainers! Jamie complained strenuously, feeling he'd been betrayed and hornswoggled yet again. We assured him that it was only a short-term thing, and we reminded him how terrific he had been about his braces, and we renewed the promise of Slim Jims Yet to Come. And so Jamie went back to the orthodontist for the forty-ninth time (or thereabouts) and had an impression of his teeth made. He hated that. Who wouldn't? Who gets up in the morning and says, "You know what, I hope I can lie back in an orthodontist's chair and have my mouth filled with pink goo today"?

Janet and I felt sheepish that we hadn't told Jamie what wearing his retainers would entail. Actually, we didn't know ourselves; Janet thought he'd need retainers only at night, and I was completely ignorant of everything, including when to take them out and when to leave them in. I suspect you know where this part of the story is going, because almost every teenager who has ever had retainers has lost them at some point. Here it goes.

Part the First. One day I picked Jamie up from the Y and discovered that his upper retainer was missing. He said maybe it slipped out when he was swimming. "While you were swimming?" I asked. "I don't know," he shrugged. "I'm not sure." Oy. Would it be at the bottom of the pool, perhaps? So one of the Y staff and I searched the entire building, looking for a little black plastic thing with a small metal strip in the front. Why were Jamie's retainers black, you ask? Because he'd rejected all the more colorful designs as "too weird," that's why. He hadn't wanted colored brackets on his braces, either. He's just a basic-black kinda guy. Finally one of the YMCA staff remembered that Jamie had taken out the retainer during lunch and put it in a napkin. So I started to comb through the lunchroom garbage can—the nice, full garbage can—musing as I did so on the fact that his retainer was very like the color of the Hefty bag . . . when I found it! I took the opportunity to teach Jamie the phrase "needle in a haystack," because he used to have trouble with idiomatic expressions. He thought that was very amusing. But I also took the opportunity to tell him, sternly, never to lose his retainers again or he'd have to go back to the orthodontist for another round of pink goo. So he learned his lesson and never lost his retainers again. His parents, however, were not so fortunate.

Part the Second. A few months later, Jamie and I went out for pizza and a movie (pizza and popcorn: crucial five-servings-a-day components of the USDA food pyramid). I told him he could leave his retainers out for a while, and I'd carry them for him. Why did I do such a stupid thing? Because I was being smart. I thought ahead and reasoned that it would be a bad idea for him to be popping out his black retainers in a dark movie theater. So at the pizza place I wrapped the retainers in a napkin . . . and by the end of our meal, the table was covered with napkins. This was some seriously unctuous pizza we were eating. I tossed the whole mess into the garbage. And even though Jamie was, by this point, vigilant about putting his retainers back in, he didn't say anything as we left the mall, precisely because I'd told him not to worry about them until after the movie.

I realized what I'd done when we got to the octoplex parking lot and found that I hadn't, after all, put the all-important napkin in my pocket. Panicking, I told Jamie we were driving back to the mall and that I wanted him to stay in the car while I ran to the pizza joint, because I'd lost his retainers and it was all my fault. "I'll just look through the garbage again," I assured him. "I won't be long." "Like a needle in a haystack," Jamie replied.

But this time the Force was not with me. I told the guy at the pizza joint that I'd lost my son's retainers by throwing them in the trash, and he hoisted the garbage bag into the back of the kitchen and sifted through it with me, but, alas, his extraordinary helpfulness was offset by the fact that he didn't speak much English and seemed not to have a very clear idea of what he was looking for. I tried to insist that I could go through the mess by myself, but to no avail, and he kept tossing things from one garbage bag into another while I tried to unwrap napkin after napkin while sifting through paper plates, pizza crusts, half-eaten calzones, and discarded salads. "You don't understand," I wanted to say. "If I don't find these damn things, my kid has to do the pink goo in the mouth thing again, through no fault of his own, just after I threatened him with having to do the pink goo in the mouth thing should he ever lose his retainers." And I thought again of how he had had to return to the hospital after his tonsillectomy-and-tooth-extraction even though he had been a good kid and listened to his mother about drinking plenty of Gatorade.

We reached the end of the garbage. I wanted to give a second look to some of the garbage the pizza guy had ripped his way through, but he insisted, "No, is not here," so I gave up, paid him five dollars for his time, and sprinted back to the car, near tears. "Jamie, I'm so sorry," I said when I climbed into the driver's seat. "I couldn't find them. I looked and looked, but I couldn't find them, and it's all my fault."

Sweetly, Jamie tried to console me, just as he had when I'd forgotten his backpack. "It's OK, Michael. It's not your fault."

"Oh, yes, it is my fault," I said. "I threw your retainers in the garbage, and now we have to get new ones." Jamie nodded, but then that little light bulb went on and he asked about the goo. "Yes, we have to do the goo again," I replied, "and I'm so, so sorry. . . . You didn't do anything wrong. . . ." Well, this was just unbearable. Jamie had become too mature, at fourteen, for any squalling or fussing or acting out, but he was stunned. Betrayed yet again! Would the Dental Drama never end?

"Look," I said. "I'll tell you what. I'll call the doctor, and we'll ask for new retainers, and after you have the goo, I'll buy you that Slim Jim we talked about. Is that a deal?" It was a deal. Still, I kept apologizing all through the rest of the day (and of course there was a fresh round of apologies to be made when I told Janet what happened), to the point at which Jamie finally said, "It's not your fault, Michael. It's my fault."

"What?" I exclaimed. "It's not your fault at all! You did everything I asked, and I threw your retainers in the dang garbage. It's completely my fault."

"No, it's my fault," he insisted, and this went on for a while.

Now, I didn't believe he really understood the concept of "fault" at stake here. In those days, he and Janet and I had an odd little routine in which I would say, "I think this is *Lucy's* fault," he would laugh, turn to Janet, and say, "Janet, say it," whereupon Janet would say, "Michael, you can't blame Lucy; she's just an animal." Jamie loved this routine and often embellished it by telling me that I couldn't blame Lucy because she was, as he put it, "an animal companion" or, sometimes, "an animal companionship." I wasn't entirely sure that Jamie got the joke behind this routine—which is to say I wasn't sure he understood why you can't "blame" an animal, which is also to say I wasn't sure he understood that the concept of blame relies on a whole host of other concepts having to do with probability, risk, responsibility, consequences, right and wrong. But as it turned out, Jamie did indeed understand what he was saying when he claimed that it was his fault the retainers got tossed in the garbage. He was saying, as he has since explained to me, that he should have kept better track of his retainers. Which is true, but the fact remains that I didn't bring along the bright-orange retainer case to put them in while he took them out, and I put them in a napkin and tossed them in the garbage. So really, in the end, it's completely my fault.

We got new retainers. Jamie hated the goo, of course, but he did much better with it the second time, and I promised promised promised we wouldn't be doing it again. And then I bought him a good, chewy Slim Jim. "How is that stuff?" I asked skeptically as we drove away from the convenience store, the one that stocks dozens of varieties of Slim Jims and beef jerky, right next to the big display of dozens of varieties of chewing tobacco. "*Really* great," Jamie replied. I told him he couldn't get black retainers again, just in case they ever wound up in the garbage. But he once again rejected all the day-glo colors as too weird and insisted on black. So we compromised. We got camouflage-colored retainers. At least they had patches of green, brown, and yellow in them.

I learned that our family dental plan only covered one set of retainers, so the final tally for that exceptionally expensive day was this:

Chicken Little matinee: $12

Popcorn and soda: $10

Tip for the helpful pizza guy: $5

Pizza and new retainers: $400

Jamie: priceless

Part the Third. Yes, despite all my promises to Jamie in Part the Second, there is a Part the Third. How shall I put this? Ah, yes, I know: #@$%&*@%$#@&! In the summer of 2006 Janet taught one of her four-week courses in Ireland. Jamie and I flew to Dublin to join her for the final two or three days, and then we all flew to France for a week's vacation. To catch our flight out of Dublin, we had to get up at 3 a.m. Somehow, in our stupor, we packed everything except Jamie's retainers.

Jamie tells that story to this day. It is The Story of When My Parents Forgot My Retainers, and for Jamie it is part of the trip-to-Dublin saga, which began with The Morning I Had Coca-Cola for Breakfast. (There literally was nothing else in the Dublin airport for him to drink.) When we returned to the United States, there was more pink goo, and another Slim Jim. And then, only then, did our long Dental Drama come to a close. Retainers 3.0 were the last edition; Jamie wore them for a full year and he has been unencumbered since the age of sixteen.

□   □   □

Braces and retainers are ordinary. Pneumonia is not. Not long after he got his braces, poor kid, he developed a persistent cough. Janet had a bad feeling about this, and her bad feeling was confirmed when a savvy young doctor ordered an X-ray and discovered a telltale white blotch on his lungs. We will always be grateful to her for ordering that X-ray, because it made us watch Jamie very carefully. And when he seemed to be in trouble that night, we packed him up and took him to the emergency room.

It was a rainy Monday night. In the back seat, Jamie was muttering, "I don't wanna go to the ER" and a wide range of variations thereon, like "No ER, try other kind" and "Maybe go someplace else instead of ER." In his younger days he had lots of idiosyncratic ways of expressing aversion, the first of which I heard when he was six years old. I took him to the rainforest room at the Indianapolis Zoo, which was filled with uncaged birds and snakes, and he cried out, with all the eloquence a young disabled child could muster, "How 'bout try exit." I learned that day that he had a visceral fear of birds. Apparently he was bitten by a bird as a very young child, but he's never given us the details. He is much calmer around them now, as evidenced by his careful retreat from a large, uncaged macaw in an Omaha zoo (he was seventeen at the time), saying softly, "I mean you no harm. I mean you no harm." But on this rainy late-summer night, when Jamie realized that his mild, reasonable objections weren't having any effect, he balled his fists and announced, quietly but emphatically, "I *hate* the ER."

He had been taught at school not to use the word "hate," so this was roughly the equivalent of dropping an F-bomb. Jamie waited a few long seconds to see if we would react in some way. We didn't. How could we? We don't care much for the ER either. And, as it turned out, we were in for an especially wrenching ER visit in which Jamie had to be restrained to a bed while he got his IV—and once again, he was not yet capable of understanding why any of this might be necessary.

Then we heard from the back seat, in a markedly different voice, "Oh! You hate the ER. OK, then, we'll go someplace else."

Janet and I exchanged looks. "Jamie," I said at last, "are you making up words you want us to say?"

"Yes."

I told him that he was very clever. And I thought this might be a good strategy for general use: when all else fails, try making up things you want your interlocutors to say! You might even fool your parents into thinking that one of them is actually speaking! Or you can try it with creditors ("Really, it's OK if you skip this month—we won't mind") or political opponents ("Why, that's true, my administration *has* been incompetent and corrupt!"). But though this desperate stratagem marked a new stage in Jamie's verbal and cognitive development, it did not work.

When he woke up in his hospital bed the following morning, Jamie got it into his head that it was now time to go home. He insisted his breathing was fine and that he had no more coughs.

"That's great, Jamie," I replied. "But there just isn't enough oxygen in your blood right now." At thirteen, he knew enough about the circulatory system to know that it ferries oxygen from the lungs, so he knew what that meant. "Here, look at this," I said, pointing to the pulse oximeter. "This machine measures how much oxygen is in your blood, just by that little red-light thing on your finger. It is the same machine you had when you were a little baby! And right now what does it say?"

"Ninety-two," Jamie read.

"Right, ninety-two. That's kind of low for you. You need to be up around ninety-seven or ninety-eight to be really OK." Jamie took this in very carefully and would check the pulse oximeter periodically throughout the day, in between watching TV and playing with stuffed animals, all of them now garlanded with more fanciful names. Suddenly, late in the afternoon, he announced, "Ninety-seven! We can go home now!"

He was really getting the hang of this thing.

But just as Jamie had to learn that you don't get all better mere minutes after taking your medicine, now he had to learn that his O-sats needed to stay high over a long period before he could be discharged. We would be in the hospital for one more night, just to be safe. And Jamie's understanding of oxygen saturation levels was secured a few hours later that evening, when I said or did something that cracked him up. I don't remember what it was; all I remember is that within seconds, the pulse oximeter reading plunged into the low eighties, the alarm went off, and Jamie totally understood what had happened. Here he was, gasping for breath with laughter, and the machine was registering it with machine-like accuracy. So *that's* what this whole oxygen-in-the-blood thing is about.

Jamie has not been hospitalized since. I now have his power of attorney (with his informed consent), so I have the legal authority to make medical decisions for him as an adult, and the right—though I hope I will never have to use it—to override his wishes. I think this puts me in a paternalistic relationship with regard to Jamie, which is somewhat justified, perhaps, insofar as I am his father. And, in fact, that paternalistic relationship extends to all aspects of his health. I think of Andrew Solomon, quoting Harlan Lane's complaint that "the relation of the hearing parent to the young deaf child is a microcosm of the relation of hearing society to the deaf community; it is paternalistic, medicalizing, and ethnocentric," and replying, "This is true, but Lane seems not to recognize that parents have a definitional license to be paternalistic."

One afternoon, when Janet and I found that Jamie had somehow consumed four cans of Coke in the course of half a day, we gave him strict limits: two sodas per day and no sodas before noon. (This is why it is so memorable to him that he had Coke for breakfast in Dublin.) Admittedly, there are many parents out there who restrict their children to zero sodas per day, and we admire them even as we admit we don't have their resolve. And that one time at the bowling alley when Jamie ate *eight slices* of pizza, as reported to me by the people in charge when I came to pick him up? That's not gonna happen again, and Jamie knows it. The first few times he was away from parental oversight, he indulged himself with abandon—as when he went on an overnight trip to Villanova University with the Special Olympics volleyball team and decided to splurge on shovelfuls of ranch dressing. Now he knows he has to have self-control.

This is true of any child, and of any parent's paternalistic relationship with his or her children. But again, it has special resonance for people with intellectual disabilities, especially for people with Down syndrome, who are susceptible to obesity. Jamie is in relatively good shape on that front, but it always bears watching carefully. When I think of Jamie's health and hygiene, I always think of the scholarly article that has my very favorite subtitle in all of academe. The title is boringly straightforward: "Balancing the Right to Habilitation with the Right to Personal Liberties." The subtitle is totally awesome: "The Rights of People with Developmental Disabilities to Eat Too Many Doughnuts and Take a Nap." Jamie never eats donuts and almost never naps, but you get the point. He is an adult now, and he is entitled to somewhat more autonomy than he had as a child. How much more, it's hard to say. We—Janet, Jamie, and I—decide these things day by day.

You may have surmised by now that we have exceptionally good health benefits at Penn State, even if we have to fork over $400 every time we lose a set of retainers. And we do. But we recently moved Jamie, now an adult, off our medical plan and onto the plan that (we hope) will serve him for the rest of his life, Medicaid. That was the time I asked Jamie to sign over his power of attorney, and that was when I created a special-needs trust for him, with Nick as the administrator. I had already taken care of Jamie's Supplemental Security Income, so between that and Medicaid, he cannot own more than $2,000 in assets.

But, you may be asking, Jamie has parents who can afford the care he needs, so why should he be part of the machinery of (what remains of) the social-welfare state at all? To answer that question, dear reader, I offer you the little rant I promised at the outset of this chapter.

□ □ □

If you follow national debates about health care, surely you remember the story: It was the fall of 2007, and then president George W. Bush had recently vetoed an expansion of the State Children's Health Insurance Program (S-CHIP). In response, the Democrats tapped a twelve-year-old, Graeme Frost, to deliver the response to Bush's weekly radio address. Frost had sustained significant brain injuries in a 2004 car crash (his family's car hit a patch of black ice) and was a beneficiary of S-CHIP—as was his sister Gemma, whose brain injuries were still more severe. After their horrific collision, both children had fallen into comas—Graeme for days, Gemma for weeks. Gemma had an open skull fracture, shattering her left eye orbit, and when she emerged from her coma, doctors planned reconstructive eye surgery on her eye—but cancelled it, according to the Kennedy Krieger Institute in Baltimore, where the Frost children did their rehabilitation therapy, "when they discovered an abscess filled with shards of wood and glass."

The Kennedy Krieger Institute's *Potential* magazine wrote up the Frosts in 2005 in a determinedly upbeat essay titled "Dynamic Duo." It is, as the strictures of the genre demand, a story of arduous and painful recovery: "Graeme's injury primarily affected his motor skills. He could not walk or swallow and relied on a naso-gastric tube for nourishment for nearly five months. Gemma's core issues were cognitive; she could walk, but couldn't remember how to talk, what many words meant, how to dress or how to brush her teeth. 'She had to relearn everything,' says the children's mother, Bonnie." But precisely because the article was written in 2005, it couldn't tell the triumphant end of the story—in which little Graeme Frost walks the long road back to something like normal health, all the way to the point at which he can step up and respond to Republican attacks on so-called socialized medicine by presenting himself and his family as the public face of public health care.

And surely you remember what happened next. Graeme's appeal touched even the flintiest hearts among the conservative commentariat. Michelle Malkin, founder of the *Hot Air* and *Twitchy* websites, broke down into uncontrollable sobs. Former *National Review* contributor Mark Steyn vowed to give up drink and bile, and solemnly pledged to devote his life to the sick and the poor. And Senate Majority Leader Mitch McConnell, his voice cracking on the Senate floor, uttered the words that have since come to define his career as a public servant: "God bless us, every one."

Well, actually, that didn't happen. What happened instead was one of the vilest episodes in the history of conservative commentary, which is really saying something. The right-wing blogosphere launched an all-out attack on the Frosts, spreading misinformation about their very modest financial status. Malkin herself actually traveled to Baltimore to snoop around the Frosts' house, which turned out to be one in a block of row houses, and the website *Free Republic* helpfully posted the Frosts' address for anyone else who might want to explore the matter further. Senator McConnell, for his part, issued an e-mail that repeated many of the conservative talking points and asked publicly, "Could the Dems really have done that bad of a job vetting this family?"

It was one thing when Rush Limbaugh attacked Michael J. Fox, accusing him of exaggerating the symptoms of Parkinson's disease; we have come to expect that of Limbaugh. But Michael J. Fox, whatever the degree of his frailty, was an adult. The Frost children were twelve and nine. You would think they would be granted a Children's Exemption from that kind of vitriol, but then you would think wrong.

In *Life as We Know It*, I marveled at conservatives' antipathy to health-care and social-support services for children with disabilities: "It is a strange land, no doubt," I wrote, "adequate only to the imagination of Dickensian satire, where leading politicians and self-appointed moralists talk endlessly about 'family values' while kicking the crutches out from under Tiny Tim." In response, one of my former high school classmates, a conservative Catholic long associated with the *National Review*, wrote to me to complain about the characterization. No one, he said (and I paraphrase), is kicking the crutches out from anyone, and I should acknowledge that there are people of good will on both sides of the aisle. Today, I wonder: Did I go too far? Did I substitute caricature for reasoned political debate? Or perhaps did I underestimate the sheer viciousness of some people on the Right, failing to anticipate the possibility that, after they had kicked the crutches out from under Tiny Tim, they might try to harass and smear the entire Cratchit family? For now, I'm going to go with "underestimate the sheer viciousness."

And yet that wasn't what struck me most about the S-CHIP debacle. What that national freak-out crystallized was something really remarkable about our debates about health care in the United States: nobody—not liberals, not conservatives, not libertarians, not the thirty remaining socialists in the country—ever says the word "disability." We simply do not think about disability when we talk about health care. And yet Graeme and Gemma Frost were children with disabilities. They were not described that way, but the fact is that they were children with disabilities. And you know what else? Some of the people on Medicare and Medicaid and Supplemental Security Income are people with disabilities. Your parents, your cousins, your grand-nephews, your neighbors—some of them are people with disabilities. They have autism or Alzheimer's or arthritis or achondroplasia or carpal tunnel syndrome or Crohn's disease or Parkinson's or Huntington's or cerebral palsy or MS or Down syndrome or traumatic brain injury; they are deaf or blind or paraplegic or schizophrenic. Some of them don't have a diagnosis at all, or, if they do, it is "pervasive developmental delay," which means "we have no idea what's going on." Some of them came into the world that way; some inherited a genetic anomaly; some caught a virus; some, like the Frosts, simply happened to be in a car that hit a patch of black ice one winter night. And you might be one of them yourself—if not now, maybe later. One never knows.

So why don't we talk about disability when we talk about health care? If the previous paragraph gave you pause, if you stopped for a moment and shuddered at the thought that you or a loved one might lose your faculties, physical or cognitive, then that's probably a good indicator of what's going on here: individually and collectively, we are in denial.

And, of course, in a sense we have to be. No one of sound mind and body can wake up every day and make the coffee with a visceral awareness that their soundness of mind and body is a happy accident. None of us wants to start up the car in the knowledge that a random patch of invisible ice can put us or our children into comas, none of us wants to think that we could lose a foot in an indoor track facility, and none of us wants to make our retirement plans on the assumption that we will be too infirm to enjoy most of our retirement.

I emphatically include myself in this. I have been healthy for most of my life, barring a few years of depression, a couple of broken fingers, some recent high blood pressure, and an array of the usual minor illnesses. I played "adult league" hockey into my late forties, and because so many hockey injuries in recent years have been brain injuries, I worry especially about my brain. I rely on it often, and in fact am using it right this very minute. I am every bit as horrified by the idea of becoming mentally incapacitated as anyone else; I like my present mental capacities as they are. I can't even think the thought of not being able to think the thoughts I'm thinking. I would also like my feet, and Jamie's, to remain uncrushed.

When we think about the uninsured, for some reason we tend to think of the healthy twenty-five-year-old who doesn't see the point of buying insurance he or she mostly doesn't need. Sometimes we think of families like the Frosts, who couldn't afford private insurance before their car crash and couldn't get it when their children acquired serious disabilities. But apparently millions of Americans think of health insurance as a personal calculation, like putting only *just so much* change in parking meters. You make that gamble: You leave your car too long, you get a ticket, it's your problem. Or you make that decision: You go without insurance, you get sick, fine, you knew the risks. And since the Frosts were struggling but not utterly destitute, they shouldn't get any assistance from government. It's all on them.

Quite apart from the cruelty of this devil-take-the-hindmost approach to health care, what's really stunning is how profoundly foolish it is. Sure, people know (or know that they have to pretend not to know) the risks of smoking, or drinking heavily, or eating bacon double cheeseburgers with a side of ranch dressing, or riding a motorcycle without wearing a helmet. But most disabilities don't work that way. They're not the result of calculations and risk management. Only the most sociopathically callous among us would say, "Jack totally deserved that brain injury from falling off that ladder. . . . He knew the risks when he went up to clean the gutters." And to this day, no one has ever said to me, "You knew what you were getting into when you had Jamie. . . . You pay for him."

But the question of what I was getting into with Jamie opens onto a most curious political conundrum. No one has ever blamed me or Janet for bringing Jamie to term (OK, she did that part), for loving him fiercely and raising him among his nondisabled peers. On the contrary, many people assume that if we have a child with Down syndrome, we must be pro-life across the board (as, no doubt, did the family that dropped us when they saw the Kerry/Edwards sign in our yard). And the reason they make that assumption—even though we display all the social markers of Liberals in Good Standing, being pinot-grigio-drinking, *New York Times*-reading, gay-friendly college professors—is that there is, after all, one area of American political life in which people talk about disability and health care in so many words. And that is when the Sarah Palins and Rick Santorums among us take to the podium to accuse liberals of aborting fetuses with disabilities. I will say more about this in my final chapter, in which I explain once and for all the meaning of life, but pregnancies—and terminated pregnancies—are a critical part of how we think about how we talk about health.

For the claim that liberals are all about eliminating Down syndrome from the population is a popular meme among the conservative punditocracy, as well. Michael Barone covered himself in glory in 2008 when he remarked, "The liberal media attacked Sarah Palin because she did not abort her Down syndrome baby. They wanted her to kill that child. . . . I'm talking about my media colleagues with whom I've worked for 35 years." Barone later apologized, saying he "was attempting to be humorous and . . . went over the line." (Which is totally understandable, because that joke could have been really funny with the right delivery.) In more decorous language, every few years *Washington Post* columnist George F. Will writes a touching column about his son Jon, who has Down syndrome and a deep love of baseball to rival his father's; but I have yet to see a column on Jon Will that does not take a swipe at pro-choice liberals who are allegedly responsible for some kind of "moral regression." The reason people abort fetuses with Down syndrome upon receiving a "positive" result from amniocentesis, according to Will, isn't that they are making difficult moral choices for themselves and their families; it's all due to "baby boomers' vast sense of entitlement, which encompasses an entitlement to exemption from nature's mishaps, and to a perfect baby."

It's an interesting turn of phrase, that bit about "nature's mishaps." But for some reason it applies only to mishaps in utero. After you're born, health care and health insurance is a personal matter, and your encounters with nature's mishaps are nobody's business but yours. That's why you haven't heard from any American conservatives with the honesty or integrity to admit that the Affordable Care Act, known in some quarters as "Obamacare," prohibits insurance companies from denying coverage to disabled children under nineteen. Or that, as of 2014, the law has prevented insurers from excluding anyone from coverage on the grounds of disability.

As I explained in *Life as We Know It*, Janet and I didn't want an amniocentesis in 1991, when she was pregnant with Jamie, partly because we knew that it induces miscarriage once in every two hundred procedures and partly because we didn't think Down syndrome was worth screening for. (We still think that, and I'll say more about why in the final chapter.) So, in the intervening twenty years, we've tried to persuade people that prenatal screening isn't all it's cracked up to be: it certainly won't guarantee you a perfect baby, since it doesn't detect autism or cerebral palsy or just plain cussedness. We've tried to make the case that people who want prenatal screening should have access to it—but that the medical profession shouldn't oversell it, let alone recommend it across the board. Most of all, we've tried to argue that if you want prospective parents to go ahead and raise children with significant disabilities, you should promote that agenda by way of persuasion rather than state coercion. And finally—this should go without saying, but it never does—you should be prepared to support the social-welfare programs those children will need as they grow.

In 1996 Tucker Carlson wrote an essay on prenatal screening and Down syndrome for the *Weekly Standard* titled "Eugenics, American Style." In 2012, in the wake of then presidential candidate Rick Santorum's remarks about how liberals hate and kill babies with disabilities, the online magazine *Slate* republished Carlson's piece, calling it a "classic," "powerful" essay. There is no accounting for taste, I suppose. I found Carlson's essay intellectually dishonest in 1996, and I haven't changed my mind since. Carlson writes:

> It would be unfair to single out organized Down Syndrome groups
> for their unwillingness to confront the subject of abortion, since
> the willful blindness runs much deeper. In *Life as We Know It*, his
> recent book about raising a son with Down Syndrome, Michael Be-
> rube describes the typical response on an Internet discussion group

when the subject of prenatal testing and abortion arises: "Every time someone brings up the question on the listserv, he or she is met with dozens of e-mail responses reading, 'NO! NO! NOT ON THIS LIST! Please don't have this discussion here! There are plenty of other newsgroups for this debate. This is about children with disabilities.'"

Why do I call this piece intellectually dishonest? I don't toss around that phrase lightly. But here Carlson speaks of "willful blindness" to the ethics of abortion by citing a passage from my book—a passage that is immediately followed *by fourteen thousand words on the subject of selective abortion for fetuses with disabilities.* (Yes, fourteen thousand. I went back and counted.) The whole point of that chapter, "Humans Under Construction," is that we absolutely have to confront those questions, difficult and wrenching though they be. And yet Carlson's pretense here—echoed since by Will, Barone, Santorum, Palin, and a cast of thousands—is that liberals don't debate these things, that we don't agonize over whether to bring children into the world. But of course we do. And some of us see disability as something intrinsic to the human condition, something ineradicable and ineluctable. In fact, some of us think that an awareness of the ineluctability of disability should inform our discussions of health care and national policy. Because otherwise we would wind up with a world in which people debate issues of public health without thinking how those issues are shaped by disability, and a world where people talk about disability only until certain fetuses with disabilities are brought to term, as if the social contract need not accommodate them after they are born. And that kind of world wouldn't make any damn sense whatsoever.

So the next time we talk about health care in the United States—which should be today, tomorrow, and every day thereafter—we should take a moment to think of people like Jamie and of all the people who have helped him along the way. Jamie has needed some help in order to reach the point at which his parents can start granting him more autonomy; he has not needed as much help as we'd expected or feared, and certainly not as much as many other young adults, with or without disabilities. And of course, we all need some degree of help in order to become independent: that's one of the paradoxes by which we live. But in Jamie's case, dear reader, if you are one of our fellow Americans, then some of that help was provided by you. You should be proud of that, and you should know that Jamie and his family are ready and willing to return the favor, should any of nature's mishaps happen to you.

Brainstorming

□ □ □ □ □

In 2011, in his senior year of high school, Jamie wrote a short essay with the help of his teachers and aides. Note that it includes the trip-to-Dublin saga and the story of the Cambodian restaurant in Pittsburgh:

I believe traveling is my very favorite thing in the world. When you travel, you have to make plans. You go to many places. You can go to other states or even countries. You need a passport to enter another country.

When I travel with my father, he takes me to many different states. We have good father and son times. We go to water parks, museums, concerts, plays, zoos, aquariums, basketball, baseball, and even hockey games.

We go to restaurants and diners of all kinds to try new foods—like Myanmar food in New York, and Cambodian food in Pittsburgh!

We have even gone on wildlife safaris in Canada and caves in Texas.

One summer I went to Dublin, Ireland when my mother taught in Ireland with Penn State students. My father and I left on the night of the Fourth of July and took an overnight flight. When we arrived the next morning, I went with my father to the baggage claim in the airport. It was early, around 7:00. I was really thirsty, but I saw there was no juice, no lemonade, and even no water. But I noticed there was Coca-Cola, and my father let me buy one. So that was the day I had Coke for breakfast!

> I have gone to France two times, in 2004 and 2006. I have been
> to the Eiffel Tower and Notre Dame and the Louvre. I also went to
> Monaco to see sharks in a big aquarium named after Jacques Cous-
> teau. My favorite place I have gone to is San Antonio, Texas. But I like
> traveling everywhere with my mother and father. And sometimes with
> my brother.
>   I think people should go traveling because they can see different
> places and meet different people. They will have a great time and their
> memories will last a life time. I believe traveling is great for my heart and
> my brain, and I learn so much every time I travel.

I began traveling in earnest with Jamie in the summer of 2003, when he was eleven. It was the first summer that Janet taught in Penn State's summer Ireland program, and Janet initially assumed that Jamie and I would accompany her for the month. This was, unfortunately for all concerned, a thoroughly unrealistic expectation. At that age, Jamie was not capable of entertaining himself for hours on end with atlases, DVDs, his iPod, and the Internet, and I could not imagine how I was going to keep him occupied all day every day when the Ireland program got to the wild rural areas of Allihies and the Beara Peninsula.

So I came up with another plan. Jamie would stay in the Y summer camp, and every weekend while Janet was gone, he and I would take a weekend trip. Overnight in Pittsburgh (zoo, baseball), overnight in New York (at a friend's house in Brooklyn), overnight in Ocean City, Maryland (at a friend's timeshare). In those days, Jamie was invariably awake at the crack of dawn, which meant (since he could not be left alone for long periods of time) that his bleary, night-owl father would also have to be up at the crack of dawn. And we would learn, by trial and error, how to travel together.

I liked this plan for three reasons. One, it allowed me to travel with Jamie; that much should be obvious. Two, it would come in handy for some of my professional travels. I travel for business five or six times a semester, mostly but not exclusively for speaking engagements, and I didn't want Janet to have to hold down the single-parent fort every time I had an out-of-town gig. At first this arrangement required me to pay local

students to watch over Jamie while I did my meeting-and-speaking business, but within a few years, Jamie became capable of sitting through my
lectures and even visiting classes with me. (He now regularly contributes
to my class visits on various campuses, if the classes involve disability
issues or discussions of *Life as We Know It*.) And three, it would enhance
Jamie's sense of the world—and, I hoped, his ability to tell his own stories. The first time I ever heard him describe his travels, he was telling
his mother (still in Ireland) about our trip to Ocean City. "We went to a
waterpark," he said into the phone. "All the girls screamed." This was
Jamie's truncated way of saying that every time this enormous barrel of
water tipped over and drenched everyone underneath it, there was much
adolescent-girl shrieking to be heard. By itself, it's not much of a story,
but I had never heard Jamie try to narrate his experiences before. (Janet
disagrees, insisting that "we went to a waterpark / all the girls screamed"
is a perfect short story, with all the precision of a haiku or an Imagist
poem.) And travel, I thought, always provides a ready-made framework
for narrative: first we went here and did that, then we went there and did
that. Sure enough, the more Jamie traveled, the more adept he became
at talking about his travels—to the point at which he was able to write, at
the age of twenty and with a teacher's editorial help, a short essay about
his travels.

Along the way, Jamie and I have had some epic journeys that produced epic tales. OK, not literally. But whenever I could bring him along
on a business trip, I did—and that is how we came to be in the Omaha
zoo on a November afternoon, the only people in the place on a 35-degree
day, with the sea lions staring at us and nudging each other, *Look at the
crazy humans in the cold. They have no food for us—what are they doing
here?* That is how we wound up in a funky roadside attraction in Cer-
rillos, New Mexico—the Casa Grande Trading Post, Turquoise Mining
Museum and Petting Zoo, where Jamie fed the llamas and asked if he
could buy an antelope skull to give to his French teacher, Madame Eid.
I said no to the skull, fearing that it would be damaged in transit on
the way home. But how cool is it that Jamie saw an antelope skull and
thought, *Hey, that would make a great gift!?* (My refusal to let Jamie give
his French teacher an antelope skull from New Mexico is now one of

the minor regrets of my life.) And that is how we wound up in the African Lion Safari in Hamilton, Ontario (yes, you read that right—it is the "wildlife safari in Canada" Jamie mentioned in his essay), one day after the Canadian Down Syndrome Society conference, at which we were wisely advised not to drive our rental car into the safari lands because the baboons would strip it of every piece of rubber they could pry off the car.

I have already told the Vancouver story. Here I'll share the Las Vegas story, partly because it was not a business trip; it was pure vacation, a reward to Jamie for being so helpful after his mother had neck surgery. That surgery, in late August 2007, involved fusion of vertebrae C3 through C5 to stabilize Janet's spine where it had come so perilously close to the spinal cord that the doctors were using phrases like "imminent danger of paralysis." The surgery had been spectacularly successful, leaving barely a scar (Janet's surgeon, James Fick, also a parent of a child with Down syndrome, called me three times during the procedure to update me on its progress), but the aftermath was rocky, because Janet is susceptible to migraines and you can't take ibuprofen after this kind of spinal surgery because it inhibits bone fusion. Knowing this, the Furies whose spirits take the form of migraines descended upon Janet with a vengeance, twice sending her (and her worried husband) to the ER. Through all this, Jamie was always patient and solicitous—and, just as important, willing to be dropped off at a friend's house at a moment's notice.

Within a month of the surgery, we all went to see Cirque du Soleil's *Saltimbanco* show at the Bryce Jordan Center in State College. Janet reported that the incredible acrobatics made her neck hurt in sympathy— and Jamie fell in love with Cirque du Soleil. He had never wanted to go to the circus as a child: a good instinct, that, because those "circuses" are so often utterly miserable affairs featuring mistreated elephants and assorted sad animals. Cirque du Soleil, however, had somehow managed to save the circus from itself, devoting its repertoire entirely to human feats of skill, athleticism, and derring-do, eschewing the sad animals altogether. Right around that time, a family friend gave Jamie a copy of the Beatles' *Love* CD, the acclaimed collection of mashups and remixes that formed the soundtrack of the equally acclaimed Cirque du Soleil tribute to the Beatles. Well, when Jamie heard that CD, and heard that there was a Cirque du Soleil show devoted to the Beatles, his head practically asploded. "They could *come here!*" he exclaimed. I checked it out online. No, it did not seem that the *Love* show was a traveling show—it was strictly a Vegas operation, with highly elaborate sets that could not easily be moved around the country. Ever the optimist, Jamie suggested that someday we might go to Las Vegas. I said I would look into it.

Airfare, hotel, tickets—it all came to just over two thousand dollars. "I'm sorry, Jamie, it's just too expensive," I told him. He took this in for a moment and then came back with, "Maybe if we try Motel 6."

I laughed out loud. "That is such a great idea! Jamie, where did you hear about Motel 6?"

"On TV," he replied. But of course. Motel 6—they'll leave the light on. It was a very clever suggestion, but I explained to him that if we went to Vegas, we were going to stay in a "nicer" hotel. I didn't say more than that, and I didn't explain why one should avoid discount hotels in Vegas, though by the end of this story, you'll find that I did have to give Jamie some general idea of what Las Vegas can be like.

A few months later, I came upon a package deal that made the trip plausible. Jamie was thrilled. Planet Hollywood! An outdoor pool! Tickets to Cirque du Soleil *and* front-row tickets to *Stomp!* A tour of the Hoover Dam! This was going to be awesome. We circled the dates: three days in late June, 2008.

Except that when we arrived, somewhere 'round midnight, we found that everyone else on our plane had gotten the same package (or something similar), so that the rental car plaza consisted of ten or twelve counters, only one of which featured a line of over fifty people. That was our line, of course. I was tired, and I knew our hotel was only a ten-minute cab ride away, so I suggested to Jamie that we take a cab to the hotel and come back in the morning to get our car.

"Michael! We have to get our car *right now,*" he replied. "We have no other options."

I smiled indulgently. "We certainly have other options, Jamie. For example, we can get a cab tonight and come back and get our car tomorrow. That is totally another option."

No dice. He was determined to stick it out and get our car that night. At which point a pleasant young woman in front of us turned and said, "I've been on this line before—it's not that bad. Probably half an hour?"

I put it to Jamie: "OK, Jamie, is that all right with you? We wait on this line for half an hour?"

"We have *no other options*," he insisted. The pleasant young woman laughed pleasantly.

So I decided to spend some of that time—it wound up being forty-five minutes—explaining to Jamie what kind of world we would be walking into. "You have never seen hotels like these," I told him. "They are *huge*. You *must* stay by me—because if we get separated in one of these places, I just don't know how we would ever find each other again. OK?"

Jamie nodded seriously.

"Now, these aren't just hotels. They're also casinos, and they have restaurants and theaters and shopping malls. Seriously, they are *enormous*. There's a hotel designed like Venice in Italy, and a hotel designed like New York, and a hotel designed like ancient Egypt, and a hotel designed like ancient Rome that even has people walking around dressed like ancient Romans, OK?"

Jamie was getting into this. "And people dressed like Christians!" he added, at which the young woman in front of us burst into delighted laughter. It *was* a pretty good line, and we have repeated it often.

But it was outdone later that evening, after we checked in to Planet Hollywood and found ourselves walking through the casino on the way to the elevators. "Jamie," I asked, "tomorrow night, would you mind if I came down and played roulette for a little while after you fall asleep?"

I was not prepared for his answer. Loudly and indignantly, he cried, "Michael!! Don't you *dare* gamble!!"

Well, *that* was awkward. To everyone within earshot, it must have sounded, from his tone to his use of my first name, as if he had been abducted by his creepy uncle with a gambling problem. I assured him, quietly, that it was no big deal and that I would not be gone long and would not lose a lot of money. Playing for about an hour each evening, I won seventy dollars the first night and dutifully lost it back the second night, which is only right and just, and Jamie slept soundly throughout.

He loved both shows. He was beside himself at *Love* and insisted that we return to the Mirage hotel the next day to buy a program and some merchandise. But he had a great deal of trouble getting around in Las Vegas, and at first I could not understand why. He was dragging, he was irritable, he was *fussy*—he was a pain, honestly, and he was not himself. "If you keep this up," I warned him at one point, "it's the McDonald's kids' meal for you." We were not going to McDonald's—we had very good Mexican food in our hotel—but he got the point. He was acting immaturely, and since this was his big extravagant Vegas vacation, his reward for being so good with Janet the previous fall, I was vexed. I imagine that many people act immaturely on their big extravagant Vegas vacations. But I expected better from Jamie.

I finally realized that he was dehydrated. The brutal desert sun, beating down on us in the deepest days of June, was almost visibly draining moisture from his body. I have a picture of Jamie at the Hoover Dam, looking utterly depleted in 118-degree heat; he had never experienced such a thing (I had been to Vegas once, eight years earlier, speaking at UNLV), and it was rendering him incapable of enjoying himself whenever he was outside. Fie on me for taking a full day to see the obvious, but once I did, I hustled Jamie into the nearest CVS and bought him a couple of Gatorades.

He revived almost instantaneously, and I cursed my cluelessness. I suggested we return to our hotel and take a dip in the pool, Gatorades at the ready. He agreed—and as we emerged onto the strip, a moving billboard drove by us, its ad promising that you could have babes in your room within twenty minutes.

This struck Jamie as hilarious. "*Babies* in your *room?*" he cried incredulously, and when you put it that way, yes, it does sound pretty funny.

I could have let it go. As it stood, we had ourselves a Cute Kid Moment, and there was no need for me to tell Jamie that he had misread the billboard or explain to him what a more accurate reading of it might entail. But I thought to myself, goddamn, he's almost seventeen. I owe him an account of this aspect of Las Vegas.

So I turned to him and said, "Well, Jamie, that sign didn't say 'babies.' It said 'babes.' Babes in your room in twenty minutes."

This was just as puzzling to him. "*Babes* in your *room?*" Jamie asked, as if there were no significant difference between babies and babes.

"OK, it's like this," I said. "You know how some people, like us, come to Las Vegas for the shows." Jamie nodded. "You know that some people come here to gamble, even though you did not want me to gamble." Jamie nodded again, smiling wryly. "And then there are men who come here for sex, and they pay to have women come to their rooms." I said it just like that, matter-of-factly, as if it were simply a matter of choosing among options A, B, and C.

Jamie furrowed his brow and nodded slowly, seriously. Did he get it? Reader, he got it. All the way back to our hotel, as hawkers of strip clubs and "escort" services tried to give us cards for their businesses, Jamie held up one hand and said, "Not for us, not for us."

I don't think I have ever felt a stranger combination of pride and amusement.

□   □   □

When Jamie and I visited the College of Charleston in September 2011, we did so at the invitation of Alison Piepmeier, herself a mother of a young girl with Down syndrome (Maybelle by name). I knew Alison as a thoughtful and passionate writer in the feminist blogosphere; I now know her also as a searingly honest chronicler of her own battles with brain tumors and seizure disorders. And she was the first person to insist that if I were going to give a talk about Jamie, that Jamie himself should deliver part of it. I eagerly agreed, and Jamie, Janet, and I set about practicing his speech, which consisted of the short essay with which I opened this chapter.

Jamie is much more stilted when he reads from a prepared script than when he talks *ex tempore* (he is not alone in this, I know). But he improved with practice, and at some point I told him that when he was done, he should say "thank you" to let everyone know that his remarks had concluded. The plan was to have me speak for about twenty minutes, then to let Jamie take five, then back to me for another twenty minutes. We would both participate in the question-and-answer period.

The event was packed. It was sponsored by the College of Charleston's REACH (Realizing Educational and Career Hopes) program, a visionary initiative that offers students with intellectual and/or developmental disabilities a four-year certificate program. As Alison explained it to me, the REACH students live in an integrated setting with their nondisabled peers, and they all live like ordinary college students, which means (in Alison's words) that everyone learns together that Thanksgiving is the time for taking your laundry back to your parents' house. Over one hundred students came out to hear Jamie and me, and when Jamie took the microphone, they were rapt. Until, that is, the very end, when Jamie said, "I learn so much every time I travel," and then . . . and then . . . closed not with "thank you" but with "merci beaucoup."

He brought down the house. *Brought down the house.* I mean, the eruption of applause was electric. I mean, I mean . . . now how was I going to follow that? I did, because the show must go on, but I know when a show has been stolen.

The trip to Charleston had gotten off on a weird foot. Jamie and I packed one suitcase for the two of us, and we put his personal paraphernalia in a backpack, just as my personal stuff went into my briefcase. As we were about to leave for the airport, Janet reviewed the contents of his backpack, and was startled to see one of Jamie's large encyclopedias in it. "Jamie, you cannot bring this on the airplane," she said. "It is much too big."

Jamie clearly felt blindsided. "Michael said I could!" I had, too. It was a very large book, but if he was willing to carry it, that was OK with me. I simply had said he could not spread it out on the seatback tray table in the plane; he could certainly have it with him at the hotel and on campus. But this did not sit well with Janet. "Well, if Michael said you could, then I guess you can," she conceded, "but you are not being a very good traveler."

I discovered how much this stung Jamie when we got to airport security. The screening line at the State College airport is rarely very long, but no matter how short or long the line, in any airport, Jamie is always ready. He is not quite as crisp and efficient as George Clooney in the dazzling opening sequence of *Up in the Air*, but he's close. Shoes off, pockets emptied, laptop in bin—he's on it. As Jamie placed his backpack on the conveyor belt, an impressed TSA official told him that he was a very good traveler. Jamie didn't say thank you. He said, "But my mother says I am not a very good traveler because I have a big book." (I told him he was indeed a very, very good traveler. And that Janet thinks so too.)

Now, why am I telling these stories about a couple of key moments in Jamie's life as a young-adult traveler? Because I am so impatient with debates about how or whether we can "cure" or "mitigate" Down syndrome and enhance the cognitive capacities of people with Down syndrome with drug therapies. I know that the connection isn't obvious, so let me spell it out for a bit.

In January 2010, Lisa Belkin posted an article on the *New York Times*'s *Motherlode* blog. Its provocative title: "Should Down Syndrome Be Cured?" Belkin opened with a recap of a story that had appeared two days before the posting:

> The guest post here on Friday—about the birth of Cash Van Rowe during a blizzard, and the jolting news that he had Down syndrome—led many of you to leave comments for his parents, assuring them that the road ahead was a journey they would cherish.
>
> But what if Cash's Down syndrome could be cured—or, more precisely, be mitigated?
>
> News out of Stanford University late last year hinted that this might one day be possible. Researchers from its medical school and the Lucile Packard Children's Hospital explored why children born with Down syndrome do not start life developmentally delayed but rather fall behind as they get older. By using mice that were genetically engineered to mimic Down syndrome, they found that neural memory deficits prevent such children from collecting learned experiences, and that they could improve memory and cognition by medically boosting norepinephrine signaling in the brain.

Belkin goes on to quote Stanford neurologist Ahmed Salehi, who had claimed that this testing "could lead to an improvement in cognitive functions in these kids."

Two things should set off your spider sense here. The first is the promise of the miracle cure, every bit as sensational—and sensationalized—as the claims that research team X has discovered the gene for Y. The second, more elusive and more vexatious, is the slippage between "cure" and "mitigation." Belkin's second paragraph muddies the waters from the get-go, suggesting that "mitigation" is a more "precise" term than "cure." No. It is not. It is a wholly different term. I think of the famous 2002 press conference with the incendiary, dynamic NBA star Allen Iverson, just after his Philadelphia 76ers had been bounced from the playoffs and he had been criticized by his coach, Larry Brown, for missing practices during the season. It is available on YouTube, and it features Iverson saying again and again, with great exasperation, "What are we talking about? We're talking about practice. Not a game, not a game, not a game. We're talking about practice, man, not a game. . . . We're talking about practice." This goes on for about two minutes, much to the delight of the press corps and Internet mashup artists everywhere. And it summarizes nicely how I feel about Belkin's slippage: We're talking about *mitigation*. Not a cure, not a cure, not a cure—we're talking about mitigation, man, not a cure. . . . How long do I have to keep saying this? Mitigation. Not a cure.

But apparently this slippage is not Belkin's alone, if Dr. Salehi himself held out the possibility of improvement in cognitive functions. It is no wonder, then, that at the end of her column, despite having written that (more precisely) mitigation is the issue rather than cure, Belkin asks her readers, "If there were a cure for your child that would fundamentally change who he is, would you welcome it?" Such is the power of the discourse of the cure: it obliterates all nuance before and behind it.

Along the way, however, Belkin acknowledges that not everyone is enthusiastic about curing (or mitigating?) Down syndrome. She quotes at length a response from Jenn Powers, a Canadian mother of twin boys with Down syndrome, Josh and Jacob:

As you know, I have many years of history supporting people with intellectual disabilities. Through my connections with these remarkable people, both personal and professional, I have become more and more convinced of the fundamental human dignity present in each person, the vital importance of diversity among the human race, and the particular and irreplaceable role that folks with intellectual disabilities play in creating a more humane, compassionate, and hospitable society. It is clear to me that, as a society, we need what people with intellectual disabilities have to offer.

Before we welcomed Josh and Jacob into our family, I might have had a much easier time responding to this particular piece of research. *But as a mother of two little boys with Down syndrome, boys whose identity, personality, appearance, is linked to that extra chromosome, my ability to rationally argue my point is seriously compromised.* I find it hard to read this article without hearing a judgment on the value of my children, children who have transformed my life and the lives of many others—for the better—with the help of an extra chromosome. [Emphasis mine]

I'm going to break into Powers's response here, because even though I agree with it—and I will continue agreeing with it below—I think she makes a very serious mistake in the second paragraph. There is no sense, I believe, in which her ability to rationally argue her point is "seriously compromised" by the fact that she is a mother of children with Down syndrome. As you'll see in a moment, her argument is solid from start to finish: it is rational, persuasive, and thoroughly humane. But this belief that one is "compromised" by being closely involved and invested in a subject is part of what German philosopher Hans-Georg Gadamer called "the Enlightenment prejudice against prejudice," and it is amazingly pervasive in Western culture. I'll explain briefly, with the proviso that my ability to rationally argue my point is not seriously compromised by the fact that I went to graduate school in the humanities.

In decrying the prejudice against prejudice, Gadamer wasn't saying "go ahead, be racist." He wasn't using "prejudice" in its customary, pejorative sense; on the contrary, he was arguing against understanding it in its pejorative sense, which he believed had become customary in Enlightenment and post-Enlightenment thought. He argued instead that one can come to knowledge precisely because one is interested in a

subject, and that there are forms of "pre-judgment" that do not necessarily lock one into a narrow dogmatism about that subject. Jenn Powers's
response provides a perfect example of the phenomenon. Because of my
own history, my own choices, convictions, and experiences, I approach
Powers's response sympathetically. I too can say that because of my connections with people with intellectual disabilities, I have become more
and more convinced of the fundamental human dignity present in each
person, the vital importance of diversity among the human race, and the
particular and irreplaceable role that folks with intellectual disabilities
play in creating a more humane, compassionate, and hospitable society.
And yet my sympathetic "pre-judgment" of Powers's argument does not
prevent me from disagreeing with a more meta-philosophical aspect of
it, the claim that it is logically compromised because its author is a parent with Down syndrome.

No doubt there are many people who cannot argue a point rationally
because they are too emotionally invested in their beliefs to reflect critically on them; this phenomenon, I have found, is especially prevalent
among people who root for sports teams and athletes I disapprove of.
(Kidding. Kidding.) But there are also plenty of people whose ability to
argue a point is *enhanced* by their intimate personal knowledge of what
they are talking about—in this case, years of experience, personal and
professional, dealing with people with intellectual disabilities. Powers's
argument is not disqualified by that experience; it is authorized and
underwritten by that experience. And parents of or caseworkers with
people with intellectual disabilities need to own that experience and lay
claim to that authorization. Rather than demurring by saying we are too
close to the subject of intellectual disability to be rational about it, we
should be arguing that we know and care about people with intellectual
disabilities precisely *because* we are close to the subject.

That said—though it needs to be said—let me get back to agreeing
with Powers, who proceeds to make one great argument after another:

In the debate surrounding disability—prenatal screening, euthanasia, etc.—there is an assumption that we all agree on a definition
of what is good, what is better, what is the ideal. Who decided that

smarter is better? Who decided that independence takes precedence over community? Who decided that both the individual and the society are better off without Down Syndrome? I would assert that something important is lost as our genetic diversity diminishes.

I would also assert that people with disabilities may not themselves choose to be "cured." Bioethicist and disability activist Gregor Wolbring, who happens to have no legs as a result of the effects of thalidomide, asserts that, if given the choice, he would want to remain "disabled." He feels it gives him an evolutionary advantage, even, as it allows him to weed out the "jerks" who treat him differently as a result of his disability. He poses the compelling question, "What exactly is the problem? Is the problem that I have no legs, or is the problem that I live in a leg-dominated society?" Similarly, what exactly is the problem with Down Syndrome? Is the problem that my boys have a low IQ, or that they live in an IQ-dominated society? . . .

In the end, for me, this all comes back to people. Josh, Jacob, Mary, Cathy, Kate, Janet . . . [Ellipsis in original] these people have Down syndrome. These people are my family, my friends, my teachers. Without the benefit of that extra chromosome, they would not be who they are. Their intellectual "impairment" gives them an insight and an emotional intelligence and maturity that I can only aspire to. They do not need a needle in their brain to make them more functional, to help them find their car keys. What they need is a society that values what they have to offer. I would like to think that I can be a part of creating that society.

Belkin, for her part, responds to this argument with equanimity, half-endorsing the Gadamerian grounds for granting the cogency of Powers's perspective by suggesting that there is a relatively benign sense in which Powers's position is self-serving, but that Powers's experience constitutes legitimate grounds for that argument. Writes Belkin:

On the one hand, parents of children with disabilities are emotionally well served to find a silver lining in that disability. It makes it easier to get through the day if you focus on what life has given TO your child, rather than what has been taken away. On the other hand, optimism is not merely denial. It is based on an intimate familiarity with a condition and a firsthand knowledge of what life looks like from inside the disability, looking out.

They say you should never read the comments to anything published online. I can never seem to follow this advice, so when I read this column, a day or two after it was published, I went to the comments section and found to my dismay that the overwhelming majority of Ms. Belkin's readers had weighed in to insist that parents who are skeptical of "curing" Down syndrome are selfish, irresponsible, deluded, and even colonialist. Colonialist! That was a new one. *Down syndrome, Down syndrome rules the waves . . . the sun never sets on the Down syndrome empire.*

At this point I should probably make it clear that, as a general rule, I am not against curing things. As scholarship in disability studies has established, the discourse of the "cure" is most controversial with regard to Deaf culture, partly because of the long history of "oralism," which involved more than a century of trying to stamp out sign language, and partly because there are myriad social contexts (if you're reading, you're in one now) in which it is no disability at all to be deaf. Indeed, wherever there are Deaf communities using ASL, Deafness is a name for a linguistic minority, not a diagnostic category of disability. Nor is the resistance to "cures" exclusive to the Deaf. Gregor Wolbring, as you have just learned, does not want legs. And in *Choosing Children: Genes, Disability, and Design*, Jonathan Glover (whose work I will address in my final chapter) describes the case of a blind man who, upon having his sight restored, fell into a deep depression at the realization that the world was so much more drab and boring than he had imagined.

And yet even in the most cure-averse precincts of disability studies, there is no Polio Restoration Society, no Smallpox Appreciation League, no Cholera Pride movement. Scholars may have critiqued the March of Dimes up and down the block for its pity-laden anti-polio campaigns featuring adorable "crippled" children, but none of those scholars can be said to be objectively pro-polio. And even though I am very, very skeptical that there could ever be a cure for Alzheimer's, would I be happy if we discovered the magic Alzheimer's-B-Gon mineral on the planet Pandora? Yes, I would. I would even be in favor of mining for it, unless that involved destroying the natural habitat of beautiful tall blue humanoids. My ability to argue my point rationally may be compromised on this one, but I can't really bear the thought of Jamie, with his phenomenal memory, living through the experience of having that wonderful faculty eroded gradually and inexorably, to his complete and utter confusion. So I hope against hope for a cure. Or for mitigation.

The larger question at stake here involves understanding that disability is not disease. That distinction was driven home to me in 2006 when I taught the first graduate seminar in disability studies at Penn State. My class was reading essays on the overlap between disability activism and gay/lesbian activism—an overlap concentrated on, but not exclusive to, the history of AIDS. One of my students, a young gay man, objected to the conflation of AIDS with disability in general. He understood, he said, why disability activists have resisted the idea that disability is something that can be "cured" or "prevented" with technological advances and medical interventions, just as gay and lesbian activists have resisted the idea that homosexuality is a curable disease. He understood why people with congenital disabilities would recoil from a prenatal-screening initiative whose assumptions seem to be that the world would be a better place if they had never been born. But, he said, if a cure for AIDS were found tomorrow, would he be happy? If HIV could be wiped from the face of the earth, would he support its eradication? Yes, yes he would. Without hesitation, without a second's misgiving.

It was a decisive, clarifying moment in the course, insofar as everyone (the professor included) had to ask just how far they were willing to go in criticizing the discourse of the cure. For weeks, we'd been reading the work of disability activists who argue, justifiably, that contemporary biomedicine frames everything in terms of the cure—the scientific breakthrough that will allow the lame to walk and the blind to see. But in all that reading, we'd never come across a disability activist who saw any problem with the eradication of disease. The elimination of smallpox and polio and tuberculosis and cholera and bubonic plague seems to most people to be an unqualified good for the species. Even in the work of disability activists who would never give a moment's thought to providing all deaf people with cochlear implants, there is a common sense that there are some human conditions we are better off without.

But—and this is the critical point—deafness isn't one of them. Tay-Sachs disease is. Down syndrome is not even close.

I admit that the line between disability and disease is sometimes blurry. Some diseases are disabling, yes; others are potentially disabling (diabetes, Graves, Hashimoto's thyroiditis) but can be palliated with medication. But most disabilities have no disease etiologies whatsoever. Applying the cure/disease model to those disabilities is what philosophers call a category error, and fundamentally muddles our thinking about how to accommodate disability in society as best we can. At its worst, in the promotional campaigns of Autism Speaks, the disability-as-disease model not only focuses exclusively on the "cure," as if autism itself needs to be wiped out, but adopts all the tropes of eliminationism. As the Autism Self-Advocacy Network points out, "Autism Speaks has compared being autistic to 'being kidnapped, dying of a natural disaster, and having a fatal disease.'"

When I'm in one of my black-humor moods, I tend to say, "The reason all the T-shirts say 'RACE FOR THE CURE' is that 'RACE FOR THE REASONABLE ACCOMMODATION' doesn't fit neatly on one side of the shirt." By which I mean, of course, that the discourse of the cure is everywhere, and the discourse of reasonable accommodation, so far as I can see, is understood only by those people who already know something about disability, US disability law, ramps, kneeling buses, in-class paraprofessionals, and job coaches. It's almost like a kind of sign language, spoken only by those who are already disability-literate. In the comment thread after Lisa Belkin's *Motherlode* post, the remark that struck me most vividly—partly because it was so strongly "recommended" by other readers—was this:

> Are babies who are born with cleft palates fundamentally who they
> are so we should not use surgery to fix them? Are babies born with a
> genetic disorders [sic] such as celiac disease, Tay-Sachs or Sickle-cell

be [sic] left to suffer because to do anything would compromise "who they are?" This is ridiculous. If there's something you can do to help your children get along better in the world you do it. Anything else is about you and is fundamentally selfish.

Remember that this is a comment in response to a column *about Down syndrome*. Not about cleft lip and palate, or celiac disease or Tay-Sachs or sickle-cell or anything else. In other words, the writer clearly sees no problem with discussing Down syndrome in the terms we ordinarily apply to fatal diseases. And *this* is why it is so important for the Jenn Powerses of the world not to undercut their legitimacy by saying their perspective is compromised by their closeness to people with intellectual disabilities: so many people talk about intellectual disability without having the faintest froggy idea what they're talking about.

I assure you that I am not cherry-picking a random comment from the Internet. I am talking about something that underlies all of Autism Speaks' appeals for support—and that underlay the *New York Times*' next major discussion of cures and mitigation for people with Down syndrome, written by Dan Hurley and published in the *New York Times Magazine* in July 2011 under the headline "A Drug for Down Syndrome." In the essay, Hurley covered the work of Dr. Alberto Costa, a neuroscientist whose daughter Tyche has Down syndrome. Costa has been experimenting with the drug memantine, giving it to Ts65Dn mice, which were developed in the 1980s by Muriel Davisson and exhibit many of the traits associated with Down syndrome.

Hurley interviewed me for the essay, and I appear in its antepenultimate paragraph, trying to say some of the things I have just elaborated here. "Nobody would be against giving insulin for diabetes," I am quoted (accurately) as saying. "But Down syndrome isn't diabetes or smallpox or cholera. It's milder and more variable and more complicated. I'd be very leery of messing with the attributes Jamie has. He's pretty fabulous. At the same time, I'm not doctrinaire. If you're talking about a medication that allows people to function in society and hold jobs, how can you be against that?" The following paragraph then pivots away from my remarks, reporting that "the parents I met who participated in Costa's study expressed little of Bérubé's ambivalence." Yes, well: you could say they were a self-selecting group, since they had self-selected into Dr. Costa's experiment. But what the ambivalent-Bérubé paragraph doesn't tell you is that the insulin/diabetes analogy *was Hurley's question to me*. The reason I mentioned diabetes and insulin in response is that I was trying to push back against a leading question—a misleading question. Hurley quite clearly was working with a syllogism in which insulin is to diabetes as memantine is to Down syndrome, and in which parental resistance to the latter makes no more sense than parental resistance to the former. I learned later that Hurley had written a book on disease prior to writing this cover story on disability for the *Times Magazine*. Its title: *Diabetes Rising: How a Rare Disease Became a Modern Pandemic, and What to Do About It*. When I discovered that, I was left to conclude that when all you have is an insulin hammer, everything, even Down syndrome, looks like a diabetes nail.

Hurley has since written a book titled *Smarter: The New Science of Building Brain Power*. Personally, I am all in favor of building brain power. But on the subject of building brain power among people with intellectual disabilities, let's review some context, shall we? People with intellectual disabilities and their caretakers know that there is a long and sorry history of snake-oil "cures" for intellectual disability; the most recent, which was all the rage when I was writing *Life as We Know It*, was piracetam, the alleged-miracle nootropic drug that was claimed to produce stunning improvements in the cognitive capacities of children with Down syndrome. Its leading exponent was Dixie Lawrence Tafoya, who in 1995 was given a national-network platform on ABC-TV's *Day One* to promote her snake-oil mixture. In 1997 I wound up keynoting a Down Syndrome Society event in St. Louis with her—she was not present, but spoke to the group from her home in Louisiana—and I heard her insist, with evangelical fervor, that anyone who was not giving their kids her miracle supplement was actively harming them.

Janet and I never gave Jamie piracetam. In the closing pages of *Life as We Know It*, I referenced the debate over nootropic drugs and vitamin therapies, noting in my final paragraph that Jamie had "learned to take vitamins." This prompted a number of readers to write to me and ask whether we were going the whole nine yards with Dixie Lawrence Tafoya. I replied that we were not, and would not, but that we saw no harm in giving Jamie supplemental antioxidants, since we'd noticed that he would devour ketchup, and we had heard that children with Down syndrome love ketchup for the lycopene. That was our line in the snake-oil-soaked sand: antioxidants yes, spray vitamins yes, ketchup yes, piracetam no.

I know that contemporary experiments with molecular biochemistry are light-years away from where they were a few decades ago. And surely Alberto Costa's work with Ts65Dn mice is far more sophisticated—not to mention more legitimately peer-reviewed—than Dixie Lawrence Tafoya's homemade piracetam cocktail. But still, I have to note that the title of Hurley's essay isn't any different from the terms in which Lawrence peddled her wares: *a drug for Down syndrome.* And when I take a step back from all the reasons why parents and caretakers of people with intellectual disabilities would have good reason to be skeptical of announcements of stunning breakthroughs and miracle cures—er, mitigations—I think, *Wait a minute here.* We are talking about experiments to enhance the cognitive capacities of mice, experiments that are then approved for clinical trials in humans with intellectual disabilities. Seriously? For the love of Mike, hasn't anybody here read *Flowers for Algernon?* Build your brain power, people!

A year after Hurley wrote his cover story on Costa, the *Times* followed up with an item in its *6th Floor* blog. In Ilena Silverman's "Can a Pill Make People with Down Syndrome Smarter?," Hurley reported the disappointing news that "of the 14 cognitive measures tested before and after treatment, those taking memantine only did significantly better than those taking a placebo on a single test. And it was not one of the two 'primary' measures designated by Costa before the study began." One wonders about the amazing cognitive-enhancing properties of this mysterious miracle drug, "placebo." And yet the final word in this update is given to yet another researcher whose characterization of Down syndrome is fundamentally wrong:

> "We still do not know if we have something that will actually work,"
> said Alcino J. Silva, professor of neurobiology, psychiatry and

psychology at the University of California at Los Angeles. Even so, Silva added, "In my mind, the big story here is that for the first time we have a logical path that can take us from a mental health problem like Down syndrome into the development of targeted treatments. This is indeed a big deal."

In *my* mind, the big story here is that we still have researchers in neuroscience who think of Down syndrome as a mental health problem, almost in precisely the same terms whereby autism was once conflated with schizophrenia. Because of that fundamental category error, I submit, certain neuroscientists' ability to rationally argue their point is seriously compromised.

□   □   □

I am not kidding when I say that I take Jamie on my academic business trips and that we try to help him develop his skills as a traveler in lieu of drug therapies. For what are Janet and I doing but trying to build his brain power, to enhance his cognitive capacity? There's a reason people (including Jamie) say that travel is broadening: it happens to be true.

However, I am mindful that not everyone has, or can have, Jamie's opportunities. And when I first thought of travel as a way for Jamie to begin to tell his own stories, I did not anticipate that he would eventually run into a school aide who considered him (and his parents) the central Pennsylvania version of Eurotrash. Apparently you can tell your schoolmates stories about having Coke for breakfast in Dublin or going to La Museé Oceanographique in Monaco only so many times before someone gets the sense that you are a jetsetter who seriously needs to check his privilege. Even though Jamie's travel-and-cognitive-enhancement program began in Pittsburgh, Brooklyn, and Ocean City, Maryland.

But it's quite clearly true that there is a substantial difference in our family circumstances between the life we knew in the early 1990s, that of struggling young assistant professors in the humanities, and the life we know now, as established middle-aged academics who get speaking invitations and can afford travel abroad. We know how fortunate we are, and Jamie does too. Only once have I had to explain to him the rules about traveling with me on business: at one of my lectures, at a small liberal arts college in the Midwest, he came up to the podium as I was speaking and asked me to change the DVD in his laptop. I apologized to the audience for the interruption, changed Jamie's DVD, resettled him in his place at a table on the side of the auditorium, and resumed where I had left off. No one seemed very put out by this, but it was bad form on our part, and I spoke to Jamie afterward, telling him that when I'm giving a talk at a college or university, I am working, and if he can't take care of himself while I am working, he can't come along with me on business trips. This may sound harsh—but he was perfectly capable of changing the DVD by himself, and more generally, he needed to know that the only reason he and I had made that trip was that people at that college had invited me to deliver a lecture. That was the bargain, and we—Jamie and I—had to hold up our end of it. I am pleased to report that I have had to explain this to Jamie only once.

But traveling is only one of the ways Janet and I have tried to build Jamie's brain power. Another of our strategies involves the history of Western art and music. I know, it sounds crazy, right? So old school. So useless, so frivolous, so meerschaum-chomping humanist, so Allan Bloom (though he did not chomp any meerschaums). In Dan Hurley's *New York Times Magazine* essay, Dr. Costa makes a point of demonstrating that he has other priorities for his daughter Tyche:

> On the whiteboard at the front of the room, Costa wrote out an algebra problem for her to solve: $8x^2 - 7 = 505$.
>
> "She's one of only two people with Down syndrome who I've ever known to be capable of doing algebra," Costa said. "Normally we give her a problem before she goes to bed." As she solved the equation, taking six steps to show that x equals 8, he said, "It's basically instead of a bedtime story."

When I read that Dr. Costa knew of only two people with Down syndrome who could do algebra, I thought of Sir Arthur Eddington's famous line (though it is not so famous as Allen Iverson's "practice" rant, and it is not preserved on the Internet) when he was asked in 1919 if it were true that only three people understood Einstein's equation for general relativity: "Who's the third"? That night, I asked Jamie what x might be if $5x$ equaled 35. "Seven," he shot back, seemingly without thinking.

I admit that this very basic algebra is not as impressive as Tyche Costa's ability to solve $8x^2 - 7 = 505$. But the basic concept of the problem—the abstract understanding that x stands for a number in an equation—was not a problem for Jamie.

Bright kids with Down syndrome—and there are many bright kids with Down syndrome—can be usefully challenged with math problems. And in fairness to Dr. Costa, it is not as if he was all math all the time; Hurley's essay proceeds to note that Dr. Costa also bought Tyche the Rosetta Stone guide to learning Portuguese, and that she did well with it. All I'm saying is that bright kids with Down syndrome can be challenged with algebra *and* bedtime stories. And art. And music. And the entire recorded history of human achievement. Indeed, all kids with Down syndrome, and many other intellectual disabilities, can be challenged—or rewarded!—with exposure to any or all of the above. If a child isn't into algebra, whether because of lack of capacity or lack of interest, perhaps something else will strike her fancy.

When I wrote *Life as We Know It*, I did not imagine that I would someday be taking Jamie to museums and concert halls. Honestly, the idea would have sounded either preposterous or pretentious. With regard to cultural institutions, Jamie did the little-kid things as well as any little kid—zoos and aquariums mostly, moving up to natural history museums when he was ten years old. But he was mostly oblivious to the appeal of so-called "high" culture: When we visited Rome in 1999, when Jamie was seven and a half, doing the tourist thing at the Colosseum and St. Peter's and the Sistine Chapel, Jamie's main interests were (a) pizza and (b) chasing the pigeons in St. Peter's Square. By contrast, ten years later, when he visited Florence, he was all about going to the Uffizi (in fact, this was his idea). By that point he had developed a deep fascination with the Renaissance and could spot in an instant the difference between the bright, exuberant, religious paintings of the Italian Renaissance and the dark, secular paintings of the later Northern Renaissance. Though it took him a while to get there: he was hooked initially by the ubiquitous Madonna-and-child tableaux of the late medieval and early modern periods—but his understanding of them was a bit sketchy. At the age of fourteen or fifteen, he showed Janet's mother, Kay, one of his books on Renaissance art, pointing to a rendering of Christ and saying, "That's the dead guy." Kay Lyon was horrified: "Jamie! That's Jesus Christ!" Janet and I sheepishly admitted that we hadn't offered Jamie much in the way of religious instruction. (I mentioned this in a talk once, and someone stormed out of the room in outrage.) So we had some explaining to do, but we were following Jamie's lead all the way.

His first meaningful exposure to the history of Western art and music came in seventh grade, in one of those surveys that cover "art" from ancient to modern and "music" from Gregorian chant to Stravinsky. I know that much because one night Jamie exclaimed, apropos of nothing, "Stravinsky! That's another great composer we forgot!" This in itself constitutes a pretty powerful argument for art and music instruction in grade school, though if we Americans keep going down the path we're on, with high-stakes testing and increasingly narrow return-on-investment conceptions of education, arts and music instruction will disappear from our schools altogether. For Jamie, art and music became two more things to be fascinated by, two more things he could learn about and experience and wonder at. We got him Fandex cards, which played right into his list-making skills, giving him an array of major composers to memorize as he wished. I used to remark that he liked talking about composers but not actually listening to their work; at the time, he was a young teen, much more into rock and pop than baroque and classical, and Janet and I have almost no classical music in our CD collections. Then one night I found some Chopin on YouTube and played it on my laptop, asking Jamie if he knew what composer this was. "Chopin," he replied, with no more than a slight shrug of his shoulders. Now, Chopin is distinctive and identifiable to people who know about such things—at once meandering and intensely passionate—but I am no aficionado of classical music, and I had no idea that Jamie could identify Chopin by a snippet from an étude. "How about this?" I countered, putting on a recording of *The Goldberg Variations* (one of the few classical CDs I do own). "Bach," he said with a nod. "Wow," I said. Just wow.

I suppose this would be a good place to note that there are still some doctors out there who tell pregnant women that children with Down syndrome will never have a meaningful thought in their lives. And it might be a good place to reflect for a moment on the word "retarded." The Special Olympics has respectfully asked everyone to stop using the words "retarded" and "retard" because they (especially the latter) are so strongly associated with stigma and dehumanization. *Spread the word to end the word*, they say, and with every good reason. (When I have mentioned this on the Internet, I have invariably been met with howls of outrage from people complaining about political correctness. My usual response is something like "Uh, the year 1991 called. It wants its clichés back.") But there is another, more clinical reason to reject the term "retarded," in that it entails an inaccurate account of what "intelligence" is, by suggesting that intelligence is simply one scalar thing, a line on a graph, and that some people are higher on that line and some people lower. For the record, Jamie's IQ is somewhere in the low sixties—or so it appeared when he was tested at the age of six. But although Jamie continues to have trouble with many areas of human endeavor, there are some areas in which he spikes up into "normal" and others in which he spikes up into "holy fucking shit." The word "retarded," like its more polite relative "delayed," doesn't begin to get at the cognitive capacities and challenges of people with intellectual disabilities. It's really a stupid word, when you think about it.

Some years ago, I tried a little experiment. I called it Culture Weekend. Jamie and I took a bus to New York, stayed in a friend's apartment, and I devised a cornucopia of offerings for my then sixteen-year-old aesthete: Friday night, a visit to a midtown Brazilian churrascaria followed by games at ESPN Zone in Times Square; Saturday morning, a trip to the Metropolitan Museum of Art to check out the Rembrandt show; Saturday afternoon, down to Broadway for *The Lion King*; Saturday night, out to the Brooklyn Academy of Music (BAM) for *Ship in a View*, an experimental modern dance choreographed by Hiroshi Koike, artistic director of the troupe Pappa Tarahumara; Sunday morning, salsa music for children at Carnegie Hall. A heady and eclectic mix, I thought—and a largely spontaneous one. We got third-row seats for *The Lion King* because the Broadway wing of the screenwriters' strike had just ended, and we went to see *Ship in a View* because I read an intriguing review of it in the *New York Times* that Friday morning. It was a decidedly mixed review, warning readers that "the eventually predictable alternation between such near chaos and beached calm is the central weakness of 'Ship in a View,' inducing a glazed-eyed state somewhere between hypnosis and boredom." But I wanted to see how Jamie would respond.

Jamie reminds me now that our 2007 visit to the Metropolitan Museum of Art was his first. He raced through the Rembrandts, taking them in without really looking closely, and then was hit amidships by a hall of late medieval European art, over which he lingered long, always wanting to know how old Jesus was in each painting. I made some observations to him about the emergence of one-point perspective in the early modern era and some snarky remarks about how many infant Christs had the faces of middle-aged men. On his way out, Jamie bought a book of Caravaggio's work. Who knew that you could buy art books for under twenty dollars? Not me. Jamie has returned to the museum many times since then, always with a different aim in mind. He loved *The Lion King*—what kid doesn't?—and became a Julie Taymor fan (like his parents) when he learned that the person responsible for this fabulous staging of the Disney movie was the same person responsible for the film *Across the Universe*, which spoke to Jamie's advanced Beatlemania—and his love of fun. The evening's dance at BAM was, as you might imagine, a bit too much; we both wound up in a glazed-eyed state somewhere between hypnosis and boredom. And in fact, six people walked out, two of them only minutes before the end of the piece (did they have a train to catch?). Jamie, for his part, entertained himself during the less interesting moments of *Ship in a View* by flipping through his Caravaggio book.

The salsa performance the following morning was delightful, and tickets were nine dollars each. And it was in Carnegie Hall, in the basement performance space. Dancing was encouraged. A fine way to wrap up Culture Weekend!

From that weekend on, Jamie has been a culture vulture. The *Mostly Mozart* show in Lincoln Center—that was his idea. The Museum of Modern Art was Janet's idea (Jamie loved it). The New Museum of Contemporary Art was my idea (Jamie liked it). The Outsider Art Fair in New York was Janet's idea (Jamie loved it, and I hope someday he will exhibit his work there). The IFPDA (International Fine Print Dealers Association) Print Fair in the Armory at 67th Street and Park Avenue was a friend's idea (Jamie liked it). The Whitney Museum of American Art was his idea. We happened upon an Edward Hopper show. I pointed out a few obvious things about Hopper's clean lines, dramatic shadows, and urban settings, and then we stumbled onto early paintings like *The Bridge of Art* (1907) and some renderings of the river Seine that look as if young Hopper had been taking lessons from Cézanne. "Hm. Or maybe Monet," Jamie added, drawing startled looks from people within earshot. The Smithsonian Museum of the American Indian—also his idea (he loved it). The Guggenheim—his idea (he liked it). The Cloisters—my idea (he didn't care for it).

Understand, this sophisticated cosmopolite and accomplished museumgoer is also a young man who loves contemporary country music, particularly Jason Aldean and Luke Bryan, and who can sit rapt for hours in wonderment at professional wrestling. (I got him two tickets to the Jason Aldean show when it came to town in 2013, for Jamie and another country-western-loving young man with Down syndrome, and did so again in early 2016. I have not yet taken Jamie to live professional wrestling, but I will.) He is not a snob. His tastes are ecumenical, ranging from Michelangelo to thriller/action movies. He is a huge Austin Powers fan, and has had to learn for himself that there are some jokes from the Austin Powers movies that one really should not repeat in polite company. He has also become fond of a genre of music associated with black T-shirts, skulls, and iron crosses, featuring bands with names like Onslaught Apocalypse, Rivers of Blood, and Excruciating Pain. (I can't bear to listen to it.) He just thinks that there is a great deal of stuff in the world that merits his attention, and he happens to be right about that. And because of his phenomenal cataloguing memory, he is capable of telling me (as he did in the course of talking through this chapter with me) that Caravaggio died in 1610, "very similar," as he put it, to El Greco, who died in 1614. And he loves drawing analogies among the things he loves, whether it's remarking that Andrea del Sarto is "very similar" to Michelangelo or observing that the young-adult SF film *Divergent* is "very similar" to the film version of *Ender's Game*. You can see why he would be a great resource for anyone preparing to compete on *Jeopardy!*

Last but not least: if you are not inclined to try to enhance your child's cognitive capacities (regardless of where he or she might be on the spectrum of human variation) by way of travel, art, or music, I have one more card to play: an animal companion, who can provide animal companionship.

At first blush this might not sound like the kind of thing that builds brain power in the way that travel, art, and music do. A pet seems cuddlier and cuter, not only cuddlier and cuter than teaching your kid algebra but also cuddlier and cuter than Caravaggio. But there is no question in my mind that Jamie's animal companions—Lucy, who was with us from 1997 to 2011, and Becca, who joined us eight months after Lucy left—have enhanced his cognitive abilities. As I noted above, Lucy gave him someone to talk to, someone who never misunderstood or misheard him, and many of the first complex sentences he uttered, at the age of six, were *about* Lucy. Lucy was the object of Jamie's first understanding of simile, when he grasped with delight his mother's observation that *Lucy is the color of leaves in the autumn.* Likewise, when Jamie was seven and I pointed out to him (at the Detroit zoo) that some animals, like the ostrich or the human, have two legs, and some, like the camel over there, have four, he nodded and added, "Like Lucy."

Lucy was a present for Jamie's sixth birthday, a clever mutt from the pound whose previous family was apparently horrific enough to have shot a BB pellet into her back. She knew immediately that there was something special about Jamie, and Jamie became almost preternaturally attentive to her moods and desires. For as long as I have memories, I will never forget the night Jamie and I were doing his homework for seventh-grade science class, going over the components of the gastrointestinal tract, when we came to the pancreas. "We can skip this one," I said to him, "you don't know the pancreas." His teacher, Ms. Pelligrini, had told us that Jamie would only have to know most of the GI tract, not the whole thing. But Jamie immediately retorted, "Lucy had pancreatitis and cannot eat human food." OK. Point made. You *do* know about the pancreas.

And then there was the conversation Jamie and I had one lazy weekend as I was sitting around reading Alasdair MacIntyre's book *Dependent
Rational Animals*. I had just come upon a passage in which MacIntyre
takes Martin Heidegger to task for distinguishing humans from animals
by putting one big opposable thumb on the scales, insofar as Heidegger
justifies the distinction by emphasizing "lower" animals whose cognitive capacities are not remotely comparable with our own:

> A domesticated dog does appear early in [Heidegger's] discussion,
> but thereafter we find a welcome variety of bees, moths, freshwater
> crabs, lizards, sea-urchins, woodworms, and woodpeckers. . . . What
> we do not find are wolves or elephants or, even more importantly,
> gorillas or chimpanzees or dolphins.

The larger argument at stake here is that our attempts to distinguish
humans from other animals on the basis of our superior cognitive abilities have become increasingly suspect: We are not the only species to use
tools. We are not the only species to punish social cheaters. We are not
the only species to use language. I sometimes try to sum up the situation
by saying that there is no study of animal cognition, at any point in the
last five hundred years, whose results could be summed up by the headline "Animals: Dumber Than We Thought." The research has uniformly
gone in the other direction.

So I put down MacIntyre's book and asked Jamie, who happened to
be watching the Animal Planet channel at the time, "Can animals think?
Some people say yes and some people say no. What do you say?"

For Jamie, this was (so to speak) a no-brainer, because Lucy was
clearly among the very smartest dogs on the planet, capable not only of
determining when a family member is ill but also of reading highway
signs (Exit 242! This is where we stop for bathroom break! Yay!) and of
knowing where she is by using elementary canine calculus to fix her
position in the hemisphere.

So we talked for a bit about how Lucy can be happy or excited or worried (about the thunder, because she does not understand about weather)
or sad (when she sees a suitcase), and about how some animals have

brains that are very complicated but others have brains that are very simple. "Sharks," Jamie did not fail to say, "are one of the best predators."

"True enough," I said. "Animals can be very clever about finding food. And they can have feelings, like sadness or happiness. And complicated animals like dogs and horses can even understand humans, too."

"Or chimpanzees," Jamie added. "Or gorillas, like Koko. Or dolphins." Here Jamie did his dead-on imitation of dolphin clicking. And being disability-aware, he is fascinated that Koko learned sign language.

"But, of course, animals do not speak human language," I added.

Quick as a flash, Jamie replied, "Parrots."

"Right, parrots. Good one. And, of course, dolphins and whales can talk to each other in dolphin and whale language. So we know that animals can understand things, can talk to each other, and can figure out how to find food even when it is very difficult. But do they have thoughts about these things? Do you think Lucy can sit down and say, 'Hey, maybe I shouldn't be so worried about the thunder'? You remember when you were sad, and you thought about it, and we talked about what it is like to be sad. Do you think a dog can do that?"

Jamie mulled this over for a few seconds.

"Well . . . you can train," he said.

I thought (and still think) that was a brilliant response. What Jamie meant, I learned, was that animals must be capable of some form of thought if they can be trained. Lucy, for example, must have some reflective relation to her bodily functions in order to learn not to urinate and defecate in the house. (We talked for a bit about the rule, in the film *Babe*, that ducks and pigs are not allowed in the house.) But the fact that you can train an animal with operant conditioning isn't necessarily evidence that the animal has become, how should we say, *thoughtful*. I myself trained a white rat to respond to a variety of feeding schedules (fixed-ratio, fixed-interval, variable-ratio, variable-interval) in college. But the more radical implication of Jamie's remark—that you can train an animal to think—is really interesting. Indeed, it echoes an important passage in J. M. Coetzee's novel *Elizabeth Costello* (a passage important enough to quote at length):

Sultan [a chimpanzee] is alone in his pen. He is hungry: the food that used to arrive regularly has unaccountably ceased coming.

The man who used to feed him and has now stopped feeding him stretches a wire over the pen three metres above ground level, and hangs a bunch of bananas from it. Into the pen he drags three wooden crates. Then he disappears, closing the gate behind him, though he is still somewhere in the vicinity, since one can smell him.

Sultan knows: Now one is supposed to think. That is what the bananas up there are about. The bananas are there to make one think, to spur one to the limits of one's thinking. But what must one think? One thinks: Why is he starving me? One thinks: What have I done? Why has he stopped liking me? One thinks: Why does he not want these crates any more? But none of these is the right thought. Even a more complicated thought—for instance: What is wrong with him, what misconception does he have of me, that leads him to believe it is easier for me to reach a banana hanging from a wire than to pick up a banana from the floor?—is wrong. The right thought to think is: How does one use the crates to reach the bananas?

Sultan drags the crates under the bananas, piles them one on top of the other, climbs the tower he has built, and pulls down the bananas. He thinks: Now will he stop punishing me?

The answer is: No. The next day the man hangs a fresh bunch of bananas from the wire but also fills the crates with stones so that they are too heavy to be dragged. One is not supposed to think: Why has he filled the crates with stones? One is supposed to think: How does one use the crates to get the bananas despite the fact that they are filled with stones?

One is beginning to see how the man's mind works. . . .

At every turn Sultan is driven to think the less interesting thought. From the purity of speculation (Why do men behave like this?) he is relentlessly propelled towards lower, practical, instrumental reason (How does one use this to get that?) and thus towards acceptance of himself as primarily an organism with an appetite that needs to be satisfied. Although his entire history, from the time his mother was shot and he was captured, through his voyage in a cage to imprisonment on this island camp and the sadistic games that are played around food here, leads him to ask questions about the justice of the universe and the place of this penal colony in it, a carefully plotted psychological regimen conducts him away from ethics and metaphysics towards the humbler reaches of practical reason. And somehow, as he inches through this labyrinth of constraint, manipulation and duplicity, he must realize that on no account dare he give up, for on his shoulders rests the responsibility of representing apedom. The fate of his brothers and sisters may be determined by how well he performs.

When we got Lucy from the animal shelter for Jamie's sixth birthday, we also wound up giving Jamie—and Lucy—a great deal of food for thought.

Toward the end of Lucy's life, her increasing ill health weighed heavily on nineteen-year-old Jamie, not only because of her impending death but because her illness manifested as an inability to eat. In her final weeks she was skeletal, often shaking with pain. "You may *not* let this animal starve," our vet told us, and we agreed: starvation is a terrible way to die, and we would never allow our beloved Lucy to undergo that torment. Desperate, we made one last effort to keep her with us, with the vet's blessing: baby food. Jamie and I visited the baby food aisle of the supermarket for the first time in almost twenty years—a nostalgia-inducing experience for him, one that I was happy to indulge as we sorted through the pureed plums and peaches and sweet potatoes he dimly but warmly remembered (or claimed to remember) from his early youth. But over the next day, we found that Lucy couldn't eat that human food either. Tearfully, Janet and I returned to the vet and had her put to sleep that afternoon. I picked Jamie up from his intramural bowling game that evening and broke the news to him. "Lucy didn't make it, sweetie. She couldn't eat. She died this afternoon, very peacefully, and we will have to keep her in our memories."

Jamie took this in calmly, saying "shoot" and nothing more.

At first I thought this was testimony to his maturity—and, perhaps, to the careful way Janet and I had tried to prepare him for Lucy's eventual death. Only a few months later did I realize the depths of his loss. When Janet and I first broached the subject of getting a new dog, Jamie shut us down. He would not hear of it. There could never be another dog! Right there on the refrigerator was the card some of Nick's friends had made for us—LUCY, ALWAYS IN OUR HEARTS. If Lucy is always in our hearts, how could we possibly betray her memory by replacing her? Jamie did hold out one alternative possibility as a conciliatory gesture: perhaps, he suggested, we could get a tarantula.

By autumn, as the leaves were turning the color of Lucy's soft brown fur, Janet had made an executive decision. After months of what she called "online dog dating," she had picked a comely Jack Russell mix named Becca, who was listed as being six years old. We decided to take her for a trial period, figuring that Jamie would overcome his resistance and bond with her once he actually met her. For my part, I switched rhetorical tactics on Jamie. Since "it would be nice to have another dog, and Lucy wouldn't mind" wasn't getting anywhere, I pointed out to him that, as he well knew from his volunteer work at PAWS, a local animal shelter, there are many animals out there who need good, loving homes, and ours is definitely a good, loving home. Jamie made no reply to this argument, because there is no reply; it is simply incontrovertible. And so, when we picked up Becca one crisp fall day near Thanksgiving, Janet took the dog home to feed her and acclimate her, and I went to tell Jamie, who was, at the time, working at a bingo fund-raiser. But Jamie had one last form of resistance, involving a very clever deflection of the "good, loving home" argument. When I told him that we had gotten a lovely little dog whose family could no longer afford her and who needed a new home, Jamie, rather than passively acceding to a done deal, went from table to table, asking the assembled bingo players if they needed a dog for their home.

I confess that I found this perversely delightful, even as I was struck by how profoundly loyal Jamie could be to his beloved Lucy. But as events unfolded, Janet's hunch turned out to be right: Jamie bonded with Becca almost immediately, and Becca, like her predecessor, sensed something special about Jamie. As their relationship has developed, Becca has become sensitive to every nuance in Jamie's life. Most recently, in the weeks prior to my writing this chapter, she has scurried into my study from the sofa downstairs every time she hears me call Jamie on his cellphone to make sure he is on the 3 p.m. bus on the way home from work. (I was calling him only because the bus schedule changed at the end of the school year, necessitating a change in his daily routine.) Somehow Becca knows that I am talking to Jamie, and she surmises as a result that I am talking about picking him up at the bus stop downtown; exuberantly, she is asking me if she can come along to get him. And because she has abandonment issues, understandably enough, the words that make her happiest are "you can come with us," which Jamie always utters with a glee to match Becca's excitement.

Jamie is right: traveling is great for his heart and his brain. So are art and music, Lucy and Becca. And even though Becca is Jamie's dog now, we all know that Lucy will be forever in his heart, having helped him grow his brain.

On the Fields of Play

□ □ □ □ □

Something bad happened to Jamie at a summer camp in 1998, when he was six and a half. For many years we didn't know what it was; only when Jamie and I started talking about this chapter did he tell me that it had something to do with a diving board. Up through the summer of 1997, he loved going to the town pool in Champaign. He started out as a little aquatic mammal who would jump into practically any body of water, from the bathtub to the Arctic. The following year, though, whenever we proposed going to the pool, he wouldn't hear of it. I have to assume that he had attempted a dive and had gotten a mouthful of water or worse—though the camp staff never mentioned any unfortunate pool incidents. Whatever may have happened in 1998, I decided in 1999 to make this one of my life's projects: getting Jamie back into the water.

I started small, holding him on my hip and easing him into the pool. At first we simply walked around bouncing a little, so that Jamie's "swimming" experiences consisted of hanging onto my shoulder like a rhesus monkey in water three feet deep. After a few weeks of this, I began a game. I held him away from me, my hands under his armpits, facing me. In a singsong voice, bouncing more strenuously, I said, "He's my guy and my guy and my guy and my guy, and his name is Jamie B."—which is what his classmates called him. I gave the "B" two syllables, be-eee. On the second repetition of this line, I slowed down the last bit. And. His. Name. Is. Jamie . . . B! One short, staccato syllable for the "B" this time, and I flung him backwards over my head. (Yes, I always made sure there was no one within twenty feet of us.) Splash!

He *squealed* with delight. I spun around and gathered him to me, lest he go under for too long. "Again!" he chortled.

As you might imagine, we did it again. And after a few reps, I had him swim to me, to my back, and wrap his arms around my neck. I then proceeded to pretend that I did not know where he was. "Jamie? Jamie?" This elicited waves of laughter. "I'm *right here,*" he would say, just as he said on the day I lost him at Illinois's IMPE building. I would turn my head this way and that, but of course, since Jamie was attached to me, I was unable to see him. Laughter, and more laughter.

And gradually, Jamie got used to the pool again.

It wasn't that simple, but that's what started him on the road to re-covering from whatever diving-board misstep had put the Fear of Pool into him the previous year. By the time he was nine, I had gotten Jamie to the point at which he was willing to play by himself in shallow water. Toward the end of the summer of 2001, after we had moved to State College, I thought he had enough confidence to join me—as I held him—in the deep end of the Welch Pool, a few blocks from our house. Jamie ten-tatively came down the steps, leapt into my arms, and quickly realized that he was nowhere near touching bottom. Indeed, we were in twelve feet of water. "Is deep," he protested, ungrammatically. "I would sink."

"It is deep, sweetie," I replied. "But you will not sink. Just hold onto me." All we did, that day, was hang out at the pool's edge for a few min-utes. All I wanted was for him to be in the deep end, not to try to swim on his own or, perish the thought, go off the diving board.

The following year we joined a health club, the one we eventually left in frustration at its irregular hours. But I will always think of it fondly in one respect, because it is the place Jamie learned to swim. And he learned to swim because, unlike the municipal pools across the coun-try that have been challenged by a combination of attorneys, insurance companies, and grieving parents losing their children to water-wings drownings, this club permitted flotation belts. In fact, they *provided* flo-tation belts. So, every weekend, Jamie and I would head to the club. We had a ritual (I had forgotten it, but Jamie reminded me as I was writing this): We would burst out of the men's locker room and Jamie would cry, "We're out!"—citing the scene in *A Hard Day's Night* when the four lads from Liverpool burst out of the television studio in which they have been rehearsing and run away to gambol and frolic on a field as "Can't Buy Me Love" soars on the soundtrack. Jamie would then grab a flotation belt—at only 4 feet 5 inches, he could not stand up even in the shallow end—and we would proceed to play in the water for about an hour, mostly by tossing a racquetball back and forth and making spectacular diving catches (or not making them). Gradually we stepped up to jumping in the deep end, flotation belt securely on. Sooner than I would have imagined, Jamie ditched the belt, even in the deep end. By that point, in spring 2003, he had developed an idiosyncratic swimming stroke in which his arms never broke the surface of the water. He would undulate, like a sea lion or a manatee, thrusting forward with his arms under his chest and kicking his legs in a breaststroke-esque fashion. It was ungainly, but it worked, and before I knew it, Jamie had decided to dive and touch the bottom of the deep end, eleven feet down. He was down there too long, I thought, but he made it, and he was thrilled with himself. "You had no trouble holding your breath?" I asked, nervously.

"No way, José!" Jamie replied.

"Your chest does not hurt? Your lungs do not hurt?"

"No way!"

And now we were off to the races. Not literally: I could not have imagined in 2003 that Jamie would begin his career as a Special Olympics swimmer only six years later, at the age of seventeen. But bit by bit, almost too slowly to perceive, his confidence grew—and so did his competence. That summer, he considered going off the diving board at the outdoor pool of the Penn State Natatorium and actually got out on the board and thought about it for about two full minutes while standing at the edge of the diving board. You can picture the scene, I'm sure—and thankfully, there were only one or two people waiting behind him (though it sucked to be them). Finally he decided to inch carefully back to dry land, whereupon he jumped off the side of the deep end and swam half the length of the pool (a good twenty-five meters) before hauling himself out and announcing to the world, "I am a brave and very good kid." Which he was. He was simply frightened of the board's bounciness, because he likes to have a nice steady surface under his feet.

And now I know he must have been thinking of that fateful attempt on the diving board five years earlier.

When the Natatorium's outdoor pool closed on Labor Day, we moved to the Nat's indoor pools. In 2001, Jamie had found these too intimidating: one is a fourteen-foot-deep diving pool, one is a six-to-ten-foot-deep lap pool, and one is a three-to-five-foot-deep lap pool. In 2001–2002, he could only manage the shallow end of the last of these. But by 2003, he could jump right into the deeper lap pool, which I (sneakily) called the "big kids' pool," and within a few years he could manage—with minimal, but crucial, urging—to swim four laps back and forth. We punctuated these with experiments in how to touch the bottom at both ends, and Jamie was thrilled to discover that when you're five feet tall, six feet of water isn't very intimidating at all.

And then one day, in 2006, not long after his fifteenth birthday, we were playing around the sides of the diving pool alongside six or seven students. I asked Jamie, for the hundredth time, if he wanted to go off the diving board, and for the hundredth time, he replied, "I don't think so." As I did on the previous ninety-nine occasions, I said, "OK, then, just checking." But this time I added, pointing to five lithe and rambunctious young men who were taking turns flying off the board, "You know, they're not much older than you are, those guys. They're maybe nineteen or twenty, I think." And that did it! Before I knew what was up, Jamie was striding over to the board, declaring, "I will do it *by myself*." I asked the lifeguard whether Jamie would be allowed to wear his goggles (the outdoor pools in State College forbid this), and he said, "Sure. He'll probably lose 'em when he hits the water, but that's OK if you can get 'em." And then *splash!* Without the slightest hesitation, Jamie had walked right to the end of the bouncy board and flung himself off. He swam to the ladder, goggles still snugly on his face, where I met him with "nice jump!" and a big high-five, and he—you knew this was coming, right?—announced that he would do it again. And then again. And then again.

By 2010 he was brave enough to attempt a jump from the three-meter platform at the outdoor pool. I was on line for the platform diving—I go off the 5-meter platform, but I will leave the 7.5 and the 10 to younger and more supple folk—when suddenly Jamie joined me. "Do you really want to jump off the platforms?" I asked. "Michael! I can do it," he replied.

"OK, then, are you going to jump off the one-meter like you did last year?"

"No way! I can go off the three."

I had my doubts. One of the funny things about those platforms is that they look twice as high once you're actually on them, so that when you're up on the five (which doesn't look very high from the ground), you think you're jumping off a three-story building. And though the platform is not a bouncy diving board, I worried about Jamie's fear of heights. The three is ten feet up, of course, but Jamie's eyes would be fifteen feet off the ground. I figured he would climb up to the three, flip out, and either (a) retreat to the one or (b) get stuck up there so that I'd have to retrieve him.

"Are you absolutely sure?"

"No problem!" he insisted, somewhat dismissively. So I told him that he must, must, must hit the water with his feet first. He must not, must not, must not jump forward the way he does on the spring board, landing knees-and-chest in the water. He must, must, must jump straight down. And so forth. "Michael!" he said, "I got it."

When he got to the edge of the platform, Jamie didn't waver for a second. He sized it up, took a few steps, and wooosh! He went flying into fifteen feet of water from the three-meter platform.

The following day, Jamie not only went off the three again; he also doodled around the far end of the diving well and then decided to take off from the water's surface (that is, without jumping in) and touch the bottom. For this he got a warning from the lifeguard (no playing around in the diving well!), but he was so pleased with the feat (and even the lifeguard seemed impressed) that he swam over to me bursting with glee. "I did it!"

"You did what?" I asked.

"I touched the bottom! By myself!"

"Wait, you just touched the bottom? In the deep end? Just now?" That would be *fifteen* feet down, four feet deeper than the club pool, in which he'd tried this stunt seven years earlier.

"Uh-huh!"

"With your hand?"

"Yes! And I pushed myself back up!"

"Wow." That really *is* impressive. "And you had enough air? Do you feel all right? Did you have any trouble holding your breath?"

"Michael! I'm fine!"

Let's put it this way: the movie of *Percy Jackson and the Olympians: The Lightning Thief* opens with Percy sitting at the bottom of the deep end of a pool, where, we find, he has been for an incredible seven full minutes. Now, whenever Jamie plays in a pool, he asks me how long he has been under. I am trying to discourage him from breaking Percy's record; after all, Percy is the son of Poseidon and staying underwater comes naturally to him. But I am totally thrilled at how pool-adept Jamie has become.

□ □ □

So much for Jamie's amateur diving career; he is not a Special Olympics diver. But before I get to the thrilling tale of Jamie's spectacular debut as a Special Olympics swimmer, in 2009, I have to explain how Jamie became competitive in the first place. And that explanation will take us through Challenger League baseball and the annual Geri Ryan Track Meet, held in Penn State's indoor track facility (the very locale in which Jamie almost got a foot crushed in a track practice). The Geri Ryan meet was established in 1992, after Geri Ryan, co-manager of Centre County Special Olympics and mother of a child with Down syndrome (Rebecca), died of cancer. Jamie started participating in the Geri Ryan meet in 2005, when he was only thirteen. Challenger League baseball is emphatically noncompetitive. And yet Jamie learned from those experiences to push himself physically—and, crucially, to have fun in doing so.

For me the story starts on Little League baseball opening day, April 2004. I was sitting cross-legged on the grass on the third-base side of the field. Jamie, twelve, was sitting on my lap. Jamie was technically a Little Leaguer, and was there as a member of the Challenger League, a Little League division for kids under twenty-one with developmental disabilities.

Jamie started playing Challenger League in 2002, and over his first two years I'd been struck by how pleasant an experience it was. Up to that point, he had never played any form of organized sport. And of course, Little League baseball in central Pennsylvania can be deadly serious business. Every summer we host the Little League World Series at a baseball complex that sits at the end of an unassuming residential street in a quiet part of Williamsport, a small town in coal-mining and fracking country. Jamie and I have been there a few times: it is a genuinely weird experience, driving down a tiny side street that somehow opens on to a hidden world where thousands of people are watching—and ESPN is televising—a competition that involves children from around the world.

And for many years, Little League has been notorious for eliciting aggressively bad behavior among coaches, players, and (most of all) stage fathers, who seemed determined to live their sports fantasies vicariously through their children. Youth baseball, I thought, was a world in which parents threatened and assaulted umpires, where coaches threw temper tantrums and water bottles . . . and threatened or assaulted umpires. In 2005, in a western Pennsylvania children's league, a coach actually paid a seven-year-old player twenty-five dollars to injure an autistic teammate in pre-game warm-ups so that the team would have a better chance of winning. The young hired gun, after striking his teammate in the head and the groin with a ball, eventually told police of the arrangement (after the victim's parents had investigated their child's injuries), and the coach was arraigned on a variety of criminal charges. The league president, Eric Forsythe, a friend of the coach, told the press that the incident had been "blown out of proportion." And that, folks, is how you condone and enable bullying and violence aimed at kids with disabilities.

All one can say is that these appalling incidents are not specific to baseball; parents who get involved in other sports are often worse. Hockey parents have been known to attack one another and to hurl objects at referees; my own hockey dad was mild by those standards, but he was capable of advising me never to pass to a rival teammate who was vying with me for the league scoring title. It hardly mattered, however, because my rival's parents had advised him never to pass to me, either.

But Challenger League, I thought, was a world apart. No one keeps score, no one counts balls or strikes, and everyone reaches base. The games last two innings; an inning is over after every child has batted, and after the last batter makes contact with the ball, be the ball fair or foul, everyone rounds the bases for home. Often, after a batter has struck a ball, coaches will throw a few more balls into play so that everyone gets a chance to field. It's like sport without the thrill of victory or the agony of defeat.

In every Challenger League game, Little Leaguers served as "buddies." Tweens from local Little League teams would pair up with the Challengers, and though there must have been some degree of pity or condescension in this arrangement, it was never palpable. I have no idea how any of the individual Little Leaguers, or their coaches, felt about this. It seemed, on one hand, a little too much of a feel-good "helping-the-handicapped" exercise. And who knows how many of the Little League kids thought *I have to get into full uniform and spend an hour on Friday evening with kids who have no idea what baseball is?* But if any of them thought such ungenerous things—and humans being what they are, it would be miraculous if no one ever had such thoughts—they never gave themselves away. Because on the other hand, they really *were* helping the handicapped, so to speak, and spending an hour of their time (plus travel time, plus whatever time it took to get into and out of full uniform) to incorporate Jamie and his cohort into Little League, more or less. And for what it's worth—it could be condescension or genuine admiration—the Little Leaguers who became Jamie's buddies never failed to marvel at the fact that he has a strong throwing arm and can wield a serious bat. However, he had trouble catching a thrown ball. (Though by the time his Challenger years were up, he had managed to snag a legit foul pop behind first base.)

So it was especially surprising to me, that April 2004 morning on Little League opening day, to hear sweet, mild-mannered Jamie start grousing about how he hadn't been picked to throw out one of the ceremonial first pitches. Three or four children had been selected to throw out the first pitch from each of what seemed like dozens of leagues, divisions, conferences, and associations. So I started grousing about the

ceremony of a "first pitch" that went on for over half an hour and thinking dark thoughts about what a second, third, fourth, fortieth, four hundredth first pitch could possibly mean, and Jamie was grousing that he
wasn't a part of it. I had never even heard him grouse before. But there
he was, in his cap and jersey, telling me, "I can do it better than Pete."

"Did you say you can do it better than Pete?" I asked, *sotto voce*.

"Yes," Jamie insisted. "*I* should throw the pitch."

"Now, listen," I replied, completely unprepared for this. "That's true;
you can throw better than Pete." There was no use denying this; Jamie
had the best arm in Challenger League. "But this is not a competition,
Jamie. Pete was invited to throw the ball this time. Maybe next year you
will be invited. But now it's Pete's turn, and you have to wait your turn."

This mollified him somewhat, as well it should have. But it also
produced in him a determination that, come April 2005, he would be
out there on the mound, ball in hand, all eyes on him. And that's what
happened, one year later: Jamie threw out one of the innumerable first
pitches, and he did it reasonably well. On my blog, I posted pictures
of his pitch, as well as a picture of Jamie in batting practice, with me
tossing him underhand pitches in a batting cage. In response, readers
suggested that I should throw overhand to Jamie, on the grounds that
overhand pitches are easier to see coming in. I took up the suggestion,
and sure enough, before too long Jamie was belting line drives and hitting the ball out of the infield. This was something no other Challenger
League player could do, and it established him as the most fearsome
slugger in a decidedly non-fearsome league.

There was, as you would imagine, a downside to this new feature
of Jamie's psyche, and I triggered it a few months after his historic first
pitch when I tried to show him how to improve on his Harry Potter
CD-ROM game. Janet and I had bought him the game in the hope that it
would improve his hand-eye coordination and give him some purchase
on the world inhabited by Nick—the world of Xbox, PlayStation, and
EA Sports.

Jamie had reached that crucial point in a young intellectually disabled male teenager's development when he was no longer satisfied to
be "included" among his older brother's gaming friends by being given

an inoperative console and being encouraged to pretend he was really playing along, but was not yet proficient enough to be given a working console. So when I noticed that Jamie was having trouble using his computer mouse to trace some of the on-screen patterns that would enable him to use spells such as "Alohomora" and "Wingardium Leviosa," I showed him how to hold the mouse steady, unlock the spells, and earn extra bonus points.

That was a very serious mistake. Once Jamie saw that his scores of 51 and 52 percent accuracy—just barely good enough to squeak by—could be bested by his father's 84 and 87, he stopped playing Harry Potter computer games altogether. That phase lasted nearly six months; and when Jamie finally returned to his computer games, I made a point of telling him—quite honestly—where his gaming skills were better than mine. We quickly struck a deal: Jamie would handle all the tasks in Hogwarts and around the grounds, and I would take over for the Quidditch matches, which involved flying tasks Jamie hadn't mastered yet. That was in spring or summer 2006. Within a year or two, he had become a better flyer and a better Quidditch player than I ever was.

In the Geri Ryan meet, Jamie's events were the fifty-meter dash, the standing long jump, and the softball throw. He killed it in the softball throw, hurling the ball as far as competitors twice his age and size, and he jumped a good four feet (not bad for a kid five feet tall). But it was his performance in the 50m that impressed me most, because prior to that first meet, in 2005, Jamie did not run. At all. Not for fifty meters, not for five. He didn't have the confidence, and as I've mentioned, for too long he didn't have the orthotic supports he needed. So Janet and I prepped him for the big event by holding mock-races in the alleyway beside our house, racing perhaps twenty or thirty meters to the nearest telephone pole. But when he got out on the track, he got into the zone. He was pumped by the crowd, by the festivities, and by seeing Special Olympians from neighboring counties like Blair and Clinton. (This is where he developed his fascination with Pennsylvania's counties.) And he earned himself a silver medal in the race, running it in 14.82 seconds.

Jamie has competed in the Geri Ryan games every year since then, and the games themselves have gotten bigger and bigger, bringing in

more and more athletes from more and more counties. Not long after his debut, Jamie decided to join the Special Olympics volleyball and
basketball teams; he has since given them up, I'm sorry to say, and his
one attempt at softball didn't please him, despite his monster arm and
his fearsome slugging. But during his brief stint as a volleyballer, I did
witness him serve up two consecutive aces in that match at Villanova—
and more important, he stayed in a hotel with the team the night before
the tournament. It was in November 2005. He was fourteen, and that
was his first night away from his parents. (That would also be the occasion on which he helped himself to many servings of ranch dressing.)
I joined him the next day, flying in from a speaking engagement at the
University of Michigan, and accompanied him to his games and to the
big dance on Saturday night. Needless to say, I left him to his own devices for the dance. But I remember as we entered the gymnasium where
the dance was being held, Jamie scouted around for a few minutes and
then turned to me, asking, "Where's my group?" And all I could think
was *He has a group. And he knows he has a group.* I have often wondered
what he thought, back then, about that knowledge. Sure, I might be
overthinking this; at the time, he might simply have meant "Where are
the people I came with?" But I know that by the age of fourteen, Jamie
identified readily as a person with Down syndrome, and as a person with
a legible disability. That process had started years earlier, when Jamie
became fascinated with a calendar published by the National Down Syndrome Society. Most, but not all, of the gorgeous photos in that calendar
were pictures of young children, and Jamie was seven or eight when it
grabbed his attention. The first time he mentioned it to me, I thought
he was saying "dancing drum"; he may in fact have been saying dancing
drum, but he was referring to his 1998 NDSS calendar of children with
Down syndrome, and he knew he was part of that group. Now, he was
identifying with a group that comprised (a) the people he came with, (b)
a group of people with disabilities, and (c) people with disabilities *who
were also his teammates.*

In 2009, Jamie entered serious solo competition for the first time:
Special Olympics swimming meets at nearby universities. Now, when I
say "serious competition" and "Special Olympics" in the same sentence,

I am aware that there are people who might snicker or guffaw. I imagine that if you are reading this book, you are probably not one of them. But no matter what your degree of sympathy with or identification with or position within the disability community, you know that there are people who think of Special Olympics as the very opposite of, or at least a refuge from, serious competition—like Challenger League, where everyone scores and nobody loses. No agon, no striving, just a happy land where everyone gets a medal just for playing. One wonders just what was going through Barack Obama's mind that night on *The Tonight Show* in 2009 when he described his poor bowling scores as "like the Special Olympics or something"; he very possibly thought that the joke would sound self-mocking, but it very clearly associated Special Olympics with athletic incompetence. (Obama promptly apologized, as well he should have; interestingly, the *Washington Times* defended him in an editorial, writing, "Obama is allowed as [sic] to say impolitic things as long as they don't hurt the country. It also lent humanity to Mr. Obama.") The very funny and occasionally problematic film *The Ringer*, one of the few films in the history of the medium that attempts to be a sympathetic comedy about (and employing numerous actors with) intellectual disabilities, does a fine job of dismantling that association: the premise is that a nondisabled young man (played by Johnny Knoxville) could clean up in a Special Olympics meet by feigning intellectual disability. The film was made with the full cooperation of Special Olympics. It is also commenting wryly on the phenomenon of nondisabled actors playing characters with intellectual disabilities—though apparently many viewers, especially but not exclusively the people who objected to the movie, missed this seemingly obvious point. That premise turns out to be quite mistaken. But you should see the movie for yourself—I will provide no spoilers here.

Anyone still inclined to snicker or guffaw should read Timothy Shriver's account of the first Special Olympics, held in Chicago in 1968. Chicago in 1968 is usually remembered for something else, but this seems important too.

> All over Soldier Field, children of scorn and lonely teenagers tried their best and won. People who had so little to give gave the one

thing they had: their hearts. And those around them were given a chance to unleash their spirits, too, by cheering them on, by watching their bravery come to life, by meeting their smiles with eyes opened to loveliness. On that day, winning had nothing to do with beating anyone and everything to do with playing like no one is judging even though everyone is watching. Sports had never seen anything like it. No one had.

   . . . On July 20, 1968, for the first time in history, people with intellectual disabilities were celebrated as great individuals by others who discovered their gifts in the joy of sports. Gifts! The idea of Olympic triumph, of winning, of bravery, of being gifted—none of these qualities had ever been conferred on these human beings. But on the first day, there was something in their persistence, something in their emotional tenderness, in the uninhibited openness to others that burst to life and awakened those who could see to a different way of defining what it means to win.

In disability studies, we tend to be skeptical of the so-called "supercrip" and allergic to any suggestion that people with disabilities can be inspiring. But it really is quite difficult to go to a Special Olympics meet, of whatever size, and *not* be inspired by the passion of the athletes and the dedication of the legions of volunteers. When you realize that only fifty years ago, almost no one believed that "the retarded" could participate in athletic events, you realize just how extraordinary Eunice Shriver's vision was. And if you're me, you thank her family—and all those volunteers.

So when I say that Jamie took part in serious competition, I am not saying that Jamie's Special Olympics swimming career can stack up against the times posted by nondisabled swimmers his age, any more than I would claim that 14.82 seconds is an impressive time for a fifty-meter dash. Here's what I'm saying.

In his first meet, in April 2009, at St. Francis University in central Pennsylvania, Jamie opened by winning gold medals in the 25m and 50m freestyle. Heats included only three or four swimmers, segregated by qualifying times; there were dozens of heats. This practice is called "divisioning," and it is at the heart of Special Olympics, allowing athletes to compete at whatever level is appropriate to them. Then for his third event, the 25m backstroke, the meet officials combined his heat—consisting of three teenagers who had posted qualifying times of about forty or forty-five seconds—with that of two adult swimmers whose times were thirty-two or thirty-three seconds. Jamie's best time in practice runs had been something like forty-three seconds.

I filmed the race like a dutiful dad; in fact, I bought a digital videocam expressly for that purpose. But I noted with alarm that at the half-way mark, Jamie trailed the field. I did manage to capture the beginning of his surge, but as he got closer to my end of the pool, my camera angle focused more exclusively on him, so I didn't immediately realize that when he touched up, he did so in first place—for the third time that morning. He had overtaken the other four swimmers in only twelve or thirteen meters.

Not until later that night, after I had replayed the race a few times on my laptop, did I discover that Jamie had briefly looked around in the middle of the pool and found that he was trailing—whereupon he had reached down and found another gear, churning his arms and legs frantically to beat his fellow swimmers. He also beat his personal best time by just over ten seconds, which suggested to me that his "personal best" was a function of his relations to other swimmers—or, in more colloquial sports talk, he rose to the level of the competition. And it wasn't simply a question of winning: in the statewide games two months later, the best he managed was a silver in the 50m freestyle—but that was all right with him, because he shaved another couple of seconds off his personal best in the event. *Citius, altius, fortius.* That's what it's all about. Well, that and living apart from his parents for two nights in a Penn State dormitory. Jamie thought that was pretty great, too. And he bonded with his roommate, a talented young man on the autism spectrum.

So by 2009, I learned that I had an eighteen-year-old with Down syndrome with a fierce competitive streak. At one point he even asked me how to spell "competitive." Who knew this personality trait was in the cards? Even Jamie himself was unaware of it until he entered adolescence. It feeds his sense of self-esteem, it helps to keep him in shape, and it affords him some pride in his accomplishments. What's not to like?

But how is one to walk that line—whether one is disabled or hyperabled—between legitimate pride and satisfaction, and obnoxious, overweening hubris? Between a sincere desire to improve oneself and a brittle, bitter determination to defeat other people? One day after track and field practice, after Jamie spent some minutes enumerating all the people he had beaten, I had to remind him that although he runs well, he is not the fastest runner in his group, and that the real challenge lies in learning how to be competitive while being gracious when you run up against a better athlete. Need I add that this is a challenge many athletes fail to meet? I always said, in my days as a hockey player, that I would rather lose by one than win by ten—even though I played on many teams that won by ten or more. A one-goal game is more exciting because every loose puck matters, and one team is trying desperately to put every loose puck in the net, whereas in a tie game teams tend to play cautiously, trying not to make a game-deciding mistake, and in the closing minutes of a blowout nobody cares about anything. And then there is the gambit in which the trailing team pulls its goalie in the final minute for an extra skater. I have been on both sides of one-goal games, many times, and I really do enjoy them more than blowouts. But sometimes it is very hard to lose. Now Jamie knows that too, because we are talking about serious competition here.

□   □   □

Nobody likes hearing golf stories except for other golfers, so I will try to keep this narrative of Jamie's development as a sportsman as short as possible.

I began playing golf at thirteen on the municipal courses of Queens. In the late 1970s, if you were under eighteen and went through the trouble of getting a golf permit from the New York City Department of Parks and Recreation, you could play any course in the city for a dollar. I know that almost everywhere in the world, golf is associated with country clubs and business deals and reactionary politics and plaid pants. But not in Queens.

So I became reasonably good at the game, and by "reasonably good" I mean horribly erratic but capable of parring five or six holes in a row when the golf gods smiled upon me. I played from 1975 to 1978, then not in college or for the first couple years of graduate school, then again from 1985 to 1991, then not after Jamie was born. But in 1997, a friend invited me to resume playing as his on-again, off-again partner, and by the following year, when Jamie was six, I would sometimes bring him along with me when I played solo—both for his sake and for Janet's. He rode in the cart, we sang songs, and I got in some golf while he got some fresh air. The course we played, Iron Horse in east central Illinois, did not charge us for Jamie's presence. When we moved to Penn State, in contrast, the university golf courses informed us that Jamie could join me on the course only if I paid a fifteen-dollar "rider's fee." Since Jamie was not playing the course, and since the golf carts seat two people, the Penn State golf course was effectively charging him fifteen dollars to breathe their air. So we decided we would take our business someplace else—thirty-five miles down the road, to Belles Springs golf course. Penn State's clubhouse is very fancy, suggestive of country clubs and business deals. Belles Springs' clubhouse is a Quonset hut, and the management was completely cool with Jamie.

Sometimes, if the club permitted it, I would let him putt; by the time he was fourteen, he was ready to hit a few balls of his own, usually from the shallow rough (I didn't want him chopping up the fairways). Eventually, he got to the point where he could play his own ball from tee to green, so long as he remembered to take a half-swing. The golf swing involves some of the most convoluted bodily motions in sports, and Jamie couldn't control the club if he took a full backswing (and he still can't). But when he "found his spot" and controlled his swing, he could send the ball flying. And as every golfer knows (and every non-golfer couldn't care less about), there is nothing quite like the *thwack* of a well-struck ball. Especially when your father exclaims, after you have struck the ball well and sent it flying over a hundred and fifty yards straight down the middle, "Holy cow"—in such a way as to betray the fact that he almost said *holy shit*.

Back at Iron Horse, there was a moment when a seven-year-old Jamie took it into his head to stand on the side edge of the cart, bouncing on it in a way that made me think he might just be capable of toppling it over on himself. That was not quite a loud-voice moment, but I did tell him in no uncertain terms never to do that again. Ten years later, Jamie was capable of driving the cart himself, though I quickly learned that he did not know how to brake, so I braked for him and took the wheel, and we won't try *that* experiment again. But most important, as Jamie improved as a golfer, a crucial aspect of his character emerged. I know, it is a horrible cliché: *sports build character.* As clichés go, it is even worse than "giving 110 percent" and "leaving it all on the field," because it is the tiresome mantra of youth leagues in every sport. In Jamie's case, golf did not build character; rather, the game revealed something about the kind of person he is. And this was—and is—a very good thing.

James Lyon Bérubé is the only golfer, since the invention of the game by bored Scottish shepherds in the late medieval era, who *does not get frustrated.* He will hit ten weak shots in a row, shanks or hooks or skulled 7-irons that roll haplessly for a handful of yards, and then *thwack*, he will lace an 8-iron to the green from 110 yards out, pin high and 15 feet from the hole, just like that. He will not mutter or grumble about the ten clunkers; he will, instead, chortle with glee at the perfectly struck ball. Only once, since we began playing together in 2007, have I seen him become dejected. He had every reason to be: five holes into a nine-hole round, after an hour of plugging away, neither of us had hit a single decent golf shot. That was the day I had to draw on his lessons in tang soo do (which we will get to in a moment): you have to have *indomitable spirit*. It's not just a question of accentuating the positive, eliminating the negative, and determining not to mess with Mister In-Between. It is something deeper, something indelible about who Jamie has become: He does not get aggravated when he does not hit the ball well. He does not get down on himself. He simply finds his spot and lives for the next well-hit ball.

We don't keep score, and there are many mulligans (do-overs, for you non-golfers). Fortunately, because Jamie plays quickly, we never hold up the people behind us. This consideration kept me from making tee times with Jamie during crowded hours, and for some years I tried to make sure we could play alone. But when we do find ourselves in a makeshift foursome with strangers, I explain on the first tee that Jamie will play from the front tees, will take mulligans, and will play at a good pace. The people who have played with Jamie have discovered what I have discovered: he is genial and enthusiastic, cheerful about the game, and (gasp) capable of getting a couple of legitimate bogeys along the way.

After one especially memorable round in 2008, we came into the tiny clubhouse of Mingo Springs golf course in Rangeley, Maine, to have a couple of those scary bright-pink New England hot dogs. The course pro, himself a *gentil et sympathique jeune homme*, casually asked how we did; I reported that I shot a 41 for nine holes, five over par, and that Jamie had had three bogeys. The pro did a double-take. "Really?" he asked, wide-eyed. I assumed he was not surprised by my reasonably decent 41, so I replied, "Seriously. He bogeyed 10, 12, and 14. For real." The tenth and twelfth holes were short, easy par threes; on both of them, Jamie reached the green from the tee and three-putted. On 14, a short par 4, it took him a drive and three 4-irons to reach the fringe of the green, and as I parked the cart at a safe distance from the green and told him to wait for me before playing his ball, he went right ahead anyway and played his ball . . . and holed a fifty-foot putt. (We walked it off to get the distance. Jamie always insists that I do this when he hits a long one. Like every other golfer, he wants to tell non-golfers, especially his mother, just how impressive his best shots are.) He has gotten a couple dozen pars here and there, and even one birdie: after hitting a perfect tee shot on the 14th hole at Belles Springs, a long, downhill par three, he faced a twenty-footer for his two. He struck a decent putt with about the right speed—he can have astonishingly soft hands around the green—but it was a bit off line. Still, I do believe the USGA *Rules of Golf* permit a father to place his foot in the line of the putt in order to deflect his child's slightly errant ball into the cup, if the putt is for birdie. I don't have my copy of the rule book within reach right now, but I think I'm remembering this one word for word. (Actually, Jamie once hit a real birdie putt, in a "scramble" event in which foursomes play whichever ball is in the best position. One guy in our foursome got us onto the fairway, I got us onto the green, and Jamie canned a snaking eight-footer on an undulating green. And there was much rejoicing.)

But though Jamie's skill as a golfer is surprising and thrilling to Jamie, and to me, ultimately, it's not the point. To make the point, I have to go back to the guy who invited me to play with him in 1997, the guy who was responsible for reviving my interest in the game. He was and is a much better golfer than I am, but he was 180 degrees from Jamie as a playing partner. For the most part, we would both bogey holes: he would hit a perfect drive and good approach shot, chip onto the green, and lip out a six-foot putt; I would drive into the trees and hack an iron into no-man's-land, then float a pitching wedge over various obstacles onto the green and two-putt. He was deeply offended that my 5 and his 5 were both 5s, even though he had played the game properly and I had scrambled out of regions unknown even to Seve Ballesteros. He played slowly, deliberating endlessly over every shot: one morning we were the first group to tee off at 7 a.m., and we came into the clubhouse after eighteen holes at 11:30. I remember this because the club pro glared at us when we arrived, looking pointedly at the clock and asking, "Were you two the first group out?" Our slow play insured that every single group behind us, for the rest of the day, would have rounds four hours long or longer. By contrast, if Jamie and I have no one in front of us, we play eighteen in a crisp, clean three and a half hours.

At Belles Springs, we played often enough—perhaps ten or fifteen times in a summer—for Jamie to become recognizable to the staff. One elderly greenskeeper actually became weepy at the idea that Jamie was a regular. As Jamie and I pulled up to the first tee, he asked incredulously whether Jamie was going to play, and when I replied, "Oh yes, he comes here often, and plays from the red tees," he got visibly misty. And as the pro shop got cooler and cooler with Jamie, I realized after seeing a couple of curiously low numbers on my monthly credit card statement that they were not charging him to play. I was deeply ambivalent about this. It was so, so sweet of them to let Jamie play for free. The contrast with Penn State, where they wanted to charge him just for riding in the cart, could not have been more stark. But still. Once I realized that Jamie had been given a play-Belles-Springs-for-free card, I insisted to the pro shop that he was playing the course tee to green like everybody else, and should pay greens fees like everybody else. Jamie agreed.

With a proviso: part of our pre-game routine at Belles Springs involved Jamie putting on the practice green while I paid up and loaded the cart with our bags. Then I would hit the practice green for five or ten minutes while Jamie went into the snack shop and bought himself a Gatorade and a Slim Jim. I would give him five bucks, and he would come back with the change. That routine lasted until the year we played Belles Springs *after* Jamie had learned how to use his debit card. One humid summer day in 2013, I finished my practice putts and drove the cart to the first tee as Jamie emerged from the clubhouse with his Gatorade and Slim Jim—even though I had not given him any money. "Wait a minute, Jamie," I said. "How did you pay for those? You don't have any dollars." (Jamie refers to cash as "dollars," which makes sense enough for me.)

"In Clinton County you don't have to," he replied. I had a funny feeling that wasn't true, though I was charmed that Jamie had decided that the snacks-for-free policy was a county-wide phenomenon.

"Wait right here," I said, dashing into the clubhouse. The snack bar was closed, and all snack transactions were being handled at the bar by a middle-aged woman whose charming bartending demeanor was a nineteenth-hole version of the *Do you want more coffee with that, honey?* roadside-diner waitress.

I hailed her with "Uh, hi." She recognized me as Jamie's father. We nodded. "I'm sorry to bother you, but was my son just in here trying to buy Gatorade and a Slim Jim?"

"Oh, we don't take debit cards," she replied. "It's perfectly all right. He's fine."

"Thank you," I said, slightly flustered. "That's very kind. But really, I insist." I forked over all of the $3.50 they were willing to forgo on Jamie's behalf.

And it *was* very kind, as was the pro shop guy's decision not to charge Jamie to play. But really, if the point of this little experiment in inclusive cultural politics is to show that Jamie can participate in social and recreational activities like everybody else, then surely Jamie should participate in social and recreational activities like everybody else. I love the fact that the staff at the Belles Springs golf course welcomes Jamie. And even though I don't want Jamie to be inspirational, I was touched by the greenskeeper who was touched by the thought that Jamie could make his own way around the course. And amused that the bartender would give him a wink and a free Gatorade and Slim Jim. I don't think they were treating him as a charity case; I think they were treating him as a friend, a special friend. But in social situations like this, I'd prefer that Jamie not be "special." I'd prefer that he be ordinary. Just another golfer. A regular. Like every other golfer, he should pay for his round and pay for his snacks. Even if, unlike every other golfer, he does not get frustrated with the game.

□   □   □

From 2006 to 2010, Jamie took tang soo do classes at the local YMCA, under the direction of Master Terry Summers. From 2002 to about 2008, he took "therapeutic" horseback-riding lessons at a local farm, under the auspices of Easter Seals. Each of these activities enhanced his coordination and his self-confidence, and each of them involved what might have been serious injuries.

The horseback-riding adventure is a mystery to me, because I had nothing to do with it. I am horribly allergic to horses, having had a near-death experience in a stable at the age of twenty. It is ridiculous how sensitive I am: it is as if merely looking at pictures of horses can cause my alveoli to shut down. So Janet took Jamie to riding lessons, where we quickly learned that he had no sense whatsoever about how to guide a horse, no idea what to do with the reins. Undaunted, Janet attached strings to a swivel chair in my study and had Jamie practice pulling one string and then the another, labeling them "right" and "left." Within weeks, Jamie got the hang of it; within months he had learned how to use his feet to signal a horse as well. He could ease a horse into a trot, which was as fast as the kids were allowed to go, and he was very pleased with himself. I saw him ride exactly twice, once from a distance, once from inside the family car. He looked great. He and Janet got riding helmets and developed a protocol for their weekend visits to the farm.

Riding gave Jamie a better sense of coordination and proprioception; it also taught him how to groom and care for horses. Jamie quickly became adept at the pre-riding and post-riding rituals, and about the process by which one establishes rapport with a large, powerful animal. Jamie was fearless and sensitive; the horses liked him. But finally, the thing we feared might happen happened: Jamie fell off his horse. There were other horses and riders in the ring at the time, so quite apart from the fall itself, this was potentially dangerous. But Jamie, being Jamie, immediately sprang to his feet and cried out, "Ta-DA!"—much to everyone's delight and relief. And yet another cliché came to life: yep, when you fall off a horse, the best thing to do is to get right back on.

Tang soo do was Jamie's idea, no doubt part of his lifelong desire to *be like Nick*. From the start, Master Summers was completely comfortable with having a student with a disability, but it quickly became apparent that Jamie didn't have the coordination to execute some of the basic moves, and many of the various commands confused him. So, deep sigh, I agreed to sign up for the class as well and help him learn the ways of the martial arts.

This was not something I wanted to do, but it was so obviously necessary that I didn't hesitate. We began as white belts in August 2006, becoming members of the World Tang Soo Do Association, taking tests and getting certificates and reading the student manual. We learned the seven tenets of Tang Soo Do: integrity, concentration, perseverance, respect and obedience, self-control, humility, and indomitable spirit. (The last of these comes in handy when you have not hit a decent golf shot in over an hour, as I mentioned above. And all of them have their uses: more than once, when Jamie refused to get ready for bed or take a shower or clean up his room, I reminded him of the *respect and obedience* part. Though I did so with humility and self-control.) By December, Jamie had gotten a "most improved" award; over the next few years, he consistently scored 6s and 7s in his pretests (good to very good), except in the "overall attitude" category, where he was always a perfect 10.

What's really striking about Jamie's overall attitude, and his indomitable spirit, is that in one of the very first sessions he and I participated in, he dislocated his right knee while trying to do a back kick. Neither of us ever managed to do very convincing back kicks, and for Jamie, the combination of the turn-pivot-leg thrust proved to be a serious challenge. That night in September 2006, as we made our way up and down the gym floor doing back kicks, Jamie wiped out, losing his balance and hitting the hardwood with a thud. That was alarming enough, but when he looked at me, his face pallid and stricken with pain, and whispered, "My knee," I rolled up his pant leg and found that his patella had shifted *to the side of his leg.* I can't begin to imagine how painful that was. The class stopped dead. Other students began to gather around. Panicked, I popped the patella back into place and helped Jamie to his feet; he couldn't put any weight on the leg, so I half-carried him off the floor while someone ran to get an ice pack.

You might wonder what the hell I was doing popping his kneecap back into place. I might tell you that I'm not an emergency medical technician, but I did stay at a Holiday Inn Express last night. But I would be lying. The truth is that I remembered Janet's similar knee injury twenty years earlier: as she was about to win the limbo contest at a party thrown by the cardiac intensive care staff of the University of Virginia Medical Center (where she worked during her years as a graduate student in the 1980s), she dislocated her right knee, cracking the patella in half. A real EMT immediately rushed to her side, popping the bone into place while someone called for an ambulance. (Janet wound up in a leg cast for two months, during a time when we lived in a crappy two-family rental house built on the side of a very steep hill. Getting in and out of that place involved navigating three flights of stairs. It was not a happy summer.)

Jamie, clearly, had inherited his mother's loose-jointedness—as well as her tolerance for pain. To this day I am astonished that he did not cry out, that he responded simply by quietly directing me to attend to his knee. Janet had been the same way, collapsing on the grass and asking for help, pointing to her knee. But in retrospect, I am glad I remembered that EMT's response to Janet's collapse. I probably saved Jamie a trip to the ER, not to mention many more minutes of living with his patella out of place. Once he could manage it, I took him home and explained quickly to Janet why we were back so early. Horrified, she immediately got him onto a couch, elevated his leg, and brought a fresh ice pack. We tended to him carefully that night, getting a knee brace that he wore for the next few weeks, during which he was seen by his doctor and given the all clear. And as soon as he was ready to resume tang soo do lessons, he got right back on that horse.

In 2009, Jamie and I attended a competition held at the Bald Eagle Area High School—not to participate, just to watch, because we didn't think we were ready for competitive sparring yet. There, Jamie met Grandmaster Jae Chul Shin, the founder of the US Tang Soo Do Federation and one of the leading martial arts experts in the world. I have a picture of Jamie, in full uniform, bowing his head in respect to Grandmaster Shin, who is smiling and looking sidewise at the proud father with his camera. (Grandmaster Shin died in 2012, at the age of seventy-six, so that picture is all the more meaningful to us.) Sometime later, Master Summers took me aside after a class and informed me that Grandmaster Shin had officially approved Jamie to proceed as far as he could in the discipline. I was deeply moved. I had been wondering what might happen if Jamie got to the point at which his (and my) tests would involve weapons (namely, the "bong" forms, requiring deft manipulation of a bamboo staff) and written essays. Effectively, Grandmaster Shin was saying *bring it*. And Master Summers continued to treat Jamie just like any other student, though (I think) with a little more solicitude and encouragement than he did for most of Jamie's peers.

We never got to the weapons-and-essays point. By spring 2010, Jamie had reached his limits, so far as I could tell—though I am aware that my reading of his limits was colored by the fact that I had reached *my* limits. We had attained the rank of third *gup*, brown belt with one white stripe, having started down at tenth *gup*, white belt; we had begun practicing for the red-belt test, and if we passed that, we would be only two steps, perhaps less than two years, away from becoming candidates for black belts. I suspected that Jamie wanted to *be like Nick* and go all the way to black belt, but then, Nick's training in tae kwon do did not involve weapons. And the sparring was beginning to get wearisome to me: usually, people sparring with Jamie pulled their punches, allowing him to develop his kicks and moves without too much risk, whereas I invariably drew as my sparring partner the class sociopath, the big guy who was totally into inflicting as much pain as possible in thirty-second segments. The way I figured it, I already had enough bruises and wear from ice hockey, and I didn't need any more. But beyond that, I sincerely believed that form eight, *pyong ahn oh dan*, was too much for Jamie (you can find all the forms on YouTube; indeed, demonstrations on YouTube helped us practice), and that one-steps sixteen through twenty, which would be required for the red-belt test, involved some potentially dangerous maneuvers. He was just not learning the movements. I thought ruefully of my father's complaint about the violence of martial arts. And gradually, Jamie and I decided to call it quits.

The "gradually" part was indeed very gradual: Jamie and I spent the rest of 2010 hemming and hawing about whether to push just that much further, take the test for red belt, and *then* call it quits. One night in San Antonio that fall, where I had taken Jamie for the American Studies Association conference, I was stunned to see him practicing some of his forms in the hotel pool, and I asked him if he really wanted to get back into it. He said maybe, but we let it drop, and there it has stayed ever since.

I realize that in recounting Jamie's various athletic accomplishments I run the risk of making it sound as if Janet and I were dynamo parents who did everything and tried everything and always proceeded with perseverance and indomitable spirit. I remember the plaintive blog comment I once received from a parent of an autistic child, telling me that my narrative of Jamie's progress in golf made him feel inadequate, like he wasn't doing enough for *his* kid. All I can say is that so far as I know, *every parent of a child with a disability feels this way*, myself included. In *Life as We Know It*, I described this as the "dialectic of disability," whereby you oscillate crazily back and forth between the conviction that you are not doing enough for your child and the fear that you are pushing him or her too hard. And I know there are parents in Jamie's group who seem to have it much more together than we do: they're the ones who organize events and drive everyone to track and field meets and make sure their kids are usefully occupied as often as possible in fourteen different activities. I know also of a father who gave his son (a young man with Down syndrome, roughly Jamie's age) golf lessons that make my instruction of Jamie look hopelessly rudimentary. There is always someone who can make you feel that you're slacking: it's true outside the disability community, it's true inside the disability community. For my part, I have tried to take my cue from Jamie as much as possible. OK, I did push him a bit to get him back in the water after the Mishap of '98. But I'm glad I did, and so is he. I honored his wishes not to play Special Olympics softball and to bail on volleyball and basketball. I taught him the basics of golf when it became clear that he was no longer content merely to ride along in the cart and watch his father play. And with tang soo do, I took one for the team, because it was what Jamie wanted to do.

On top of the dialectic of disability, there is the Father Factor: what is the difference, for me, between helping Jamie along, offering him love and consolation and encouragement, and being a crazed sports parent who instills in one's child a maniacal desire to outperform others—and a concomitant fear of failure? By the time Nick reached adulthood, I think I achieved a stable equilibrium with him: he understands that I will deal him heartbreaking losses in ping-pong, and I understand that when we play darts he will wipe the floor with me. We will simply respect each other's talents in these critical indoor sports. More important (and more seriously), although I always hoped Nick would use his talents to build a career in architecture (as opposed, say, to graphic design), and although I urged him to consider Washington University in St. Louis (that worked out well), I have no idea how the field of architecture works as a profession and no desire or ability to stand over his shoulder offering advice. But I did not expect to have to confront similar questions with Jamie. I should have known better. Though I have a new respect for certain sports clichés, I have never had any tolerance for the clichés about children with Down syndrome. Jamie is not an angel among us. He is an ordinary human being, full of passions and desires that are at once admirable, contradictory, volatile, and utopian. Why shouldn't this be evident on the fields of play, just as it is in everything else Jamie does? In his various athletic endeavors he wants to feel confident, to feel proud, to feel capable. He wants to have fun. And yeah, he likes to have people cheering him on, too.

And yet that cheering has its limitations, does it not? In a searing op-ed essay written after the 2015 Special Olympics World Games in Los Angeles, Lawrence Downes wrote that when the cheering dies down, "that glow has to last, because the athletes will need it when they get home and become invisible again." Sports have been so instrumental a part of social change in America, from the career of Jackie Robinson to the passage of Title IX, that we now tend to think of the fields of play as places where struggles over race, gender, and sexuality are coextensive with broader struggles over race, gender, and sexuality in society at large. But the integration of people with intellectual disabilities into the world of sport seems not to have followed the same pattern; as we'll see in the following chapter, the past fifty years have seen tremendous successes in inclusive education for children, but not in inclusive employment for adults. Timothy Shriver, Downes wrote, "has a theory" as to why this is so:

> When members of minority groups make progress, he said, it is because "deep down most people know that they are the same as us, as me, whoever the dominant group is.
>
> "But with our group it's like, 'No, no, no, they are not the same. They are not like us. They are not going to go to medical school if we give them a scholarship. They're not going to become engineers,'" he said. "We labor under the barrier, the attitudinal barrier, that this population is too different to matter."
>
> Given those barriers, Special Olympics is sticking with gentle persuasion and the attitude-changing power of sports. It is all carrot, no stick. It is not ACT UP, and never will be; its revolution is televised, happily, on ESPN. This is a carefully thought-out strategy. Even its health programs—Special Olympics athletes tend to have serious untreated problems with vision, teeth, and hearing—are part of what Mr. Shriver called "an elaborate bait-and-switch." Its clinics offer much-needed care, but their deeper purpose is to educate doctors about such patients, who too often get short shrift and indifferent care.

This is the downside of Jamie's (correct) identification of "his group": as Shriver (correctly) notes, it is a group that is usually considered too different from other human groups to matter. And though Jamie has been very fortunate, encountering only a few medical providers who seemed to give him indifferent care, we know very well that as a group, doctors need to be educated about the lives, the well-being, and the value of people with intellectual disabilities.

Downes closes his op-ed on precisely the right note of ambivalence:

> Special Olympics is a utopian organization, and to encounter it is to enter a well-constructed bubble of acceptance and equality. A strange thing happens when you spend a week inside that bubble at the Special Olympics World Games, watching groups of young people wandering about, relaxed and confident. You stop noticing the differences. The novelty wears off, and it becomes clearer that the world is full of people of an astonishing variety of appearances and abilities.
>
> But outside the bubble, the battle for hearts and minds, and for rights and laws, is not going away.

The story of Jamie's career as an athlete is largely a story of triumphs and achievements. Those triumphs and achievements, in the pools at Special Olympics meets (cheered on by legions of volunteers) and on the links at Belles Springs (cheered on by his father), are entirely real. But now it is time for us to go back outside the bubble.

School/Work

□   □   □   □   □

Jamie doesn't like the following story, but as you'll see in a moment, it has to be told. And after we had a brief discussion of this chapter, Jamie agreed.

Jamie started public school in the fall of 1997, entering kindergarten one year "late," at the age of six. (Later, in fourth grade, he would repeat a year, so that he wound up graduating from high school in 2011, just shy of his twentieth birthday.) Janet and I assumed he would be socially adept, having mingled with his nondisabled peers in preschool programs since the age of two, but we worried that he might already be significantly behind his classmates cognitively. You can imagine our surprise, then, when his teacher and aides reported to us, at our first parent-teacher conference, that Jamie was among the minority of kids in his class who knew the entire alphabet. And he knew much else, too, especially when it came to animals or sign language. We were asked: *How did Jamie learn everything he knows? How can we help teach him more?* We replied that we try to play to his strengths—his memory and his capacity for making lists—whenever possible. And we were deeply relieved and gratified that Jamie's teachers and paraprofessionals had recognized his potential.

Then came the bad news. Jamie required some help with behavioral issues concerning peer interactions . . . oh, let me put this more bluntly: he had licked a girl on the arm, and he needed to know that this was totally inappropriate. So our first report on Jamie's progress in school was precisely the opposite of what we had expected: Academically, he was doing fine. Socially, he needed some work. Red-faced, Janet and I explained to the kindergarten staff that Jamie had just gotten a dog for his sixth birthday, and had evidently gotten it into his head that playful licking was an acceptable form of expressing affection. That afternoon, when we picked Jamie up from school, I asked him directly: "Did you lick Depeche on the arm?" His hunched-shoulders, pursed-lips reaction told us that he felt as embarrassed about this as we did. He doesn't like hearing about this episode today, and he didn't want it to be in the book. But I have assured him that of all the things you can do wrong in school, licking a classmate's arm is preferable to biting, hitting, taunting, or bullying someone—and that I will assure everyone else that Jamie never did it again.

Telling the story is necessary, I think, because the stakes of inclusive schooling are so high. For children with intellectual and/or developmental disabilities, the Individuals with Disabilities Education Act (IDEA) is an absolutely critical piece of civil rights legislation, entitling all American children to a free appropriate public education in the least restrictive environment. The law was passed in 1975, but only in the 1990s did "the least restrictive environment" become, for most children with disabilities, something other than the special education classroom. In other words, Jamie arrived at Westview School in Champaign, Illinois, just as schools like Westview were beginning to incorporate kids like Jamie into the "regular" classroom. Jamie's Individualized Education Program (IEP) stipulated that he and another classmate would have a number of "pullout" hours for special-needs instruction; for example, Jamie needed extra help with learning how to hold a pencil, thanks to his low muscle tone and small-motor difficulties. But for the most part, and for most of his life until middle school, Jamie was thrown into the mix with all the other kids. When school districts in the United States started taking the potential of the IDEA seriously, they embarked on an experiment in egalitarian democracy every bit as daunting and admirable (though not as politically volatile) as the struggle for desegregation. Jamie was the first child with Down syndrome to be "included" at Westview, and I never stopped thinking that only thirty years earlier, he and his trisomy-21 cohort were being warehoused in state asylums. Now they were being taught reading, 'riting, and 'rithmetic. It is almost enough to make you believe in progress—though if one wants to be an agent of progress, one wants to make sure that one's kid does not develop a habit of licking Depeche.

The objections to inclusive education did not come exclusively from curmudgeons such as Roger Kimball and William A. Henry III, whom I mentioned in *Life as We Know It*, and who considered it perfectly acceptable to ridicule the idea of including "retarded children [in] classrooms for normal students." Objections also came from teachers, parents, and principals worried about whether schools would become responsible for taking care of any number of new students with challenging behavioral or medical conditions. (Short answer: it all depends on what "least restrictive environment" means.) So we were especially attentive to anything that might mark Jamie as a "difficult" student. But then again, where did anyone get the idea that children with developmental disabilities have a monopoly on difficult-student-dom? They are very unlikely to be bullies, after all, and much more likely to be bullied. I recall an incident in the local gym when Jamie was six or seven. I dropped him off in the kids' room (restricted to children under ten) while I worked out, and when I came back, I was sad to see that Jamie wasn't doing much of anything, certainly not playing with other children or engaging in the "KidFit" exercises the staff made available. And then it was time for the kids to line up, and one kid decided to run at full speed into the mirrored wall while another kid took the opportunity to slam his neighbor's head onto the hardwood floor. And I thought to myself, *Maybe it's OK that Jamie wasn't doing much of anything.*

Inclusive schooling did two things above all: it gave Jamie a chance to emulate and befriend his nondisabled peers, and it gave the other kids the much-needed sense that children with developmental disabilities are part of the ordinary fabric of life. Jamie began to dream about inviting his classmates for sleepovers (this never happened, though they always came to his parties) and started making up barely intelligible scenarios, one of which involved classmates Arooj and Tom having pudgy cheeks. Somehow B. B. King was involved. No, I can't explain it any better than that. But it was clear that Jamie's world was widening—and that he was not being bullied. On the contrary, some kids genuinely liked him; in third grade, toward the end of his time in Champaign, one girl, Shelby

Peacha, actively befriended him, visiting him at our house and inviting him to hers. On one of these playdates, Shelby confided to me that
sometimes in school Jamie was hard to understand, and I told her that
sometimes even *I* don't understand what Jamie is saying. Then I told her
about two young children who'd met Jamie on a playground earlier that
week. They didn't know that Jamie had Down syndrome, but they knew
he was different in some way, and they discussed what that way might
be. "He can't hear," said one child. "No," said the other, "he can hear, but
he can't talk." I told Shelby that I'd explained to those children that Jamie
can talk . . . and hear, and *read*, too.

But Shelby was horrified that other children would think such things
of her friend. I hastened to reassure her. "Well, that's because you know
Jamie, and he is your friend," I replied. "But these kids didn't know what
to think, and they didn't know anything about kids with Down syndrome."

"I only know a little about Down syndrome," said Shelby, with a furrowed brow. "But I know there's no one like Jamie."

Now *that*, I believe, is a valuable lesson for any kid to learn at school.

For his part, Jamie learned a great deal as well: He began reading
in second grade, thanks largely to Ms. Borgeson, his teacher, and Ms.
Avellone, Ms. Hiser, and Ms. McCabe, the school paraprofessionals. He
learned to do two-digit addition and subtraction, though he clearly preferred addition; as he told me one evening when I suggested we work on
subtracting and borrowing, when you add numbers together, "you get
more." His attitude was cheery and his sense of humor infectious, but
every once in a while he had trouble following directions, either because
he did not understand the directions or because he just didn't feel like
following them (imagine that, in a child). So his teachers, Janet, and I
devised a system: When Jamie followed directions and did things right,
he would get a duck—a little yellow-paper tag in the shape of a duck that
would be pinned on the wall next to his name. If he got all his ducks in a
row (I believe three was the magic number), he would be rewarded with
an activity he enjoyed; if he disobeyed or fussed, he would lose a duck.
Jamie liked this system, though we did get one report of his attempt
to game the system by replacing one of the ducks he had lost when he
thought nobody was looking. (Penalty: loss of extra duck!)

Many parents have told me IEP horror stories—of struggling year after year with school officials and school districts that cannot or will not provide the funds for the support their children need. For some parents, the annual IEP meeting is a hassle followed by a lawsuit followed by endless aggravation. We were extremely fortunate in that until Jamie reached middle school, we avoided all hassles and lawsuits, as well as most forms of aggravation. I wondered if our status as college professors had something to do with it: K–12 schools seem to be one of the few remaining institutions in American life in which people hold college professors in esteem. Certainly, Jamie's teachers approved of our active involvement in his education, regardless of whether Janet and I were professors. Whatever the reason, our IEP meetings were almost always cordial, collaborative affairs in which everyone involved sincerely tried to figure out what would be best for Jamie and what academic goals would be realistic for him. And I was always keenly aware that we were living in reasonably well-funded school districts, whereas our fellow Americans who lived in the rural districts surrounding our college town were dealing with schools that had to hold bake sales simply to turn on the lights in the morning. I spent some time in *Life as We Know It* inveighing against the injustice of funding public schools out of property taxes, an absurd arrangement that I described as "the ideal scheme for setting the elderly against children, singles and childless couples against parents, homeowners against tenants, and homeowning parents of children in private school against everyone else." I am dismayed to note that in the twenty years since I wrote that passage, nothing has changed in the world of education funding. And so parents of children with disabilities who live in reasonably well-funded school districts have access to resources and opportunities unavailable to parents of children with disabilities who live twenty miles away, or across the river, or in the blighted areas of our nation's cities. The same is true of parents of children without disabilities. It is almost enough to make you believe that all talk of "progress" is delusional.

But for me and for Janet, the IEP was not a hassle, and our school districts—both in Champaign and in State College—met Jamie's needs: a paraprofessional and some pullout speech/occupational therapy.

Strange as it may sound, the most painful aspect of Jamie's early school career, for me, was the annual holiday concert. Even at the age of eight, Jamie was a pure ham at home, where he would put on *The Wizard of Oz* soundtrack and launch into a rendition of Ray Bolger's brilliant dancing as the scarecrow, watching himself all the while in a mirror or the reflecting surface of the oven door. But onstage, with a hundred other children surrounding him, he invariably clammed up, barely moving his lips to the words, coming in two beats late on every bit of pantomime that accompanies "Rudolph the Red-Nosed Reindeer."

Why did I care about this? Many parents suffer through their children's holiday concerts, though only Homer Simpson is so honest as to wail, "Oh, how many grades does this school *have?*" As long as Jamie was learning how to carry the ones when he added 149 and 373, did it really matter how he looked during the holiday concert?

For me, it did matter—because it mattered how other parents and grandparents perceived Jamie as part of their school community. And for most of them, the holiday-concert moment was their only impression of Jamie. I didn't want them to think that Jamie's performance in the holiday concert was an accurate representation of Jamie's relation to the curriculum, or of Jamie's relation to his nondisabled peers. I didn't want anyone to think that Jamie sat in a corner drawing circles or playing patty-cake while the other kids were learning geography. I wanted them to know that by third grade, Jamie had learned the names of all fifty states, thanks to that formidable cataloguing memory of his.

His teachers wanted the same thing for him, and they were aware of the holiday-concert problem. So in third grade, the school's music instructor, Ms. Goodwin (Jamie still remembers her name and filled in this detail for me), made a tape of all the holiday-concert songs for him, so he could practice at home. Jamie loved that tape. We still have it, somewhere in the recesses of the house where ancient audiotapes reside. He played it in the car time and time again. He bounced in his seat and sang along eagerly, as best he could. And when at last the dreaded day of the holiday concert arrived, there was Jamie, front and left of center, standing lost and bewildered, not singing a word.

□ □ □

When we moved to Penn State, we had another option—something very rare for academic couples. Stanley Fish, the brilliant literary theorist, political contrarian, and master wheeler-dealer who built the English Department at Duke University in the 1980s and 1990s and then de-camped to the University of Illinois at Chicago, had gotten wind of the fact that Penn State had made job offers to Janet and to me. Being a master wheeler-dealer, Fish put together a dual offer that exceeded Penn State's, and that held out the promise that Janet and I could move to a major city and be a part of a major department-building enterprise. Fish had already hired some of the leading figures in disability studies, such as David Mitchell, Sharon Snyder, and Lennard Davis. UI-Chicago had a PhD-granting program in disability studies—the oldest one in the na-tion and one of the few in the world—housed in the College of Applied Health Sciences.

So why didn't we take that offer? Janet, who wanted very much to move to Chicago, looked into the schooling options for Jamie. Not a single district in the city could offer real inclusion—whether because of chronic underfunding, systemic mismanagement, or lack of interest on the part of Chicago public school administrators, we couldn't deter-mine. Our friends in Chicago told us to look at Oak Park, a famously cool-liberal-progressive neighborhood just west of the city. We looked at Oak Park: their schools were cool and liberal and progressive, and they had no history of including kids with Down syndrome. Finally we asked people in the disability community, who told us that the only truly inclusive school district in the area was in Wilmette. Wilmette! Up to an hour from campus, somewhere north of Evanston, the home of North-western. "Seriously," I said to Janet, "why don't we just commute from Milwaukee?" It seemed to me a devil's bargain: I would get to work in a PhD-granting program in disability studies, but my disabled son would be consigned to some special ed arrangement from the 1960s.

There were many reasons we moved to Penn State. One was that Janet's sister Cynthia had been diagnosed with breast cancer, and we wanted to be closer to her and the rest of the Lyon family—six hundred miles closer. But another critical reason—which, we found, was intelligible only to a small subset of our academic colleagues—was that the opportunities for Jamie in the State College school district were vastly superior to anything Chicago, and even Stanley Fish, could offer him.

Jamie's departure from Champaign was bittersweet. His teachers and classmates at Westview made him a wonderful keepsake book, full of pictures and well wishes. His new classmates at the Corl Street Elementary School in State College welcomed him warmly, and his fourth-grade teacher, Mr. Hockenberry, invited me to do a Q-and-A with the class about Jamie and about Down syndrome. During that session, I mentioned in passing that Jamie had memorized the names of all the goaltenders in the NHL. One girl spoke up: "My dad is the Penn State hockey coach and even he doesn't know all the goalies in the NHL." "See," I said, "that's one of Jamie's strengths. On the other hand, when he told you all that he has eighteen monkeys at home? Uh, that's not true."

Corl Street was a good place for him, with great teachers and paras. Jamie has forgotten many of the names of NHL goaltenders circa 2001–02, but he remembers all the teachers and paras from those years, especially young Ms. Pontano, who made him a videotape upon her departure from the district, and Ms. Poorman, who provided him with gentle reminders not to touch everything in the hallway. (This gave Jamie's parents the useful mantra "Be mature just like Ms. Poorman says.") And then, after three years at Corl Street, we were faced with a decision: Mount Nittany for middle school? Or Park Forest?

OK, it was just your ordinary American parental dilemma, the choice between Middle School A and Middle School B. But it wound up having some consequences for Jamie, and these days I think of it as the one big mistake we made during his school years. We were persuaded to go with Park Forest because (as his teachers and aides informed us) most of his cohort from Corl Street would be going there, even though we had gotten a much better impression of Mount Nittany. Not until three years later, in his final year of middle school, did we realize that Jamie was allergic to something in the building at Park Forest, something that kept his nose runny all day long. Worse still, we ran into the only unhelpful paraprofessional we ever encountered, a sullen young woman who may well have been clinically depressed—and who certainly didn't like working with Jamie.

When Jamie reached seventh grade, we faced our first inclusive-education crisis. Despite his facility with math—he was now able to do two-digit multiplication with ease—he was failing to grasp the concepts of "area" and "perimeter." In other words, he could find the area of an eighteen-by-twelve-foot rectangle when someone wrote out "18 x 12," but he had no idea what the concept was. He wasn't paying attention in science class, where his paraprofessional was (sullenly) doing much of his work for him; and he didn't seem to get French at all. At the beginning of the year, we had asked for Jamie to be included in those three "regular" classrooms, on the grounds that he was good at math, fascinated with the natural world, and exceptionally curious about languages. We were also deeply skeptical of some "special ed" classes that Janet derisively referred to as "pudding pops," in which the children were given make-work tasks and intellectually challenged rarely if at all. When we discovered that the next item on the math agenda would be the area of irregular shapes, we agreed to bail out. Janet and I had discussed this possibility when Jamie was younger, wondering when it would be more useful for him to know how to shop, make his bed, and use public transportation than to know the formula for the volume of a cone. That was our way of marking the difference between "life skills" classes and "regular" classrooms, and besides, who remembers the formula for the volume of a cone, anyway? (I once asked this question aloud in a forum on inclusive education. Unfortunately, I did so in an auditorium full of high school teachers, many of whom shouted out variants of "one-third height times pi r squared." *Tough crowd*, I thought.)

So we dropped "regular" math and settled for a class that would simply keep Jamie in practice with multiplication and division. But we pleaded for French and science. "I know he's not getting it all," Janet said to his science teacher. "But he truly loves learning about the world around him, and we don't want that world to close in on him . . . just yet." This appeal almost moved the science teacher, Ms. Pelligrini, to tears (Janet was near tears herself), and she eventually became the Hero of Seventh Grade, agreeing to keep Jamie in her class and to adapt the lessons and exams for him. This meant, as the year unfolded, that Jamie learned about the circulatory, respiratory, gastrointestinal, nervous, and cardiovascular systems of the body—information he retains to this day. He learned about cells, which helped him understand what it means for someone (like his aunt Cynthia) to have cancer. He learned about chromosomes, including a curious moment of illumination in January 2006 when the class turned to the details of human reproduction, and he learned that most humans have forty-six chromosomes but that people with Down syndrome have forty-seven. "Wow, one more," he said, intrigued and a little bit impressed. I wonder if he also thought to himself, *You know, that explains a lot.* As for the "adapted" tests, Ms. Pelligrini required that Jamie be able to name only half the parts of a cell and half the GI tract in order to pass his exams. I wondered, When, between the ages of twelve and twenty-one, do the legions of his nondisabled peers forget about vacuoles and mitochondria? Probably around the same time they forget the formula for the volume of a cone.

Ten years later, I can report that there are at least two major school lessons Jamie retains to this day. One has to do with the structure of Earth—crust, mantle, and core. Since Jamie already knew that apples have cores, I decided to flesh out the analogy: the apple skin is like Earth's crust, the apple is like the mantle, the core is like . . . the core. But what made this memorable for Jamie was that it reminded him of the "onions have layers, ogres have layers" bit in the first *Shrek* movie, in which Shrek is trying to explain to Donkey that even ogres are capable of complex and contradictory emotional states. Thank you, Shrek.

The other lesson involves more silly-Dad-running-around-a room. Trying to explain the various states of matter—gas, liquid, solid—I adapted Ms. Pelligrini's explanation of molecules: I curled up on the couch and told Jamie I was a very cold solid, and then told him to put a "fire" on me by touching me. This caused me to wiggle and wave my arms because I now had more energy and was turning into liquid. This entailed a side lesson on how liquids can spill but solids cannot. Then he put more fire on me and made me a gas, hence the running around the room. "When matter gets hotter, it has more energy," I said, "and all the molecules jump around and get excited." Thus, ice, water, steam. He knows the drill. He does not have to remember the terms "vaporization," "condensation," and "evaporation," so far as I am concerned—he just has to know solids, liquids, and gases. Though some further explanation was required when Jamie asked why gas (gasoline) was a liquid and not a gas.

Madame Eid, the French teacher, had never had a child with Down syndrome in her class. She told us that Jamie did not speak when he was called on and did not understand how to write complete sentences in French. "He doesn't write complete sentences in English, either," I replied. "And he's shy about speaking up. But he already knows the days of the week and the months of the year, and he's beginning to understand about time. We don't want him to slow down the rest of the class. So if it's possible for him to take the class pass/fail, we'll do everything we can to help him."

I turned out to be somewhat wrong about time. In seventh grade, Jamie never did manage to understand why the French perversely insist on calling 7:40 "eight hours minus twenty," though I secretly agreed with him that *sept heures et quarante* would get the general idea across even if it was marked "wrong" on the test. And even though he learned what *voyager* means, he could not remember that *tu voyages* has an "s" even though *je voyage* and *il voyage* do not. But he negotiated the hyphens and apostrophes of *qu'est-ce que c'est* with élan, he mastered the form of *est-ce que tu?*, and he turned out to be a whiz with adverbs—getting them right *quelquefois* at first, then *souvent*. (Though *quelquefois* remains his favorite.) His pronunciation improved quickly, too—no small thing for a child who didn't learn to read fluently until he was eight. It was hard enough for him to master English vowels and silent letters the first time around, let alone foreign imponderables like *ils aiment* and *les yeux*. And in December 2005, he came up with his first bilingual pun: in the middle of homework, upon writing that the clock read *huit heures*, he turned to me and sang, "Huit heures meter maid." I laughed delightedly. (If you don't get it, you are probably one of the six people in the English-speaking world who has not heard *Sgt. Pepper*.) I thought, yes, he still has to learn how to shop and make his bed and take public transportation. But on the way there, it's OK with me if he has some fun with the texture of language.

One night when we were walking Lucy the Dog, I told Jamie how proud I was of all his hard work in French. But it turned out that, just then, he was in no mood for kind words. "It's too hard," he grumbled. "I always fail." He'd said something similar about science when he was briefly overwhelmed by the task of naming the parts of a cell. But despite that moment of despair, he was actually pretty good about remembering nuances like *accents graves et aigu*, including the two *accents aigu* on his name. When we asked him, *Parle-tu français?* He never failed to say, *Je parle français souvent* or *très bien*—even though those answers were not quite true. And although he failed his science test on rocks, he learned a great deal about living things—which is where his real interests lie, anyway. (Relatedly, I could never get him interested in astronomy. When we go to New York's Museum of Natural History, he is always all about natural history, and never about the adjacent Hayden Planetarium. Which makes me sad, because I am all about the planetarium.) So no, he did not always fail. He *sometimes* failed. *Quelquefois.* Like the rest of us. And yet, and yet . . . by the summer of 2006 he was capable of writing a postcard to my mother that read as follows (he had minimal assistance):

13 JUILLET 2006

BONJOUR! JE SUIS EN FRANCE AVEC MA FAMILLE. J'AI NAGÉ DANS LA LAC ET LA PISCINE.

    J'AIME MANGER LE PIZZA ET LE POULET. ET JE PARLE FRANÇAIS QUELQUEFOIS!

JE T'AIME,

JAMIE

Those of you who know your French know that he got the gender of "lac" and "pizza" wrong. But on the whole, this really isn't too bad. And most important, my mother loved it.

At the end of the year, Jamie's teachers and aides advised us that eighth-grade science and French would be too much for him. They did so with trepidation. Perhaps they feared that Jamie's parents, the double-barreled PhDs, would push their disabled kid until he broke. "Really, that's fine with us," we said, to their palpable relief. "We just wanted him to get a sense of it all, and to stay in some regular classes for as long as he could." And yet one year later, at the meeting to set out Jamie's IEP for his first year of high school, we got some great news from Madame Eid: she was willing to take Jamie back into French class, and the "adaptive" plan was that he would study French I for two years and French II for two years. During his high school years, Jamie became more and more fluent in French (he became better than I am at remembering the gender of nouns), and we hired a Penn State French major to help him with French II—an hour a week, twenty dollars a session. Jamie grew more confident with speaking up in class, though like his father, he remained more comfortable with rendering French sentences in English than with translating English sentences to French. And he grew fond of Mme. Eid, fond enough to think of sending her an antelope skull from New Mexico. His new para, Linda Walker, a charming and kindly woman, was delighted to accompany Jamie to French class, whereas his seventh-grade para had resented the task, never bothering to learn even elementary French with him. And by Walker's report (for that is how she is known to Jamie), as well as Mme. Eid's, he was doing just fine.

I am sorry to report that since high school, Jamie has forgotten a lot of his French for the same reason I have forgotten much of mine, time and time again, *encore un fois:* we have no chance to speak or hear it on a daily basis. In September 2013, however, when Jamie and I took a trip to Ottawa to speak to Reach Canada, a disability-rights organization, Jamie was fascinated with the bilingual signs everywhere he looked. We spent an afternoon in the Museum of Civilization—*excusez-moi,* Le Musée de la Civilisation—where Jamie insisted on seeing the IMAX film *L'Incroyable Voyage des Papillons* (we understood about 10 percent of the narration, but we got the general idea). On our way through the installation on the history of Canada—which we mistakenly entered through the *sortie* even though we know what *sortie* means (we didn't see the sign), so that our journey led us backwards through Canadian history—we came upon an exhibit about Québec in the decades before confederation in 1867. Jamie doesn't like reading extensive descriptions of things in museums, but he was struck by this one: "Michael?" he said, quizzically, "are these my people?"

Yes, I said, yes, they are your people, along with the Irish, Scottish, Welsh, and German peoples. He carried that knowledge with him for the rest of the trip, to the point at which he greeted a customs agent in the airport with "bonjour." She promptly replied with instructions in French, to which I had to say, "*Non, merci, nous parlons français quelquefois, un petit peu, mais nous sommes americains.*" "Really!" she replied, deftly code-switching as officials in Ottawa are wont to do. "Because Bérubé is such a French name." "It is," I said. "They are my people," Jamie added.

On the way home I told Jamie that I was sad that he does not take French anymore. We had been talking that summer about how much he missed taking classes and doing homework, and I wondered whether it would be a good idea to hire a French tutor again, this time for two one-hour sessions a week. He had no interest. "We did that already." But he had an alternate idea: how about a tutor to teach him about composers and music? That was what sent me to Penn State's School of Music in search of graduate students willing to work with Jamie, and that is how he wound up taking lessons with Mark Minnich and helping Nick study for *Jeopardy!*

Jamie's high school experience consisted, for the most part, of a lively, well-run special ed classroom (known in the school as "the Wild Dream Team") with pullout for French class and choir. For two years, Jamie also worked as the equipment manager for the high school hockey team, and that was pretty great. (The credit for that idea goes to Andy Wilson, a hockey player and high school teacher.) But there was one major disappointment during those years that can still make me upset to this day: the Best Buddies program.

Best Buddies is a very wonderful idea, yet another of the Shriver family's invaluable contributions to the project of improving the lives of people with intellectual disabilities. Because people with intellectual disabilities tend to be socially isolated from their nondisabled peers, and because almost everyone finds social isolation especially difficult to handle in middle school and high school (when Best Buddy programs begin), students volunteer to hang out with a designated intellectually disabled Buddy, attending Buddy events and arranging get-togethers outside of school, going to movies, out for meals, that kind of thing. It's a great program, and I am sure it looks great on college applications, too. But Jamie's first Buddy was a disaster. We took him out to lunch, and it seemed as if they had a good deal in common. They talked excitedly and engagingly, and he and Jamie learned that they both liked indie rockers Modest Mouse. We saw that Buddy again when he took Jamie to the annual holiday party hosted by the Arc (formerly the Association of Retarded Citizens). And that was it for the entire year. He didn't seem like a bad fellow. He was just too busy with other extracurricular activities to be a decent Buddy.

Jamie's second Buddy was better, joining him for a handful of social events. But he, too, seemed overbooked. Frustrated, we told the students running the program that they really had to assign Jamie someone who was actually willing to spend some time with him. And dammit, it wasn't as if Jamie was a drag to be around. With the exception of that one sullen, depressed para in middle school, everyone who has ever worked with him—every teacher, every aide, every therapist, every babysitter/companion—has enjoyed his company. But Best Buddies at State College High seemed to be infested with resume-builders. The exception was one Laura Lovins, a bright, friendly, reserved girl who saw Jamie often. We will always think well of her. But seriously, if you are running a Best Buddies program at your school, or you know someone who is, it's best to make sure that the Best Buddies are actually showing up to hang out with the people who are supposed to be their best buddies.

□   □   □

For many years I made Jamie a promise: "When you graduate from high school," I told him, "I will cry." As Jamie got older, he found this prospect increasingly annoying. Would his sentimental fool of a father embarrass him in front of everyone? And why was I making such a big deal about this?

At the same time, Jamie knew very well that graduation is a big deal. When Nick graduated from college, in 2008, we all trekked to St. Louis, flying Nick's grandmothers and aunt Cynthia out for the event as well.

The morning of the big day—the ceremonies began at the absurd hour of 8:30—Jamie took a line from *Babe*. In the movie, when Mrs. Hoggett wakes to the sound of the alarm clock that she hopes will stop loopy Ferdinand the Duck from crowing at dawn, she briskly taps her husband, saying, "Hoggett, dear! Church!" In Jamie's version, this became an announcement to everyone in the family. "Hoggett, dear! Graduation!" We thought this was very witty of Jamie, and we have used variants on it ever since.

But in June 2011, when it was Jamie's turn to ascend to the stage of the Bryce Jordan Center, I did not cry. *Someone* had to hold the videocam, after all, and Janet is useless in such situations because she spent two years studying camera technique with the experimental German director Hans von Schaekenhölden. Besides, how could I have known that the truly tear-jerking graduation ceremony wouldn't occur until two years later, when Jamie graduated from LifeLink PSU?

LifeLink PSU is an awesome thing—precisely the kind of awesome thing that helped us decide to move to Penn State. Created by dynamo disability advocate Teri Lindner, a State College Area School District teacher who won Disney's Teacher of the Year award in 1999, LifeLink PSU allows students with intellectual disabilities to take appropriate classes at Penn State until they turn twenty-one. Most school districts simply keep kids with intellectual disabilities in high school until twenty-one, at which point the state has no more obligation to educate them. Lindner, correctly seeing this policy as a benign form of educational warehousing, worked with Penn State to create a program in which high school students could graduate from high school on time (more or less), then spend a couple of years mingling with Penn State students in class and out. When I say "educational warehousing," I do not mean to suggest that high school students with intellectual disabilities are being kept in conditions like those of the state asylums of yesteryear; their high school careers, instead, consist largely of programs designed to help them transition from school to work and/or independent living. Jamie benefited from those programs. But even still, he wanted to learn more about the Civil War, more about the Iron and Bronze Ages, more about Martin Luther King Jr. He did that only because the LifeLink PSU program allowed him to.

The program is housed in Penn State's student activities center, the HUB-Robeson Center, and it involves hundreds of volunteer "mentors," including student-athletes (there is a waiting list), who were practically the opposite of the high school Best Buddies—Penn State students who give part of their day to accompany their LifeLink charges to their classes and hang out with them at the HUB. (Penn State also runs a competent Best Buddies program.) Jamie's first choices in LifeLink PSU seemed a little weird to me; they included classes in meteorology and criminal justice, and were influenced by his LifeLink classmates. But that was fine with us. It made sense for Jamie to attend some classes with other LifeLink students. Over the course of his next three semesters, though, his true interests emerged: tai chi and history, especially history. Life-Link PSU students don't get grades or do homework, so I am not sure how much Jamie learned in those two years. But I can say that he understands concepts like the Iron Age and the Bronze Age, and events like the Birmingham church bombing that killed four young black girls in 1964. And I can report that thanks to his memory and his keen sense of spatial orientation, he is now able to navigate the sprawling Penn State campus by himself, and never had any trouble making his way from the HUB, when his day was done, to my office at the Institute for the Arts and Humanities, ten minutes away.

In spring 2013 his time in LifeLink came to an end, and on April 25 we attended his graduation ceremony. This was not simply a matter of Jamie taking the stage briefly and being handed a diploma; it involved a seven-minute tribute to Jamie by his mentor and good friend Lindsay Northup-Moore, followed by another seven-minute speech by Jamie himself. (Lindsay's speech, and half of Jamie's, can be seen on YouTube.) "In true Jamie style," Lindsay said, she would offer a list of the things she loves about Jamie. She proceeded to talk about Jamie's determination, his powers of persuasion (no one else, apparently, could have gotten her to see *Abraham Lincoln, Vampire Slayer*), his memory, his love for food, his sense of adventure, his extensive vocabulary, his ability to make people laugh, and his stylin' dance moves. For the final two items of her Top Ten list, Lindsay pivoted from the lighthearted to the deeply serious. Remarking on "how much he has grown" over his two years in

LifeLink, Lindsay noted that "Jamie went from being a quiet, shy fresh-man in transition class to an active participant," speaking increasingly freely and openly about his opinions and feelings. I had seen this too: as he entered his twenties, Jamie was getting significantly more mature, eloquent, and self-possessed. And then Lindsay closed with her "favor-ite" thing about Jamie, "his caring nature." Calling him "one of the most sensitive and caring people I know, or I suspect that I will ever know," Lindsay addressed him directly, closing with "I want to make sure that you, Jamie, know that you are an extraordinary young man. You never cease to surprise all of us with your abilities."

I admit that my videocam work that day·was uncharacteristi-cally shaky.

There was another aspect to LifeLink, which Jamie loved as much as he loved LifeLink PSU: the LifeLink apartment. It is housed in one of the dozens of mushrooming apartment complexes in State College, and young people with intellectual disabilities, up through age twenty-one, can stay there in a four-bedroom suite for a week at a time with two room-mates of the same gender and the supervision of a 24/7 life coach. The idea is to teach and enhance independent living skills, to encourage kids with intellectual disabilities to make their own budgets and do their own laundry and cook their own meals (with some help). In fall 2009, when Jamie was eighteen, Janet and I filled out the reams upon reams of pa-perwork necessary for an application (specifying, for example, what kinds of things Jamie can and can't do independently or with minimal prompt-ing, and what kinds of activity outside the apartment—from going to the apartment-complex gym to traveling around town on his own—we would and would not permit). And by Thanksgiving, we had just started to think about the possibility of turning in an application. Which is to say, we were not quite ready to think of Jamie being away from us for a full week.

Suddenly, on December 1, we got a phone call: one of the residents of the apartment had gotten sick and gone home, and there would be only one person in the place through Sunday. Not wanting to leave that one young man alone (albeit with the usual coaches' supervision) all that time, the LifeLink people called to offer Jamie a six-day stay. Jamie's response was visceral: "Cool! Goin' to LifeLink." So was ours: "OH MY

GOD HOW DO WE PACK WHAT DO WE DO OH MY GOD." But Janet and I calmed down (a little), made arrangements to drop Jamie off at 8 p.m. (after dinner and a shower and a change of clothes), and began to put together his clothes and toiletries and necessary electronics, even programming into his (recently purchased and then rarely used) cell phone the numbers of his family members and afterschool companions. We met his roommate, a delightful young man Jamie had known for some time. And after the meet-and-greet and the bed making and the general moving in were done, we left Jamie to his own devices at precisely 8:45 p.m., Eastern time, December 1, 2009.

As we were leaving the house for the fateful ride over to the apartment, Jamie, starting down the back stairs with his iPod, stopped and said, "I have to get my suitcase." "That's OK, sweetie," I replied. "I'll get it—it's quite heavy."

"OK, sure," Jamie shrugged, and then added in a singsong voice, to no one in particular, "What are parents for?"

It was a rhetorical question, I think. But I have kept thinking about it ever since.

□   □   □

After that initial visit, Jamie became more and more adept at being a LifeLink resident, and Janet and I—as you might imagine—came to realize that Jamie's week-long stays could actually be good things for us, as well. We enjoyed one extended second-honeymoon week in New York in the summer of 2012, and I will always cherish that memory. But then, just as Jamie aged out of LifeLink PSU in the spring of 2013, he aged out of eligibility for the LifeLink apartment in the summer of that year. Jamie had prepared for this moment in the "transition class" Lindsay mentioned; professionals in special education speak of "transition," whereas many parents tend to speak of "falling off the cliff." For Jamie, all IDEA-related services would end on August 8, 2013. After that, free fall—and the search for employment.

The first time I talked to Jamie about getting a job, he was only thirteen. That may sound absurdly early, but I thought it was a good idea to prepare him, gradually, for the world that would await him after he left school. So I told him how well he'd managed the younger kids of some colleagues who'd been to our house recently. "You really are very good with little kids," I said. "You're very gentle with them, and you play very carefully, and you always try to help them. You know, you might think about doing something like that when you're a big man and you have a job—you might be a good helper someplace where they work with little kids."

"*Michael*," he said with exasperation, "I'm going to be a Marine."

I was flabbergasted. "Excuse me? Did you say a Marine?"

"Uh-huh."

Where did *that* come from? "You mean a Marine like a soldier?"

"No!" he said, even more exasperated now. "A marine *biologist*."

One always has to wait for the other shoe to drop. As Jamie explained, he was thinking of Eugenie Clark, the famed University of Maryland ichthyologist he encountered in the National Geographic film *The Sharks*. Ambitious, I thought; but even at thirteen, Jamie knew the differences between seals and sea lions, he knew that dolphins are pinnipeds, and he knew far more about sharks than most people. And despite his speech delays, he could say "cartilaginous fish" pretty clearly. Perhaps he could work at an aquarium?

In the course of his education, as Jamie realized just how hard it is to master the basics of biology, he scaled back his hopes from "marine biologist" to "marine biologist helper." And then he scaled back his hopes still further. When in spring 2007 we went over the IEP that would chart his way through high school, he was asked what he might do for a living when he graduated; dejectedly, he said, "Groceries, I guess." It was a difficult moment for him, and for us. And I'm not sure what I would have felt that day if I had known that he would eventually have to settle for less than that.

Through his high school and LifeLink PSU years, Jamie held a variety of part-time jobs, most of them on a volunteer basis. He trained in dog and cat care at PAWS; he ushered at the downtown State Theatre; he helped out in the children's science museum; he stocked the shelves at the local food bank; he washed fire trucks for the Alpha Fire Company—itself a volunteer unit. And sometimes he got paid: he worked for minimum wage at one of the Penn State mailrooms (two days a week, two hours a day, transportation provided from high school), and in the summer of 2011 he worked a five-week stint at the Penn State recycling plant. That job paid $10.50 an hour for a four-hour shift, 9 a.m. to 1 p.m., and it was good thing the shifts didn't run any longer than that because Jamie spent his first two weeks working outside in hundred-degree heat. In boots. And heavy gloves. And long pants. And a wet bandana around his forehead. His job coach, a genial British man, kept him hydrated and laughed as Jamie imitated his accent, mixing it with a more Northern inflection derived from Ringo.

Jamie enjoyed all his jobs, and his coworkers and supervisors enjoyed working with him. He applied himself fully—he is no slacker— and he always took care to do his jobs right. In the mailroom, he took very seriously the fact that he was dealing mostly with care packages from parents to students, and he listened carefully when Janet and I told him how important it was to get the right letters and packages to the right people. "How are you doing with that?" I asked him after his first week. "Good," he reported happily, then added, "Cursive is hard."

Praise for his good work means everything to him; money means almost nothing. *Almost* nothing, because he was definitely very happy with himself to be pulling down two hundred dollars a week at that recycling job. Today, he loves the fact that he has a checking account and a debit card, and that he's able to buy himself lunch, snacks, Magic: The Gathering cards, and movie tickets. He is very generous—indeed, to a fault, as I discovered one winter when I bought a snowblower, went to get the car so that we could load it into the back of the Toyota RAV, and found that Jamie had paid for it in my absence. Six hundred dollars. I paid him back—and I told him that in the future, he will need my permission (or Janet's) for anything over a hundred dollars.

But after August 8, 2013, we were in new territory, speaking a new language. And that is what took us to the ICAP intake interview at the MH/ID BSU and then the series of CBWAs.

Here's what that means in English. The Mental Health/Intellectual Disabilities office (MH/ID), working out of the Base Services Unit (BSU), is a county-level agency overseen by Centre County. The ICAP is the Inventory of Client and Agency Planning, a long quiz and checklist designed to determine not only a client's eligibility for services but also the degree of support he or she might need if he or she is determined to be employable. And the CBWA is the Community Based Work Assessment, by which it would be decided what kind of job Jamie might do. Jamie knows very well that the people in these state and county offices are trying to help him, and he is familiar with intake sessions and reams of paperwork thanks to his history of IEPs. Whenever Janet and I talked with Jamie about his employment prospects after the age of twenty-one, we assured him that he did not want to live a life of watching YouTube, wrestling videos, and *Beatles Anthology* DVDs in the basement. He always agreed; the idea of watching YouTube in the basement all day was preposterous. But the ICAP turned out to be a very difficult hurdle for him.

It took about forty-five minutes. I talked Jamie through it and answered most of the questions for him (as I was supposed to do—I was not usurping his role). And as the process dragged on, Jamie became visibly depressed and withdrawn.

First, the questions covered a very wide spectrum of behavior, including some quite severe symptoms of mental illness. They would start mildly—has this person ever been in trouble with the law? (No!)—and mount to a point at which they would begin to get scary: Has this person ever harmed someone? Has this person ever assaulted a police officer? (No! Certainly not! How ridiculous!) Since these were things that Jamie could not even conceive of doing, I could tell that he was starting to think, after about ten minutes, *Is this my group? Are these the people like me?* Worse still, far worse, were the multiple questions to which I had to answer yes. These weren't disaggregated, so that at one point the exchange went something like this:

MH/ID: Does this person talk to him/herself? Does this person hear voices? Has he/she had any episodes of violent behavior? Is he/she a danger to self or others?

ME: Yes. [Jamie cringes.] He talks to himself. But he has never heard voices or become violent.

I added, also, that he talks to himself because he is imaginative and creative, not because he is delusional. I did not add that he sometimes talks to himself because he is lonely.

Jamie's caseworker and the other MH/ID person left the room to tabulate the results and render an assessment of Jamie's eligibility for "competitive employment," which is to say, paid work. Jamie curled into himself on his chair. I had never seen him like this; even when he was sad about his brother or his hanging-out skills, he was engaged and feisty. Now he just seemed defeated.

I came over to sit next to him and put my arm around his shoulders. "Jamie, sweetie," I began, "you are such a wonderful kid, and I am so proud that you are my son. This is why I always say 'Je suis très, très fier.' Because I am. And it is OK to talk to yourself! You do, you know. You imagine entire conversations. Like last night, when you came upstairs, I could hear you saying, 'And you know who else was born in Hawaii? Obama!' 'Really, Obama was born in Hawaii? How do you know that?' 'My father told me!' 'That is so cool.' Right? You were thinking about talking to someone who was from Hawaii?"

Jamie nodded dispiritedly.

"Well, that's totally fine," I went on. "You know you are never violent and never mean—you are a good, good kid with a sweet, sweet heart. Everybody knows that. That is why everybody you have ever worked with, in school or at work, has liked being with you. You are funny and bright and full of ideas. And I am sure that when they come back, that is exactly what they will say. You would be a good employee. That test is really for people who have much more severe disabilities and mental illnesses that make them behave dangerously sometimes. It is not for you." At this he seemed to cheer up a little, but it took the rest of the afternoon for him to fully recover. And the assessment was very much what I had expected: Jamie is not quite capable of living independently and needs help with various life tasks, especially with things involving small motor skills, but otherwise he is good to go, with appropriate supervision. He was cleared for a Community Based Work Assessment. Now all we had to do was to figure out what kind of job he might be able to do.

That, indeed, was the hard part. What is Jamie capable of doing for a living? Our first checklist filled us with despair: factory work, nope; food service, nope (not fast enough); hotel maid service, nope; machine and auto repair, nope. (Though Jamie expressed interest in auto repair—*not* a moment of astonishing self-awareness.) With one agency, Jamie had two CBWAs followed by detailed five-page write-ups: one doing setup for conferences and meetings (tables, chairs, A/V), the other doing shelving at a supermarket. Neither went well. He had trouble stacking chairs, dealing with the duct tape for the A/V setup, and attaching skirts to tables. At the supermarket he had trouble with the U-boat, the device that carts dozens of boxes out into the aisles—and besides, they were only hiring on the graveyard shift.

The result? For two months, it was basically YouTube in the basement for much of the day, as Jamie gradually realized (with what I think was a kind of horror) that we hadn't been kidding about that part. Finally, the local sheltered workshop for people with disabilities, Skills of Central Pennsylvania, offered him an 8:30 a.m.–2:30 p.m. slot twice a week—and then three times a week. On top of that, I sent out a few e-mails and got him an afternoon of volunteering once a week, Wednesdays 3–5 p.m., at the children's science museum.

I was puzzled by the first CBWA. It seemed to me that the agency responsible for that one gave up on Jamie too easily. So he had trouble with his first attempt at conference setup—so what? Isn't that precisely what job coaches are for, to supervise and assist their charges? Jamie could certainly learn how to stack chairs, peel duct tape, and attach skirts to tables. Peeved, I switched to another agency, which promptly set up a trial run for Jamie as a dishwasher in a local restaurant. I liked this trial better. Unlike the conference-setup CBWA, it wasn't a one-off. Jamie had five or six stints as a dishwasher, accompanied by a job coach, and after one of them, he took his first solo taxi ride, handing the driver the note I had given him when I dropped him off:

> My name is Jamie Bérubé. Thanks for picking me up! I am going to Ihlseng Cottage—it's on the Penn State campus, on Curtin Road just west of the Pattee/Paterno Library. My father works there. You

can leave me off at the crosswalk. If there are any problems, my father's cell phone is xxx–xxx–xxxx. Please add $5 to my fare for a tip. Thanks!

That cab ride went well, but the dishwashing job did not. Jamie was in the way of his coworkers in the kitchen, and he wasn't sufficiently attentive to detail when it came to the actual dishes. Needless to say, clean dishes matter to a substantially large percentage of people who go out to eat in restaurants, as well as to a correspondingly high percentage of people who own restaurants.

So the decision that Jamie couldn't do that job seemed legit. His second CBWA with this agency, though, was more vexing. They set up a six-month trial volunteering at the Y, doing janitorial work twice a week in two-and-a-half-hour shifts. If the trial went well, he would be hired. They liked him enormously at the Y, where many of the staff remembered him from afterschool and summer programs. And the agency job coaches very generously and carefully supervised him minute by minute. But after a six-month trial, he would have only five hours of employment per week? What was the point in that?

We know many other parents in similar situations, who went through the bureaucratic gauntlet only to face the prospect of having their adult children placed in menial jobs for a few hours a week. Some have opted out of the system altogether; the parents of one exceptionally charismatic, capable young man with Down syndrome helped him get a full-time job in a restaurant kitchen, and the parents of another young woman helped her land a job in food prep at a lunch-and-smoothies place. Other parents of young adults with intellectual disabilities in our area of central Pennsylvania have begun to meet to see whether we can create our own programs to make better use of our children's independent-living skills. One mother told me she had given up on the employment system altogether: "If the people whose job it is to get our kids jobs aren't getting our kids jobs," she asked testily, "why do they have jobs?" Another surmised that the job agencies were more invested in employing job coaches than in finding paid employment for the people served by job coaches. I find these remarks not merely cynical but ungenerous; I have a good working relationship with the people who work with Jamie, and I know that they are doing their best for him and for dozens of people like him. They are frustrated not by their clients but by local employers, who are often bafflingly inflexible when it comes to hiring people with intellectual disabilities. Trader Joe's, for example, is an enterprise many liberal-lefty people like: it has all the arugula and multigrain baguettes and aromatic cheeses and frozen masala burgers we need. But our local store will not hire people with intellectual disabilities as baggers, on the grounds that every Trader Joe's employee should be trained in every possible area. Still, I understand these parents' complaints, even if they are misdirected. I had to admit that the CBWA at the Y didn't seem designed to get Jamie a meaningful job with substantial working hours. And then, a few weeks later, after Jamie nearly injured his fingers in a vacuum cleaner (I wonder whether this was the counterpart to his foot-in-the-indoor-track moment), the Y trial was ended. Jamie still did not have competitive employment. He had two hours of volunteer work and three days in the sheltered workshop during the week, and a morning of volunteer work at the animal shelter on Sundays.

Jamie takes public transportation to and from the workshop. He loves riding the bus by himself; not everyone who works at Skills can do that. He loves being a commuter and being punctual. As I write, more than two years after he started, Jamie has never been late to work. Occasionally he has companions whom we pay to hang with him for a couple of hours at a time. It is a life, and he is happy with it; I ask him about that regularly. Though it is not the life we—and he—wanted to imagine for him. We have visited a Camphill community in southeastern Pennsylvania, where adults with intellectual disabilities live in their own villages (with supervisors and assistants) and practice various trades, from textiles to dairy farming. But Jamie is not interested, and if he is not interested, then his parents are not interested.

Janet and I have followed the debate about sheltered workshops, in which nonprofits and charitable organizations (such as Goodwill, the subject of a 2013 investigative report by NBC's *Rock Center*) pay their disabled workers a tiny fraction of the minimum wage. Jamie makes about $1.30 an hour. These workshops are a relic from the 1930s, when people with disabilities were segregated from the general population—and a time when it was not considered problematic to exempt such people from the nation's new minimum-wage laws. (The relevant law is the Fair Labor Standards Act of 1938.) Jamie does piecework there, most often involving the packaging of various vials or hardware. And thanks to his Supplemental Security Income of about $450 per month, he has enough money to buy himself lunch, snacks, Magic cards, movie tickets—and the occasional T-shirt or DVD. A snowblower is really out of his range.

Obviously, if Jamie had to support himself, he could not do it: that is the point of the protests against sheltered workshops, a point that is all the sharper for people with disabilities who are not living in their relatively well-off parents' houses. But for now, that workshop is almost all he has. He does not mind the repetitive, sedentary, and intellectually unstimulating nature of the work. He likes the workplace, and he likes his coworkers. He comes home cheerful every day, happy to be a commuter, happy to be a bit more independent from his parents.

And his supervisors at the workshop, for their part, are keen and sympathetic observers/recorders of Jamie; their accounts of his strengths and weaknesses are bracingly accurate. Here is an excerpt from their June 25, 2015, report on Jamie—specifically, their responses to 055 Pa. Code § 2390.151(e)(1) and § 2390.151(e)(2), dealing with the assessment of clients in vocational facilities:

> Jamie is a delightful, ambulatory, verbal 23 year-old young man. He began attending the Skills VT [Vocational Training] 10/24/13 at 2 days a week and increased to 3 days a week beginning 1/20/2014. He also began participating in the community exploration program in January, 2014. He is friendly and polite, although there are times when he will choose not to respond to greetings or questions. Jamie has been willing to try any task asked of him and he cares very much about the quality of his work. He asks for periodic reassurance that the work he is doing is correct and he does need periodic oversight, particularly when initially learning a new task. Most of·the work tasks he has learned he has mastered and he is able to remember how to complete the steps over time.

. . . When asked what his "dream" job would be, Jamie responded that he would love to work at Ace Hardware and/or carry
heavy supplies at Lowe's. He would be interested in doing construction, plumbing, or electrical work. He mentioned that he would like
to work at a supermarket, stocking shelves or bagging goods. He
would consider working in a restaurant, doing dishes or delivering
food to people. He would be interested in learning to do automo-
tive work and change tires. He mentioned enjoying moving boxes
around and some interest in learning to use a floor jack or fork lift
to move objects. He mentioned that he really, really enjoys organizing things and would enjoy work tasks involving organization
such as in a video section in a retail store where he could "organize,
move things around and make things fit." Jamie seems to have an
amazing memory for detail within subjects he enjoys (such as geography, the counties in Pennsylvania, sharks, movies, music, etc.).
This talent would naturally lend itself to being very helpful on a job
site requiring such attention to detail.

I was surprised by this report, and asked Jamie specifically about
his ideas about working in construction as a plumber or electrician—
that requires a great deal of training, you know—and the bit about working on cars and changing tires, or operating heavy machinery. Where
did *that* come from? As for his organizational skills: on that topic, his
self-knowledge was far more grounded. But I felt a twinge of sadness at
the idea of Jamie organizing the video section of a retail store, just as I
would feel if he had expressed a desire to organize the eight-track-tape
collection at Columbia Records. And I was stunned that the category of
"animal care" scored so low in his responses. Jamie's explanation? "I do
that already."

In January 2014, I had occasion to take Jamie to the Shedd Aquarium in Chicago and could not help noticing that they were looking for
volunteers. For Jamie, that would amount to a *real* dream job, pay or no
pay. Perhaps the sheltered-workshop aspect of his life is partly my fault,
for not arranging our family life in such a way that we could live in a city
that has an aquarium. Should we have taken the jobs at the University

of Illinois at Chicago after all, subjecting Jamie to an inadequate school system for ten years in the hopes that he could someday be a volunteer at the Shedd? I don't think so. But when I watch the way he comes alive in aquariums and natural history museums, sometimes turning into a chatty docent before my eyes, I wonder.

I knew that Jamie would not grow up to be a marine biologist. And I know that there are millions of nondisabled Americans out of work or underemployed whose lives are less happy than Jamie's. For that matter, the set of fully employed people who find their work meaningful, enjoyable, and fulfilling is a subset of all working people, and as the middle class erodes under the pressure of austerity economics, the number of people who can find secure, stable jobs that will see them into old age dwindles steadily. Jamie is not the only young person looking for work, and I don't imagine that he has a "right" to a job that supersedes everyone else's needs. But I look sometimes at the things he writes in his legal pads, and I think, isn't there any place in the economy for a bright, gregarious, effervescent, diligent, conscientious, and punctual young man with intellectual disabilities, a love of animals, and an amazing cataloguing memory and insatiable intellectual curiosity about the world?

□   □   □

In 2014, I wrote an account of Jamie's search for work, and in May of that year *Al Jazeera America* published it as an essay, "For Hire: Dedicated Young Man with Down Syndrome." (The previous section is a revised and updated version of that essay.) The story was reprinted in the Penn State alumni magazine, where it caught the attention of an editor from the Penn State Press, Tony Sanfilippo. Sanfilippo was so struck by the story, and by its accompanying photographic evidence of Jamie's skill in making lists, that he offered Jamie an interview for a job in cataloguing, information retrieval, and tracking inventory and sales. Somehow I think it is relevant that Tony has two brothers with Down syndrome.

Janet accompanied Jamie to the interview, but first, she prepared him for it by going over some basic data about books: title, author, ISBN number. Titles and authors were things that Jamie knew; the world of

ISBN numbers was new to him. But he is a quick study. When Tony Sanfilippo started to explain to Jamie what information he would need to understand the cataloguing job, he started with author and title . . . whereupon Jamie flipped over a book, pointed to the ISBN number, and said, "I know, and ISBN number." Sanfilippo was pleasantly surprised and proceeded to let Jamie know that some Penn State Press books are highly specialized and very complicated, such as the books in art history and the Renaissance. "I *love* art history and the Renaissance!" Jamie exclaimed and reeled off the names of six or seven of his favorite Renaissance painters, from Botticelli to Caravaggio.

Jamie got the job. He works every Friday from 9 a.m. to 1 p.m.; I drop him off in the morning, and he usually takes the campus shuttle to my office, arriving just after 1:30. Even though Tony Sanfilippo has since moved to Ohio State University Press (damn!), Jamie is still cataloguing, cutting-and-pasting, and tracking information, two hours on his own and two hours with his job coach. The agency was a bit surprised by this development—apparently they had not considered this line of work for Jamie, ahem—but they are supporting him well. Jamie is very proud of his Penn State Press job and always insists on wearing a dress shirt on Fridays. I call it Uncasual Friday. He knows very well this is competitive employment, not a sheltered-workshop job, and he wants to look and perform his best.

Still, when I contrast Jamie's school history with his work history (as I cannot help but do), it's impossible for me not to feel dissatisfied, uneasy. Jamie's life is immeasurably richer than it would have been fifty or sixty years ago; there is no denying that. Now that we as a society are no longer institutionalizing people with Down syndrome, we have collectively learned something extremely important—not only about Down syndrome, or about ourselves as a society, but about human life in general. Nature and nurture are so deeply intertwined, so interdependent, that even so dramatic and indelible a genetic aberration as trisomy-21 is not simply "in the genes." To put this another way, in the terms I use when teaching disability studies classes, over the past century, nothing has changed about the chromosomal nondisjunction that produces Down syndrome. The biology is what it was.

So what *has* changed? Social policies. Those social policies now make it possible for Americans with Down syndrome to receive meaningful education and to achieve some degree of social integration with their nondisabled peers. Those social policies have brought people with intellectual disabilities, more generally, out of the shadows and the warehouses and into public life. Those social policies have literally changed human bodies and minds, and expanded our collective sense of human potential.

Medicine, too, has played its part: the advent of open-heart surgery allowed untold numbers of people with Down syndrome to survive neonatal heart defects, and advances in medical care have improved the quality of life (and lengthened the life expectancy) of people with disabilities. No degree of distrust in the "medical model" of disability should induce us to ignore that. But the "social model" of disability studies caught on in academe precisely because disability is not simply a matter of individual bodies and somatic conditions; it is a social relationship, mediated by social customs and social policies.

I doubt whether any endeavors in human life could make this clearer than the realms of education and employment. To take another example from the scholarship in disability studies, mild intellectual disability has not uniformly been considered a disability in all human societies. The ancient Greeks, for instance, were deeply disturbed by congenital malformation, thinking it grounds for infanticide, but do not seem to have cared much about mild intellectual disability. In many pre-industrial societies, people with mild intellectual disabilities served in the workforce without very much fuss. Henri-Jacques Stiker's monumental *A History of Disability* makes this case in great detail, though I tend to distance myself from some of Stiker's rosier depictions of pre-industrial society, which seem to me to come perilously close to the position that 1100 CE constituted the good old days. He has a point, though, insofar as for much of Christian Europe in the Middle Ages, disability was not sharply distinguished from poverty, and Christian charity was the appropriate response to both. Just as you can find radical environmentalists who not only question the costs and benefits of the Industrial Revolution but also romanticize pre-Columbian Native civilizations as living in perfect

harmony with nature, so too is there a strain, in Stiker's thought, of ro-
manticizing the community ethos of Christian Europe (and overlooking
the whole tortures-and-crusades aspect of that culture).

Jamie's struggles with employment leave me of two minds about
the world we have created over the past few centuries. It is not too hy-
perbolic, or too social-constructionist, to say that some people with disabilities were disabled *by modernity*, insofar as the organization of life
and work in modern societies gave them fewer roles in public life than
they might have had in some premodern societies. The Industrial Revolution increased the aggregate quality of life for the people of developed
countries, but it also maimed millions of workers—men, women, and
children—and inaugurated the era of the mental institution and the sciences of population management. The horrors of eugenics flow directly
from the ideas of "progress" that spread in the wake of industrializa-
tion. At the same time, modernity created new forms of disablement
among putatively able-bodied persons: I would not be capable of writing
this book without the modern device known as reading glasses, which
I have needed since my late forties. Disability is contextual: for most of
human history, the slight degeneration in my eyesight would not have
mattered to anyone, not even me; only with the advent of the modern
device known as "writing," five thousand years ago or so, and the even
more modern invention known as "fine print," did it become an issue of
some importance.

And yet I believe with all my heart that this is the best time in human
history for people with Down syndrome. I have no nostalgia for an era
in which Jamie might have been able to work alongside his nondisabled
peers as a baler of hay or a carrier of water, if he were so lucky as to have
survived childhood. But it seems clear to me that whereas the Individuals with Disabilities Education Act has changed the national landscape
for people with intellectual disabilities, the Americans with Disabilities
Act, though far better known, has been far less successful on that count.
That's not just because courts have read the ADA so narrowly—finding for plaintiffs only on the rarest occasions, looking for any rationale
to deny a plaintiff standing to sue—that Congress had to go back and
amend the law in 2008. It's also because in this world we have created,

people with intellectual disabilities are incapable of doing a great many jobs, even with all the assistance imaginable.

As for the sheltered workshops: On July 22, 2014, President Obama signed into law the Workforce Innovation and Opportunity Act (WIOA), which went into effect on July 1, 2015. The law will transform the workshops substantially, severely limiting the number of people who can legally be paid a subminimum wage. That sounds great: Who is in favor of the subminimum wage? But the law does not say what will become of people whose intellectual disabilities are significant enough to prevent them from being competitive for competitive employment. Like Jamie, they are doing piecework for a buck and change an hour. Every well-meaning person might object to a wage scale that low, anywhere in the world (including the places in the world where it would constitute a huge raise). But although the new law will strike many people with disabilities from the rolls of subminimum-wage workers, and although it provides that they receive career counseling and job preparation, it does not, because it cannot, say anything about whether employers are going to go along with the plan. So what becomes of people like Jamie, and people less suited for competitive employment than Jamie? "There are exceptions," notes the online magazine *Disability Scoop*, "for those who are deemed ineligible for vocational rehabilitation and to allow individuals already earning less than the federal minimum to continue in their jobs." But it is not clear how those exceptions will play out, state by state, city by city, workshop by workshop, individual by individual. After the state of Vermont closed its sheltered workshops in 2002, it integrated many of the former workshop workers into competitive employment, such that the employment rate of people with developmental disabilities in Vermont is now twice the national average. As Halle Stockton wrote in a 2014 investigative report, "Within three years, about 80 percent of people who'd worked in the last sheltered workshop to close found jobs. Those who didn't got other services based in the community." Here's hoping Vermont's success can be the model for the other 49 states.

On paper, here's how it is supposed to work: section 511 of the new law, "Limitations on Use of Subminimum Wage," affects employers who hold "special wage" certificates under section 14 (c) of the Fair Labor

Standards Act (the provision that exempts them from minimum-wage laws). As the Arc puts it in their summary of WOIA:

> Entities with a valid 14 (c) certificate may not continue to compensate employees at a subminimum wage unless the individual:
>
> (1) Is provided career counseling and information by the designated state agency which are delivered in a manner facilitating independent decision making and informed choice;
>
> (2) Is informed by the employer of self-advocacy, self-determination, and peer mentoring training opportunities available in the individuals' geographic area; and
>
> (3) These options are presented every six months for the first year of employment in a subminimum wage position and then annually thereafter.

So will Jamie and his group be grandfathered in as subminimum-wage workers and given counseling and training and self-advocacy opportunities that all our local employers are free to ignore? Or will Pennsylvania become gradually Vermontized? It's impossible to say. But we have been put on notice that much of Skills of Central Pennsylvania might be converted to an "activity center" as a small number of Skills employees are transitioned to minimum-wage jobs.

In November 2015, Skills held an informational session with local families. There was pizza and soda and PowerPoint, and the vibe in the room ran from cautiously optimistic to anxiously suspicious to plaintively bewildered. A substantial number of parents insisted that they like the sheltered-workshop system just as it is, especially the "sheltered" part; they didn't want their children out in the workaday world of competitive employment where they might be subject to bullying, taunting, and derision. Some of them had had bad experiences with employers and unsympathetic coworkers; one mother complained that her son's previous workplace had included people who smoked and cursed. Are these parents being overprotective, paternalistic to the point of infantilizing their adult children? Possibly. They might also be prudent.

At one point, Janet asked why the Skills employees should be doing subminimum-wage piecework labor at all; why not convert the facility into something like an arts center?

The Workforce Opportunity and Innovation Act has two objectives. One is to cut down on the use of subminimum-wage work. That is unobjectionable. The minimum wage produces a yearly income of $14,500, and it is hard to see why any American worker should be allowed to earn less than that. The other objective is to integrate people with intellectual disabilities into the community, to get them out of the workshops and into the wider world. That has been a goal of the disability rights movement from the outset— a goal, it turns out, that some parents of adults with intellectual disabilities do not share. It is a conundrum. It is true that much of the wider world does not welcome adults with intellectual disabilities, and yet how can we try to destigmatize intellectual disability unless adults with intellectual disabilities are seen as, and treated as, ordinary people—albeit ordinary people who need a bit more help? How might it be possible to combine publicly funded programs—not only counseling but the provision of job coaches and supervisors—with financial incentives for private businesses to hire and integrate people with intellectual disabilities? As a society, in our treatment of people with intellectual disability, we have survived the long dark era of eugenics and institutionalization—though not without heart-wrenching suffering and misery. We have created an era of inclusive education. But we still do not seem to know what inclusive employment would look like, or how to go about achieving it. For people with intellectual disabilities, it is the next great civil rights struggle.

The Meaning of Life

□   □   □   □   □

One thing in my world has changed radically over the past twenty years, quite apart from Jamie growing up to be big. When I published *Life as We Know It*, there was no such thing as "disability studies" in the humanities. Lennard Davis had published his groundbreaking book, *Enforcing Normalcy*, in 1995; Rosemarie Garland-Thompson published the collection *Freakery: Cultural Spectacles of the Extraordinary Body* in 1996; David Mitchell and Sharon Snyder published the collection *The Body and Physical Difference* in 1997; Simi Linton published *Claiming Disability* in 1998. These are generally regarded as some of the first major works in disability studies, and rightly so. But at the time I was writing my book, I had no idea that I might be contributing to a new academic field. I wanted to write something that would be more than just an account of Jamie's life, something that explored the political, cultural, and philosophical implications of Down syndrome and intellectual disability. But I never thought of it as a book in "disability studies," because disability studies didn't exist.

   I was also trying, in my way, to help make the world a more welcoming place for my son and everyone like him. Unsurprisingly, some readers responded to that aspect of the book by suggesting that I was "cheerleading," painting a mostly shiny happy picture of Jamie's early life. (For my part, when I go back and look at that book now, I am struck by how much sorrow and worry it testifies to.) And I suppose that people who cannot imagine the value and delight in raising a child like Jamie will inevitably think of this book as more cheerleading, this time laced with accounts of literal cheering for his accomplishments at school and his victories in Special Olympics.

The odd thing is that despite the rise of disability studies as an academic discipline, a discipline to which I now claim some allegiance and to which I hope I have made a substantial contribution in my previous book, *The Secret Life of Stories: From Don Quixote to Harry Potter, How Understanding Intellectual Disability Transforms the Way We Read,* I suspect that I am more likely to find people who cannot imagine the value and delight in raising a child like Jamie in academe than outside of it. In one way that is not *terribly* odd, since academe values intelligence (or claims to) above everything else. In the humanities, Licia Carlson writes, intellectual disability has often been treated as "the philosopher's nightmare": "Rather than promoting ideals of assimilation and normalization, many who bring the intellectually disabled into the philosophical fold mark this group out according to its departure from the normal and highlight its profound otherness, its radical alterity." We are about to see just how right Carlson is. But in another way this phenomenon seems quite strange: in American popular culture, it seems to me, the public image of people with Down syndrome is pretty good, even if their representation sometimes takes the icky form known to theorists and activists as "inspiration porn." For the most part, when someone with Down syndrome is the sibling of an athlete or a celebrity, or when someone with Down syndrome accomplishes something substantial, the press coverage goes into heartwarming mode, and we as a society give ourselves a collective pat on the back for being inclusive, caring, and sensitive to difference and diversity. Whereas in the subfield of philosophy known as bioethics, things are decidedly bleaker. Which is why, for a couple of years, I would offer an academic lecture entitled "Bioethics: Much Too Important to Be Left to Bioethicists."

Bioethicists sometimes bristled at that title, so I suppose I should preface my argument with a hashtag such as #notallbioethicists. But the people I discuss are pretty mainstream, influential figures; they are not fringe characters housed in some makeshift Quonset hut adjacent to the main Bioethics Building. And I begin with a book I have mentioned earlier, Jonathan Glover's *Choosing Children: Genes, Disability, and Design*. On the book's opening page, Glover asks:

> Progress in genetics and in reproductive technologies gives us growing power to reduce the incidence of disabilities and disorders. Should we welcome this power, or should we fear its implications?

The answer turns out to be something like "welcome this power, with some reservations"; notably (and sensibly enough), Glover rejects the idea that there is a bright line between using genetic technology to restore or maintain a person's "normal" level of functioning and using genetic technology to enhance functioning well beyond that level. His book can thus be seen as a reply to (or, at the very least, I teach it alongside) Michael Sandel's *The Case Against Perfection*, which makes precisely that argument against "designer babies." For Sandel, going beyond that "normal" level, blurry as the line might be, violates something important about our humanity; instead, Sandel insists that we must retain our "openness to the unbidden" and that the attempt to extend our mastery over uncertainty paradoxically diminishes our freedom. Glover, by contrast, argues that

> it is common to say that genetic choices are acceptable when they are to avoid a disability or disorder, but objectionably "eugenic" if they are to enhance "normal" functioning. The medical boundary may seem the obvious line to defend against "designer babies." But making some enhancements may add to flourishing as much as eliminating some disabilities. If we are not motivated by the ugly attitudes [toward disability], if what we care about is really not disability but flourishing, the medical boundary may be impossible to defend.

The medical boundary may be impossible to defend no matter what the rationale, because Sandel's argument unfortunately relies on an unquestioned and highly problematic idea of the "normal." I was struck by this reliance the first time I taught Sandel's book to undergraduates, precisely because they unanimously agreed with Sandel: genetic and

medical interventions are OK if they are a means to restoring someone to a baseline of normal, but not if they are used to enhance our
abilities and take us into the realm of comic-book superheroes. "Now
I find this curious," I said in one class. "For ten weeks in this course
you've challenged and historicized and deconstructed the idea of the
'normal.' You've learned how the idea of the 'normal' has served as the
primary tool of oppression not only for people with physical and intellectual disabilities but also for gay, lesbian, bi, and trans populations. And
suddenly now you want it back? Seriously?" Besides, what norm are we
talking about? I have mentioned my need for reading glasses. Can I have
restorative surgery that brings me back to the species norm for eyesight?
And is 20/20 the species norm or the species ideal? And what of the fact
that in my prime, my eyesight was closer to 20/15? Do I get *that* back
instead of the species average? And as for the students who complained
that we are "playing God" with these genetic and medical techniques, I
presume they are not taking that attitude toward antibiotics.

Two things strike me as remarkable about Glover's book. The first
is that he does not come to his pro-enhancement conclusion without
taking into consideration a wide variety of accounts of the lives of people
with disabilities. For instance, even though Glover begins a discussion
of blindness by writing, "Since sight enriches our lives so much, it is
hard not to see blindness as an obstacle to flourishing," he proceeds to
recount the stories of John Hull, whose terror at going blind was gradually replaced by a wholly new and surprisingly pleasant sense of himself and his world, and of "S.B.," who became severely depressed after
an operation restored his sight. "When blind he had lived with energy
and enthusiasm," writes Glover, "but when given sight he lost his peace
and self-respect." Glover's opening chapter begins from the premise that
"since the 1980s, ethical debate about disabilities and disorders has been
transformed by the participation of those who have these conditions,"
and he credits the disability rights movement with having "brought out
the extent to which society's response to a medical condition contributes
to whether or not it is a disability."

The second remarkable thing is that despite this seemingly careful
consideration of the disability studies critique, Glover can nevertheless

write, in a later chapter, "In this book disability has been contrasted with human flourishing." Obviously, if your goal is to enhance human flourishing, and you see disability as inimical to flourishing, there is no way to account adequately for the ways in which some people with disabilities might enjoy their lives more fully and thoroughly than some people without disabilities.

How does *Choosing Children* do this? How does it credit people with disabilities for having transformed the debate and then wind up back in the pre-transformation position of arguing that disabilities are to be contrasted with human flourishing? I think there are two distinctive problems with the book. One is that, like so many discussions of disability and bioethics, it conflates disability and disease at a key moment in the argument. The other is that it relies, at other key moments, on thought experiments and hypothetical questions that make no sense except in the "what if" world of bioethicists.

The first key moment involves Glover's dismissal of what is known as the "expressivist" argument: "Choosing to have a child without certain disabilities need not come from any idea that disabled people are inferior. Nor does it entail that the world, or the gene pool, should be cleansed of disabled people." This much is true; some prospective parents might feel, reasonably enough, that they are ill-equipped to raise a child with certain disabilities, and that this is more a judgment on them than on anyone with such disabilities. Moreover, Glover argues that we can contest the "ugly attitudes" toward disability so that such decisions about childbirth are not motivated by fear, prejudice, or stigma. Here, however, is where the argument gets knotty.

> I think that, other things being equal, it is good if the incidence of disabilities is reduced by parental choices to opt for potentially more flourishing children. But we should not deny the potential cost to which the expressivist argument draws attention. And we should try to reduce that cost as far as possible.
>
> To do this, we need to send a clear signal that we do not have the ugly attitudes to disability. It is important to show that what we care about is our children's flourishing; that this, and not shrinking

from certain kinds of people, or some horrible prospect of cleansing the world of them, is what motivates us. To think that a particular disability makes someone's life less good is not one of the ugly attitudes. It does not mean that the person who has it is of any less value, or is less deserving of respect, than anyone else.

There are two ways in which we can show this. One is by making the comparison with other medical programmes. We want to defeat cancer, not because we lack respect for cancer and want to rid the world of them, but because of what cancer does to people. The existence of doctors, hospitals, and pharmaceuticals is not an insult to the sick, just a sign of the platitude that illness impairs human flourishing. And the same goes for programmes that aim to reduce the number of children born with HIV. The harm the expressivist argument points to comes through communication. And so, if we have the right attitudes, clear communication should reduce or even eliminate the harm.

One might reasonably question whether thinking "a particular disability makes someone's life less good" is not one of the ugly attitudes toward disability—or, if not "ugly," at least "unjustified." But what I want to point out is that the analogy to cancer and HIV construes disability as disease—indeed, as life-threatening disease. This seems to me to be a decisive mistake. Are we racing to "cure" autism because it is like cancer? Do we want to "defeat" Down syndrome the way we want to "defeat" cancer? Glover argues carefully against many of the ugly attitudes that would stigmatize or seek to eliminate people with disabilities, but the idea that disability is best thought of as analogous to cancer cannot be called an "attractive" attitude.

As for those thought experiments and hypothetical questions: In his chapter "Parental Choice and What We Owe to Our Children," Glover relies on the work of influential bioethicist Derek Parfit. At one point Glover discusses a hypothetical question in the context of determining what counts as a life worth living. In the course of asking whether "prospective parents [should] be under some moral pressure, at least, to consider whether it is right to bring into the world a child whose life is, by a small margin, just worth living," Glover argues against the "zero-line view"—in which a life is just barely tolerable—in favor of a "minimum level" of flourishing. First, he poses an open-ended ethical question. "Some victims of horrendous abuse as children may later still find their lives worth living and be glad to have been born. Does this mean that a couple with a persistent record of terrible child abuse should still be serious candidates for fertility treatment? Should there not be some minimum level above the zero line?" This should make us squirm: Who among us wants to approve that couple for fertility treatments? But wait. How do we apply that question to matters of genetics and prenatal screening?

By way of bioethicists' thought experiments:

> Many think the zero-line view sets the standard far too low. Where should the minimum level be set, and on what basis? Frances Kamm has suggested the line be normality. She discusses a hypothetical case (introduced by Derek Parfit) of a woman who knows that, if she conceives now, her child will have a life worth living but will be mildly retarded. The woman also knows that, if she waits, she will be able to have a normal child. Frances Kamm accepts that, having a life worth living, the child with mild retardation will not be harmed by being created. But she thinks the woman will still have done wrong by not waiting. This is not just a comparative point, based on the fact that the alternative child would have a better chance of flourishing. She says "even if she could produce no child except a mildly retarded one, it might be better for her not to produce any" and that the woman "would do wrong to produce a defective child when she could have easily avoided it."

There are three things to be said about this passage. The first is that Kamm is saying, in so many words, that it may be better that children with mild retardation—children *who have lives worth living*—not be born. (See how blinkered and destructive the concept of the "normal" child can be?) The second is that the Parfit-induced hypothetical that leads Kamm to this stunning conclusion is totally implausible. There is no scenario—I repeat, no scenario, none whatsoever—in which any woman knows that, if she foregoes conception now, she will have a normal child later on.

Earlier in the chapter, in the course of demonstrating that some children's disabilities truly do place crushing emotional burdens on parents, Glover had presented the case of Julia Hollander, mother of a child with significant brain damage: "The cause of her problem was not genetic," Glover notes. "When she was born, the placenta peeled away early, and this destroyed her cerebral cortex."

> Imogen has fits, and will never walk or talk. She will need help with feeding. She will be in and out of hospital all her life. She cannot smile or make eye contact. She cannot communicate except by crying. Her expectation of life is about twenty years.

Imogen Hollander was sentenced to a life of much pain and many limitations—and Hollander had almost no social supports for her child. Glover is right to conclude that "such a severe disability brings out how the thought that a parent is 'selfish' to hope for a child without disability can be cruel and unfair. No one should be criticized for wanting to escape the problems faced by Julia Hollander"—or, for that matter, the problems faced by Imogen. But this example of severe disability caused by birth trauma should give pause to bioethicists who concoct scenarios in which women decline to initiate a pregnancy now in the assurance that they will have a normal child if they only wait.

The world in which bioethicists propose such things, the world in which Kamm can chastise a woman who produces a "defective" child "when she could have easily [!] avoided it," is a world without birth trauma, without conditions undiagnosable before birth (autism, pervasive developmental delay), without any sense of contingency—let alone an openness to the unbidden. Such what-if hypotheticals profoundly distort what it is like to contemplate having a child who may have a disability; indeed, they distort what it is like to have a child.

So the third thing to be said about this discussion is that bioethics is much too important to be left to bioethicists.

□ □ □

I focus on Glover—and I teach his book—not because he is the most emphatic of the pro-enhancement bioethicists but because he is one of the most moderate. It is not hard to find, in the "let a thousand enhancements bloom" camp, people who not only advocate unregulated genetic engineering but deride skeptics as Luddites and superstitious fools. And then there is the "transhumanist" group, who can't wait until we all fuse with computers and solve everything. That sounds like a party I will be happy to miss.

None of the advocates of enhancement are deterred by counterarguments that their programs and visions amount to a form of eugenics. For them, the evil aspect of eugenics, from the early days of social Darwinism to its culmination in the Holocaust, was that it involved state coercion—not that it promoted deeply mistaken and ultimately catastrophic beliefs about genetics, evolution, and disability. *This* time, we are assured, we have the science all figured out, and we owe it to ourselves and to the future of our species to let people choose whatever enhancements they desire—more or less. This position is commonly known as "liberal eugenics," and the term is not meant as a criticism. It accurately expresses the position that for its proponents, eugenics would be perfectly all right—indeed, a great good—if only it did not involve state officials, laws, and institutions. Glover does not go quite that far; he endorses Joel Feinberg's idea that, as a species, we have "a right to an open future," one key component of which is the permission for individual parents to choose what they believe to be best for their children. (This might also be part of Glover's response to Sandel, even if Sandel is not explicitly addressed in Glover's book: *You want an openness to the unbidden, you say; all right then, I'll see you an individual's openness to the unbidden and raise you a species' right to an open future.*) But Glover acknowledges that an untrammeled, free-market liberal eugenics might be undesirable:

> Could leaving people free to choose genes for their children at the
> genetic supermarket have serious social costs? If so, we may need
> a regulated market, on a European model. On this system, there

would be no state plan to change people's genes or to improve the gene pool, but there might be limitations on genetic choices thought to be against the public interest. Social intervention would act only as a filter. Which choices, if any, should be excluded would be part of democratic debate.

On one hand, this position is considerably more circumspect than that of famed biologist James Watson, who reliably embarrasses himself every few years by delivering himself of the opinion that African people are inferior to the rest of the species, that it would be desirable to screen for "pretty" girls and to abort fetuses found to be gay, and that "you would have to be crazy to say you wanted" a child with Down syndrome, "because that child has no future." As Watson put it in 2003, "I am against society imposing rules on individuals for how they want to use genetic knowledge. Just let people decide what they want to do." Glover cites this remark and takes his distance from it—hence his admission that we may need "a regulated market, on a European model." But on the other hand, Glover's position is remarkably vague—and remarkably naive, politically. Apparently, the mechanism that will determine which enhancements are acceptable will be democratic deliberation— not just on a European model, but everywhere on the globe, in order to thwart "genetic tourism" as people shop for enhancements their own nations forbid.

Glover acknowledges the difficulties of regulating such a market. Surely we would find ourselves in the world of *Gattaca* before we knew it, screening not only for all "major inheritable diseases" but also for things like myopia, baldness, obesity, and addictive susceptibility—all of which are mentioned, and treated as unambiguously undesirable, by the film's genetics counselor, who just happens to be black (the surprising implication is that he lives in a society obsessed by genetics but utterly indifferent to race)—and, as no one but me seems to have noticed, bald. Lest I sound like one of those wearisome scolds who wanders into genetics debates from their homes in the humanities armed with nothing but copies of Huxley's *Brave New World* and Hawthorne's short story

"The Birthmark," I assure you that the *Gattaca* scenario is well within the realm of possibility in Glover's book. He writes:

> Sometimes disabilities arouse a special revulsion, creating a desire to cleanse the world of them. But, without this special revulsion, the case for reducing the incidence of disorders and disabilities is that they are obstacles to people having flourishing lives. And this is equally a reason for making other choices, including genetic ones, to remove non-medical impediments to flourishing. Eliminating a genetic disposition to shyness or laziness might help someone flourish, as might making them more cheerful or boosting their ability to sing or to learn languages.

Shyness? Laziness? These are traits to be eliminated from the species now? But some of my best friends are shy and lazy! Why, I myself spent the first twelve years of my life being shy, and the next twelve being lazy!

I joke, but this is very serious business. I should make clear that I have no problem with people taking medication for severe shyness or social anxiety—or for a wide range of psychiatric conditions from depression and PTSD to schizophrenia. (Indeed, my late mother once refused to believe that I was the only member of our family *not* taking some form of medication.) I strongly suspect that such medications are overprescribed, especially to parents of unruly children, but I have no doubt that the underlying conditions they seek to mitigate are real and that palliative measures are not to be rejected merely because they might be applied too widely. I do, however, have grave doubt that ordinary shyness or laziness constitute threats to human flourishing so substantial that we as a species would be better off without them. And I note that this anti-shyness-and-laziness position follows, curiously, from Glover's conflation of "disorders and disabilities," which is very close to the conflation of disability and disease entailed in the analogy between disability and cancer. It appears that once you start enumerating human traits you find undesirable, and once you start thinking of them as if they constitute disorders or diseases, you just can't stop yourself from imagining what it would be like if we could "cleanse the world" of them.

Again, there are many diseases I would like to see disappear, and I can say this without sounding like Victor Frankenstein, dreaming that he might "banish disease from the human frame, and render man invulnerable to any but a violent death." And one of the traits enumerated by *Gattaca*'s genetics counselor, and targeted for screening, happens to be a propensity for violence—something whose elimination I would find relatively unproblematic, though I strongly doubt we will locate a genetic sequence for violent temper, and I tend to think that some forms of violence (though not all) are responses to severe social injustice. But thinking of shyness and laziness in these terms, as obstacles to flourishing, seems to me another category error. It's not quite as bad as thinking of disability as something that is to be contrasted with human flourishing, but it's still not a good thing to think with.

In 2012, I had the good fortune to meet someone who could explain for me exactly why: Glenn Treisman. It was at the Conference on World Affairs in Boulder, Colorado, an extraordinary week-long festival of panels on "everything conceivable" (as it quite accurately bills itself). I was assigned to eight panels in four days, on subjects ranging from Shakespeare to sports to "Ethics and the New Genetics," for which my copanelists were Joseph McInerney, director emeritus of the National Coalition for Health Professional Education in Genetics; Vivian Siegel, director of Scientific Education and Public Communications at the Broad Institute of MIT and Harvard; and Treisman, professor of psychiatry and behavioral sciences and internal medicine at the Johns Hopkins University School of Medicine. The presentations of my copanelists were every bit as terrific as you might imagine, and unlike every academic conference I have ever attended, everybody kept to the strict time limit. (In every panel!)

Treisman's talk swiftly and decisively put to rest the claims of "liberal eugenics," pointing out not only that we have no idea how to go about eliminating things like shyness or laziness but also, and more important, that we have no idea whether some of the traits we now consider undesirable or harmful actually have survival value for us as a species. In other words, for all we know, our capacity for depression is what got us through the Pleistocene. Likewise, for all we know, shyness and laziness are, in evolutionary terms, two of our saving graces.

Just over a year earlier, in January 2011, I had a similarly instructive exchange, this one online, courtesy of the National Humanities Center's On the Human project. My contribution to that multiyear project was a version of the critique of Glover I have offered here, and it drew this response from Tom Shakespeare, one of the founders of the disability rights movement in the United Kingdom (and yes, a distant descendant of *that* Shakespeare). I will quote it at length, because it underlies much of my thinking in this book:

> To me, disability is not neutral, it is a decrement in health. Not a tragedy, granted, but not just another difference like sex or ethnicity. Disability may sometimes open one up to other possibilities (as might poverty, HIV and divorce) but that does not make it less of a predicament. Of course, environments contribute mightily to the burden, and it is a matter of justice for us to try and lessen those physical and attitudinal barriers. People are indeed disabled by society—but by their bodies too. (I also find the distinction between illness and impairment ultimately unhelpful.) Those of us born with our disabilities are used to our form of life, and we rarely bother worrying about it—we cannot imagine any other way of being. But ask any disabled person how they would feel about losing further abilities, and most would be less sanguine, I think. (I was broadly happy to spend forty plus years with restricted growth. But I regret deeply spending the last couple of years as a paraplegic, despite the fact that I am probably as happy today as I have ever been.)
>
> I would like to deconstitute the disability category a little. I think there is a danger in equating disability, as some utilitarian bioethicists do, with all the worst and most difficult forms of life—Tay Sachs or Lesch Nyhan or other profound limitations in which the possibility of flourishing seem[s] truly remote. But I also think there is a danger, as some disability advocates do, of equating disability with the other end of the scale—with Deafness, or dwarfism, or Down syndrome, conditions which hardly diminish flourishing at all.

> Where I part company with Jonathan Glover is his perfection-
> ism—his hope that we can not only put disability behind us, but that
> we can, and should, improve on average human nature and human
> embodiment. My messy, possibly incoherent, position is that we
> should accept a measure of diversity and difference, because human
> frailty is unavoidable, but that where the balance tips into suffering
> and restriction, we should do whatever we can to avoid it. While still
> valuing, supporting and including all those individuals who end up,
> despite our efforts, with profound disability.

Shakespeare misreads me in one important respect, attributing to
me the position that disability is never a decrement in health (my actual position: sometimes it is and sometimes it isn't). And his critique
of the "social model" of disability, expressed here as skepticism about
the usefulness of the distinction between illness and impairment, will
be troublesome for many people in disability studies. (Shakespeare was
one of the people who developed the idea of the social model of disability decades ago; he now finds that model inadequate for people with
intellectual disabilities and psychiatric conditions, and I think he is right
about that.) But I love the rest of this rich and thoughtful response.

Shakespeare's comments on "additional disability" strike me as salu-
tary reminders not to romanticize disability or to pretend that all disabilities are merely "differences" like other identity categories. (Think again,
as I have, of Jamie almost losing a foot.) And yet even Shakespeare's
description of his paraplegia is ambivalent: he regrets being paraplegic
after living his life happily with achondroplasia . . . and yet he remains as
happy as he has ever been. As for his final paragraph, I agree with every
word. But it's the middle paragraph I cherish most, for its enumeration
of conditions that "hardly diminish flourishing at all"—Deafness, dwarfism, and Down syndrome. That is the whole enchilada, right there. If you
see things like Deafness, dwarfism, and Down syndrome as unremark-
able aspects of human diversity and difference, part of ordinary intraspecies variation, you will never make the mistake of thinking that their
eradication constitutes an unambiguous species-wide good. You will
never make the mistake of thinking of these conditions in the terms you

would apply to fatal diseases. And you will never embarrass yourself in public by proclaiming that people with these conditions have no future.

Yet I know there is not a chance in the world I will ever be able to win universal support for this position among my fellow humans. For every Tom Shakespeare who says, "Meh, Down syndrome, no big deal," there will be dozens of people, some of them prospective parents, who think of Down syndrome with horror and revulsion and who will seek prenatal testing precisely to ensure that they will not give birth to a child with trisomy-21. Over the past twenty years, I have taken every available opportunity to say two things about this: the right of a woman to terminate a pregnancy must be respected, regardless of the reason (this is an especially important argument in states whose legislatures are trying to outlaw abortion when the fetus has Down syndrome); and people shouldn't be snookered into believing that prenatal screening can catch every kind of significant disability. I realize, however, that for some people this second argument amounts merely to kicking the can down the road a piece. Yes, yes, screening can't catch everything, they will say. But it can very well catch Down syndrome and other genetic anomalies, and that's precisely why we're availing ourselves of it—because we don't want our children to have anything like *that*.

In my contribution to the fourth edition of the *Disability Studies Reader*, edited by Lennard Davis (an essay on genetic screening and democratic deliberation), I mention the work of Rayna Rapp, whose 1999 book *Testing Women, Testing the Fetus: The Social Impact of Amniocentesis in America* has been such a huge influence on the way I think. Indeed, one reason it has made such an impact on my thinking is that it introduced me to a wide array of people who do not think as I do. Some of them go ahead with pregnancies that I think might warrant termination, as when one woman received a diagnosis that the fetus had partial trisomy-9; some of them decide that other anomalies might be fine but Down syndrome is not, because, as one woman puts it, "If I had this baby at 44, and it had Down's, who would inherit it? Oh, not Alex, not Stephan—it's always the girls, the girls who get caught. If I had that baby, it would be Livia who inherited the family problems." Still others decide, "Meh, Down syndrome, no big deal," while others tell Rapp,

"Having a 'tard, that's a bummer for life," and that if the baby "can't grow up to have a shot at becoming the president, we don't want him."

That last remark comes from prospective parents whose fetus was diagnosed with Klinefelter syndrome, a trisomy involving an extra X chromosome. It is even milder in its effects than Down syndrome; here's the Genetics Home Reference description of it, courtesy of the National Institutes of Health.

> Affected individuals typically have small testes that do not produce as much testosterone as usual. Testosterone is the hormone that directs male sexual development before birth and during puberty. A shortage of testosterone can lead to delayed or incomplete puberty, breast enlargement (gynecomastia), reduced facial and body hair, and an inability to have biological children (infertility). Some affected individuals also have genital differences including undescended testes (cryptorchidism), the opening of the urethra on the underside of the penis (hypospadias), or an unusually small penis (micropenis).
>
> Older children and adults with Klinefelter syndrome tend to be taller than their peers. Compared with unaffected men, adults with Klinefelter syndrome have an increased risk of developing breast cancer and a chronic inflammatory disease called systemic lupus erythematosus. Their chance of developing these disorders is similar to that of women in the general population.
>
> Children with Klinefelter syndrome may have learning disabilities and delayed speech and language development. They tend to be quiet, sensitive, and unassertive, but personality characteristics vary among affected individuals.

Personality characteristics vary among *all* individuals, one might add, including people who will abort a pregnancy if they believe their prospective child does not have a chance of becoming president of the United States.

I have thought long and hard about that remark as Jamie has grown, precisely because I never expected him to become president and never imagined that as a criterion for a life worth living. In my *Disability Studies Reader* essay, I wrote, "I remain unpersuaded that there are transcendent moral virtues to be advanced by compelling such parents to bear children with disabilities, even though the disabilities in question are relatively benign; indeed, I shudder to think how such parents will treat their disabled children if they are compelled to bear them against their will." On my blog, I was somewhat more colloquial, as befits the discourse of blog posts: "In both the deontological and utilitarian traditions," I suggested, parents who say such things "are technically known as 'assholes.'" But the underlying point should be clear: one reason I argue that prospective parents should be trusted to make their own decisions about prenatal screening is that some of them may decide that they cannot be enlightened, humane, and welcoming parents if it turns out that their child has a disability. And one reason I argue that people should have access to prenatal screening but not to genetic enhancement is (you guessed it) that some of them do not, in fact, have enlightened, humane, and welcoming attitudes toward children with disabilities.

At the same time, I agree with Tom Shakespeare that Tay-Sachs and Lesch-Nyhan are "profound limitations in which the possibility of flourishing seem[s] truly remote," and I do not see any reasonable grounds for preventing prospective parents from screening for those conditions. I think they are more accurately described as diseases rather than disabilities, and I place them in the category of diseases whose eradication would constitute a species-wide good. This position has earned me sharp criticism in some disability studies circles. I remember a forum at Columbia University in 2010 at which I was told that my advocacy of screening for Tay-Sachs was indistinguishable from the Nazi designation of "life unworthy of life," *Lebensunwertes Leben*, which underlay Hitler's extermination of the disabled. It is never a pleasant experience being likened to Hitler, though analysts report that on the Internet, someone is likened to Hitler three thousand times every minute. (Perhaps I exaggerate, though Godwin's Law clearly states that any long comment thread on the Internet inevitably produces a comparison to Hitler.) I replied, calmly (I hope), that I was not saying that children with Tay-Sachs disease were unworthy of life. I was simply acknowledging that children

place we entered. You could say that the real problem is that people leave their goddamn gum under countertops and tables in practically every public place, and you would be right. But it still required us to carry hand sanitizer for Jamie at all times. Another was his occasionally inappropriate behavior in crowded public spaces. On one trip to New York when he was eighteen, I had to stop him from swinging a glass bottle around a busy midtown street, and when I took him to the culinary mecca that is Katz's Deli on the Lower East Side, he very maturely ate only half his gargantuan pastrami sandwich, leaving the rest for later—and then got up and pranced to the men's room, nearly colliding with a waiter laden with a tray of many, many pastrami sandwiches. That time, I took him by the shoulders to stop him in his tracks and hissed, "*Be! An! Adult!*" No doubt some of the diners in Katz's that evening thought I was a Bad Dad haranguing his disabled son. But Jamie had to learn that there are some places in which it is not OK to cavort, just as he had had to learn, a few years earlier, that it is not OK to laugh when someone falls down and gets hurt. These are some of the indices of his maturity as a young man: he does not laugh at others' misfortunes, he is circumspect in public places, and he has weaned himself from his interest in touching other people's wads of gum. And then there are other difficulties and challenges that, like the story of the day Jamie was sad, will always be Jamie's private business.

I realize that such incidents and issues can arise with almost any child, and that we are very far indeed from talking about the soul-devouring struggles of a Julia Hollander or an Emily Rapp—or, for that matter, a Marianne Leone, whose brilliant, searing memoir, *Jesse: A Mother's Story*, offers an unflinching look at what it is like to be the parent of a child with a seizure disorder, a wonderful child who dies in his sleep at the age of seventeen. No one, I suspect, not even the biggest assholes in the whole wide world of parenting, thinks, "I will terminate this pregnancy if there is a reasonable chance that my child might someday collide with a waiter in Katz's Deli." I should add that Jamie's moments of inappropriate behavior are relatively rare, and that he himself is faintly horrified by children who misbehave egregiously in public. I recall the dinner in a Friendly's restaurant near Harrisburg in 2005, just after Jamie's volleyball tournament and his first night away from us, during which he and I watched a toddler crawl all over his family's table, squealing and wreaking havoc with the meal. Jamie looked at me questioningly: he seemed to be asking, *Is this a thing? Can people really do this?* To which I replied, "Jamie, believe me, you were never like that. You were such a well-behaved kid in restaurants; you always were." More recently, one night twenty-two-year-old Jamie announced to us out of the blue that "crying babies piss me off." ("He was very clearly trying out the phrase," Janet said as we talked this over that night.) A few days later, when we saw *L'Incroyable Voyage des Papillons* at Le Musée de la Civilisation in Ottawa, we endured one of those crying babies for the final five or ten minutes of the film. When the family was out of earshot, I asked Jamie, "Did that crying baby piss you off?"

He turned to me with a raised eyebrow as we got on an escalator. "You *know* it," he shot back.

Or take the classic parental struggle of trying to get your kid to wear appropriate winter outergear. Once again, we are in the realm of the ordinary, the mundane, the quotidian; we are not in the world of Julia Hollander, Emily Rapp, or Marianne Leone. Me, getting Jamie ready to head out to work one morning: "Jamie, it's 28 degrees outside—you need to wear your puffy jacket."

Jamie, blowing me off: "Leather jacket will do."

Me, sighing, having gone through years of this with both children: "Jamie, the leather jacket will not do. It is freezing outside."

Jamie: "Michael! It is not freezing."

Me: "Excuse me? It is literally freezing. It is 28 degrees. You know water freezes at 32."

Jamie, snorting: "That's a hoax."

So much for the lessons of seventh-grade chemistry! Somewhere along the way, Jamie had become a climate change denier, at least with regard to the freezing point of water. But the only notable thing about this exchange, involving a young adult with Down syndrome who has the same resistance to prudence in cold weather as any number of his nondisabled peers, is that it represented Jamie's first use of the word "hoax."

There is no question that Jamie is relatively easy to take care of, as people with disabilities go. I have lost track of the number of times I have been told that Jamie is not representative of people with Down syndrome because he is "high-functioning" (a phrase I can't abide, since it evokes a hierarchy that makes some people with disabilities more "acceptable" than others). But I have never argued or imagined that Jamie is representative of people with Down syndrome. I have insisted only that Jamie is Jamie. In fact, I strongly endorse Shelby Peacha's suggestion that there is no one quite like him. And yes, he is really quite bright. He has his limitations, but within those limitations, he can astonish. As his mentor Lindsay said, he never ceases to surprise all of us with his abilities. A case in point: On a vacation in Scotland in 2015, Janet, Jamie, and I stopped into a lovely pub in the Highlands town of Stirling. We were hoping for lunch, but the wait was half an hour. Janet clearly wanted to stay and spend a pleasant half hour at the bar; I demurred, saying I just couldn't manage to play animal hangman for thirty minutes at the bar and then another round at a table. (I was a bit grumpy that day. So was Jamie.) So that's the "limitation" part: He has his routines, and most of the time, they must be honored. Within that limitation, the animals Jamie would ask us to identify, letter by letter, would include creatures like the lowland anoa, the Sumatran muntjac, and, your favorite and mine, the Indian crested porcupine. That's the "astonish" part.

So if I were faced with Emily Rapp's question—*I love my son, but would I have him again, knowing what I know, or would I have terminated the pregnancy?*—I would answer in a fraction of a heartbeat. I would do it all over again, joyfully. I am grateful for Jamie's presence in my life, I take pride in his accomplishments, and I enjoy his companionship. I can say the same of Nick, in precisely the same terms—which, for me, settles the question of Jamie's value as a human being.

□ □ □

I have no regrets about having Jamie; quite the contrary. But at one point in our lives together, I did feel a pang of regret about the way I was raising him. It was at the 2005 conference of the Canadian Down Syndrome Society, and one of the keynote speakers was talking about how and why we need to attend to the "spiritual development" of children and young adults with Down syndrome. One of her examples involved bringing a young man with Down syndrome to the cemetery in which his grand-parents were buried, so that he could come to terms with their death.

I caught my breath. Jamie's maternal grandfather, Bradford Lyon (known to his four grandchildren as "Duke"), had died the previous autumn, and Jamie had watched attentively as Janet grieved through Duke's final year. He had also comforted his aunt Cynthia as she sobbed through the funeral service. But I had not spoken to Jamie about Duke since his death. I had done what I could to prepare him for the fact that his beloved grandfather, with whom he got on so famously from infancy to tweendom, would no longer be with us. In the seven months between the funeral and the conference, though, I had not brought it up. Jamie very clearly had taken his grandfather's death hard, and I did not want to make things any harder for him. He and Duke were exceptionally close, as Jamie's response to this fifth-grade writing assignment can attest (he composed it with the help of his teachers):

> If my parents went on a trip, I would like my grandfather to stay with me. We could go to the movies and eat pizza. We could go out to lots of restaurants. He could take me swimming and we could go shopping. We could go to Lowe's and buy Christmas gifts. We could go to Target and buy socks and underwear. We could shop at Best Buy and get videos. After we are done eating and shopping, we could go to see the fish at the Hub at Penn State. He could also take me to the playground.

To that point in his life, Jamie had never experienced the death of a family member. Then, too, there is the fact that I do not often speak or think of our "spiritual" development. I do not often speak or think of spiritual *anything*. I am a devout agnostic, though reasonably literate in Catholic intellectual and religious traditions, and I fear that if I say the word "spiritual" my tongue will cleave to the roof of my mouth.

But this was a form of "spiritual" development I recognized, and I immediately regretted not being more aware of Jamie's possible needs in this respect. I had told him, quite honestly and accurately, that no one knows what happens after we die: some people believe in a heaven and hell, some people believe in a less punitive afterlife, some people believe we return as other humans or forms of life, some people believe we become part of the universe, and some people believe that there's nothing after death, that we just die. I had not dared to ask him what *he* thought and felt about all this.

So at some point during the conference, I asked Jamie what he thought about Duke—and the fact that Duke was no longer with us. He did not want to talk about it.

Fair enough, I thought. I told Jamie he could talk to me about it anytime (just as he could always talk to me about being sad, a potentially related subject), and I left it at that.

Later that summer, he wanted to talk about it. Without warning, without context. We were in the men's locker room at Welch Pool (and why have so many of our heart-to-heart talks taken place after swimming? Is there something about swimming that is tied to Jamie's spiritual development?), and as we dried off and put on our clothes, Jamie said, "You know . . . maybe Duke could come back."

I fought back tears. "Oh, oh, Jamie," I said. "That's the hard part. That's what everyone has so much trouble with. We don't know what happens after people die, but we do know that the people don't come back. It really is final, for once and for all. And that is why we have religion, and beliefs about God and the universe—to help us deal with the fact that the people we love die and don't come back, and that every living creature dies and doesn't come back. I hope you can understand this. I hope you are not waiting for Duke to come back. He can't come back, Jamie. I am sorry. I am so, so sorry."

Jamie waited patiently through this little disquisition on mortality. Today, I like to think of him tapping his foot and whistling, but I know he did no such thing. He was just waiting quietly for his father to stop talking. And when I stopped talking, Jamie put his hand on my shoulder, tilted his head, and gently said, "Michael. I said *maybe*."

I'm not sure how I retained my composure, but I had the presence of mind to remember that Jamie and I had just made our way through the scene in *Harry Potter and the Half-Blood Prince* in which Harry and Dumbledore encounter the Inferi, dead bodies reanimated by dark magic.

"Are you thinking of the Inferi?" I asked. Jamie nodded.

"Oh no, Jamie, that's not something you would want. You would not want Duke to come back like that."

"Or like zombies," Jamie replied, totally getting the point.

"Or like zombies. Yes. Because zombies are just dead bodies with no spirit"—I said the word! And I was not smitten!—"like ghosts are spirits with no bodies. Jamie, we make up stories about ghosts and zombies *because* we do not know what happens after we die. But you would not want Duke to come back as a zombie."

"No way," Jamie agreed.

Suddenly I realized how to revive a cliché—if not a dead body. *Duke lives in our memories.* "Duke had a very lively spirit, Jamie," I said. Jamie nodded again. "And you have his spirit too."

"I do?"

"You do. Duke had a sweet, sweet heart, just like you. He was friendly to everybody, just like you. And he was a total goofball, just like you."

Jamie laughed. This is, in fact, a completely accurate description of Bradford Lyon.

"And that is why you two loved each other so much. You have the same spirit. So in a way, Duke's spirit lives in you."

Jamie straightened up. It was almost as if I had promoted him to colonel. "It does?"

"It does. And of course we will always remember him, and as long as we remember Duke, his spirit is alive in our hearts."

Jamie nodded emphatically. It was an impromptu sermon in a men's locker room at a local pool, but it was the best I could do.

□ □ □

On that summer day in 2005, Jamie was asking some of the fundamental questions about what it means to be human. Why do we die? Can we come back? And he was expressing one of the fundamental emotions that make us human—love for one's goofy, genial grandfather.

It is a truism, among people who love and care for humans with intellectual disabilities, that our interactions with people with intellectual disabilities lead us to startling and valuable perspectives on the meaning of human life. That truism is a truism because it happens to be true. But it has some profound and unsettling corollaries for everything else we think we know. I am going to have to put this bluntly: I have become convinced that societies that incorporate and accommodate people with intellectual and physical disabilities are better than societies that exclude, ostracize, and seek to eliminate people with intellectual and physical disabilities.

I am aware that this belief disqualifies me from membership in the campus Cultural Relativist Club—and I am aware of why cultural relativism exists in the first place. For most of human history, the determination that X society is "better" or "more advanced" than Y society has not taken the form of the belief *your society is superior to mine and I seek to emulate it,* but, rather, that of *my society is superior to yours and that is why I rule over you.* It has also been made overwhelmingly by Western societies seeking to justify their domination of the rest of the peoples of the world, though the belief in one's own racial or ethnic superiority can also be found in the East and any number of areas in between. And the toxicity of this attitude is matched by its persistence, as William Henry demonstrated when he wrote, "It is scarcely the same thing to put a man on the moon as to put a bone in your nose."

But I am getting old and crotchety, and increasingly impatient with people who spend their lives justifying inequality and oppression, no matter where on the globe they might happen to live. After decades of thinking about the question, I am still failing to see why limitations on the sexual and political freedom of women or gays and lesbians are any less objectionable in one geographical location than in another; nor do I understand why the lives of people with intellectual and physical disabilities should be less valuable at one latitude and longitude than they are at another latitude and longitude.

This is not, you should note, grounds for American triumphalism and chest-thumping. In the twentieth century, the United States was among the very worst offenders against the principle of treating the disabled with respect and dignity. We embraced eugenics wholeheartedly, to the point at which our Supreme Court could craft a rationale for the involuntary sterilization of the so-called "feebleminded." We created hellish institutions that shocked our colleagues overseas—and eventually shocked us, after a series of exposés and investigations forced us to acknowledge what we were doing. Even today, we have not really come to terms with the atrocity of MIT and Quaker Oats teaming up to feed irradiated oatmeal to children with intellectual disabilities at the Walter E. Fernald State School in Massachusetts. (If you haven't heard about that experiment until now, that's probably because we have still not really come to terms with it. Though in the late 1990s, MIT and Quaker Oats did agree to pay the experiment's subjects $1.85 million in compensation.) Even today, we have not really come to terms with the killing of Ethan Saylor, the young man with Down syndrome who was wrestled to the ground and asphyxiated by police as he called vainly for his mother. (In fairness, the police were dealing with a hardened criminal: Saylor had tried to remain in a movie theater and watch a film twice without paying for the second showing.) And even today, we are failing to acknowledge how many people harmed or killed by tasers are people with disabilities—sometimes deaf people, who are punished for not complying with police orders they cannot hear.

I am weighing the United States by the same measures I would use with any country—not holding it out as a shining example. And by those measures, a capacious and supple sense of what it is to be human is better than a narrow and partial sense of what it is to be human, and the more participants we as a species can incorporate into the determination of what it means to be human, the greater the chances that we will enhance our collective capacities to recognize each other as humans entitled to human dignity—and the greater the chances that we will devise an adequate understanding of our profound interdependence with the nonhuman world, as well. As Jamie has reminded me time and again throughout his life, most Americans had no idea what people with Down syndrome could achieve until we'd passed and implemented and interpreted and reinterpreted a law entitling them all to a free appropriate public education in the least restrictive environment. With the help of that law, as well as with the help of his teachers and aides and family members and animal companions, Jamie got to the point at which he could meditate on life and death with the rest of us.

And I got to this point with the help of two feminist philosophers. One is Nancy Fraser, whose theory of democracy, derived in part from the German philosopher Jürgen Habermas, involves the idea of "participatory parity" and the imperative that a democratic state should actively foster the abilities of its citizens to participate in the life of the polity as equals. Fraser's work does not address disability, and in one way, it shows: she writes as if the promise of democracy entails the promise to enhance participatory parity among citizens, which it does, and she writes as if we know what "participatory parity" itself means, which we don't. This is why the promise of disability rights is so open-ended. Jamie has his place at the table, as I had hoped at the end of *Life as We Know It*, but who knows what will happen when *everybody* gets a place at the table?

The idea of participatory parity does double duty in Fraser's work, in the sense that it names both the state we would like to achieve and the device by which we can gauge whether we're getting there. For in order to maintain a meaningful democracy in which all citizens participate as legal and moral equals, the state needs to judge whether its policies enhance equal participation in democratic processes. Yet at the same time, the state needs to enhance equal participation among its citizens simply in order to determine what its democratic processes will be. This is not a theoretical quibble. On the contrary, the point is central to the practical workings of any democratic society. One of the tasks required of egalitarians is to extend the promise of democracy to previously excluded individuals and groups, some of whom might have a substantially different understanding of participatory parity than that held by previously dominant groups and individuals.

Put it this way: Imagine a building in which political philosophers are debating the value and the purpose of participatory parity over against forms of authoritarianism, monarchy, oligarchy, plutocracy, or theocracy. Now imagine that this building has no access ramps, no Braille or large-print publications, no American Sign Language interpreters, no elevators, no special-needs paraprofessionals, no in-class aides. That may sound horribly self-contradictory, but it's a reasonably accurate picture of what contemporary debate over the meaning of democracy actually looks like. Only when we have fostered equal participation in debates over the ends and means of democracy can we have a truly participatory debate over what "participatory parity" itself means. And the meaning of participatory parity, in turn, sets the terms for more specific debates about the varieties of human embodiment. These include debates about prenatal screening, genetic discrimination, inclusive education, stem-cell research, euthanasia—and, with regard to physical access, ramps, curb cuts, kneeling buses, and widened doorways.

The other philosopher I'm relying on is Eva Feder Kittay, who has written so compellingly about her daughter Sesha—and about what her life with Sesha has taught her about life and about the practice of philosophy. Sesha is not (cough) "high functioning." She is nonverbal and needs assistance with most things, including eating. And precisely because she needs assistance, she has taught her mother that we are all interdependent to one degree or another (especially at the beginnings and ends of our lives), and that the ideals of independence and autonomy, essential as they have been for both liberal social theory and the disability rights movement, inevitably set performance criteria for being human—performance criteria that some humans will not meet.

I first met Sesha in 2008, when Eva and her husband, Jeffrey, invited Jamie and me to spend a weekend at their house in upstate New York. It struck me vividly, at the time, that I was hanging out with Sesha and observing her keen enjoyment of her surroundings, her companions, and the music of her favorite composers (Bach and Beethoven) just a few weeks before Eva and I would speak at a conference she had organized, "Cognitive Disability and Its Challenge to Moral Philosophy." (Jamie still asks about Sesha, and he remembers who her favorite composers are.) Utilitarian philosophers Peter Singer and Jeff McMahan had also agreed to speak at that conference, where they would explain to all and sundry why people like Sesha do not meet their performance criteria for being human. Eva had put together the conference, she told me, as the result of her years of frustration over philosophy as an academic discipline and its inattention to, or outright revulsion at, people with intellectual disabilities. She had considered leaving the field altogether but then, inspired partly by Sesha, decided to stay and fight.

I discuss Singer and McMahan briefly in my 2015 book, *The Human-ities, Higher Education, and Academic Freedom: Three Necessary Arguments* (written with Jennifer Ruth), in which I take issue with their conviction that a creature's moral worth is directly proportional to (their estimates of) that creature's cognitive capacity. I won't reprise that argument in full here, but I will cite again the passage of Singer's talk I found most ludicrous:

> If it happens that one of you is an alien who has cleverly disguised yourself in a human shape, but you are capable of understanding this argument, I am talking to you just as I am talking to members of my own species. In important respects, I have much more in common with you than I do with someone who is of my species but, because he or she is profoundly mentally retarded, has no capacity for verbal communication with me at all.

I dutifully pointed out, in that book, that Singer could be having these pleasant interspecies-bonding thoughts about creatures who, like the aliens in the *Twilight Zone* episode "To Serve Man," do not share Singer's aversion to meat eating and cannot wait to cook up a juicy batch of Singerburgers. But I did not tell the story of how, listening to Singer's talk in the spillover room while Jamie played a Harry Potter game on my computer, I burst into laughter when Singer said this. "What's so funny, Michael?" asked Jamie. "It's hard to explain," I replied, "but this man just said something very silly. He thinks he has more in common with some space aliens than with some of his fellow human beings." "*That* is weird," Jamie agreed. By the time the conference speakers gathered for our group photo late that afternoon, I was ready to address Singer's ar-gument, however informally. I announced to the gathering that I am in fact an alien who has cleverly disguised himself in human shape ("That explains a great deal," said someone), that I was capable of understand-ing Singer's lecture earlier in the day, and that I saw no reason whatso-ever to believe I had anything important in common with him.

I try to carry this kind of thing lightly, but of course it is no laugh-ing matter that one of the world's foremost philosophers, a passionate defender of animal rights and blistering critic of economic inequality, is so cavalier about the lives of some of the most vulnerable humans on the planet—and so woefully, willfully underinformed about the capabilities of people with intellectual disabilities.

As for McMahan, his paper the following day made much of the fact that there seems to be an enormous and obvious difference between kill- ·
ing a human being and killing a squirrel: clearly, therefore, there must be some correlation between cognitive capacity and moral standing. But this argument proves nothing, as I replied in my contribution to the question-and-answer period. Not very long ago in human history, there seemed to be an enormous and obvious difference between killing a no-bleman and killing a slave. It is entirely possible that, in the future, we will shudder in horror at the killing of a squirrel. And why, if we should want to grant some rights and some sense of dignity to certain sentient animals, should we do so at the expense of any humans? Every attempt to boot some people out of the human family has been disastrous, and with regard to people with intellectual disabilities, those attempts in-volve brutal mistreatment on a massive scale *within living memory.* Mc-Mahan and Singer are right to argue that we have undervalued the lives of many animals. When they argue that we have somehow overvalued the lives of people with intellectual disabilities, they are as wrong as it is possible for a person to be.

And so, when I think about life and death and everything in be-tween, I think about Peter Singer and Jeff McMahan on the one hand, and Jamie Bérubé and Sesha Kittay on the other. I think of Jonathan Glover and Rayna Rapp and Eva Kittay and Tom Shakespeare and Em-ily Rapp and Nancy Fraser and Marianne Leone. I think of everyone I know, everyone I have ever met. I know that Jamie and Sesha are not able to express themselves as eloquently as most people, but I do not think that is important. I think, instead, that maybe it would be a good idea if we humans stopped trying to come up with reasons not to treat each other as equals. I think that maybe it would be a good idea if we tried instead to treat people with intellectual disabilities, mild to severe, as if they are people who matter, people worthy of attention, support, and care. And I think maybe it would be a good idea to try to create societies, here, there, and everywhere, in which all humans, no matter what their individual characteristics, can flourish to the greatest extent possible. *You never know.* We might just find out that people with intellectual disabilities have something to teach their fellow human beings about being humans.

I know it sounds unlikely. It might even sound impossible. But I said *maybe.*

Afterword

□   □   □   □   □

How this book was written

This book was mostly written on a laptop manufactured by Asus, typed furiously by someone with good typing skills, but that's not what I want to explain. I want to explain that I wasn't sitting alone in a garret, typing away while Janet and/or a series of paid companions took care of Jamie. And it is not as if I have spent my life with Jamie with a tape recorder in one hand, taking notes from 1997 to 2016 on his every milestone and significant life event. For many of the details of his teen years, I have drawn on a variety of things I wrote at the time—most of them on my now-defunct blog, which was, among other things, a running record of his development, some of them short pieces for newspapers and journals (the *Norfolk Virginian-Pilot*, the *Globe and Mail*, the *Times Higher Education Supplement*, *Dissent*, *Literature and Medicine*). The account of Jamie's search for work was published in *Al Jazeera America* and substantially revised for inclusion here; the pleasant rant on American health care first appeared in *Salon*. I have also included and revised two posts from the academic group blog *Crooked Timber*.

There is, I know, something absurd about taking time away from caring for your child in order to write about your child. And I admit that, at times, I was writing and revising this book while Jamie was at work or while he amused himself with videos and YouTube in his basement lair. His basement lair is something I have to regulate, I have found, because left to his own devices, Jamie will cover the floor with dozens of DVDs, none of which have any clear relation to the DVD cases also strewn around the floor. After one particularly arduous cleanup, I told Jamie that he could have five DVDs out at any one time—and that I did not build him all his DVD-storage units (courtesy of Target, "home storage" cheap furniture department) only to have to spend hours on my hands and knees matching stray DVDs on the floor to stray DVD cases.

As for Janet's role in all this, those of you who have read *Life as We Know It* will probably notice that she is somewhat less present in this book than in that one. That has everything to do with the trajectory of Jamie's life and with the areas of competence and expertise Janet and I bring to the task of being Jamie's parents. Janet is a former intensive care nurse whose knowledge of medicine and health care remains razor-sharp; I defer to her in all matters medical. That knowledge was of critical importance when Jamie was young, and it undergirded the major decisions we made back then—including the most important decisions I mentioned in *Life as We Know It*: not to subject Jamie to abdominal surgery in order to feed him with a gastrostomy tube, and not to fix his torticollis and head tilt by cutting the muscles in his neck and resewing them. (I have never had a moment of doubt as to whether we—and by "we" I mean "Janet"—made the correct decision in either case.)

Janet spent innumerable Saturday mornings helping our teenaged Jamie to paint and innumerable hours helping him to do food prep for things like pizza, casseroles, and fish tacos. But when it comes to things like special-needs trusts and powers of attorney and navigation of the legal-social support system and Special Olympics and employment, I have usually taken the lead. More important, on a day-to-day basis, is the fact that once Jamie entered puberty, many aspects of his life became my domain. At one point in the early 2000s, Janet told me, "I'm not teaching him how to shower and shampoo. You're doing that." I had no quarrel with that, and spent a few months in early 2003 helping a reluctant and bewildered tween shower and shampoo after a Saturday morning in the pool. (We quickly solved the problem of soap-and-shampoo-in-the-eyes by keeping Jamie's swimming goggles on during the shower.) By the age of fourteen, Jamie was capable of showering and washing his hair on his own, thanks to his father's expert instruction. Though I often have to remind him not to cut corners on hygiene (he is, in that respect, very much a teenager, even in his mid-twenties), and I regret his preference for Axe body products (he is, in that respect, very much like every American male teenager and twentysomething).

And Janet does not travel alone with Jamie, because of the awkward business of sharing a hotel room with him. That is why all the travel stories here are episodes in what Jamie and I have come to call "The Jamie and Michael Show." To get the full effect of that, you have to sing it to the tune of *The Simpsons'* "Itchy and Scratchy Show," as we do. This is but one of many ways Janet and I have tried to devise some work/life balance as an academic couple. Whenever I can take Jamie with me on a speaking gig, I do. (I pay his travel costs, of course; I do not ask my hosts to cover him.)

But emotionally, psychologically, Janet is and always has been our rock. We have embarked on this journey together fearlessly ever since she uttered those decisive words in the birthing room, upon hearing that Jamie might have Down syndrome: *We can handle this.* That remains the single most important utterance in my life, guiding me for a quarter century through territories known and unknown.

□   □   □

When I talked with Jamie about my plans for the book, I told him that this book, unlike *Life as We Know It,* would be mostly about his experiences growing up—and I told him that I hoped he would be able to help me write it. I closed *Life as We Know It* with the hope that Jamie would become his own advocate, his own author, his own best representative. In many ways, my hope for him has been fulfilled: He is indeed his own best representative, a goodwill ambassador from the World of Jamie, spreading cheer to everyone he meets. He is eager to become an advocate, and he talks excitedly about being "on panels" and maybe even "on the radio" when this book is published. (I have cautioned him that he will need to speak slowly and clearly if he is on the radio. And I will try to remember to do so, as well.) But he has not become his own author in the sense that he writes his own narratives. And I recall the theologian Stanley Hauerwas reminding me that in a Christian sense, none of us can be our own author. I invited Jamie to write down a story or two, but

it's just not how he's wired. He did, however, consult with me exten-
sively throughout the composition of the book, shoring up lapses in my
memory, offering key details, and, at one point, editing. In my account
of Jamie's decision to jump off the diving board in 2006, I wrote that
he quietly muttered, "I will do it *by myself*," that day in the Penn State
Natatorium. When I read that passage to him, he objected. "I was not
muttering," he said.

"Oh, OK," I replied, surprised. "Do you think that 'muttering' makes
you sound too angry or something?"

"No," Jamie said, "I was not muttering, that's all."

I was perfectly willing to concede the point, and besides, he knows
what he was about better than I do. I suspected that he wanted a verb
that conveyed the decisiveness behind his decision, rather than a verb
that suggested he was like unto a grumpy old man. So I asked: "How
about 'declaring'? Would that work?"

"'Declaring' is good," Jamie agreed, and lo, "declaring" it is.

He has also made dozens of suggestions for material—"Sea lions in
Omaha! That has to be in the book!"—and with very few exceptions, I
have taken them. And finally, in lieu of a narrative episode from "The Jamie and Michael Show," I asked Jamie to write a list of some of the things
he likes. He presented it to me one evening, and I told him I would copy
it down letter for letter (keeping his erratic spelling and all-caps delivery
intact) and explain each item as best I can. So, without further ado, we
close with a classic Jamie List. Here are a few of his favorite things:

THE WOODY PARTY

This was a game that occupied us for many an hour on winter weekends
when there wasn't much else to do in central Pennsylvania. Not long
after we moved here, Jamie renamed all his stuffed animals, as I have
mentioned. The Woody Parties were the events at which the animals
met on Jamie's bed and were introduced to each other—by Woody of *Toy
Story*, the only one of Jamie's creatures who retained his own name (by
contrast, Buzz Lightyear was renamed Nick Hamilton). Woody would
welcome the animals to the party one by one, introducing each of them
to the already assembled guests—Tony Falion, Leon Reel, Jaws of a Tiger,

Lauren Morrow, Zokie, and so on and so on until the bed was hosting somewhere between fifty and sixty guests. How did I remember all the names in order to do the introductions necessary for a Woody Party? The same way you get to Carnegie Hall: practice, practice, practice.

BEEF JERKEY

I think this is self-explanatory. Jamie did correct me, however, on one detail in the story of Jamie and His Retainers: I thought his reward was beef jerky, but he assured me it was Slim Jims, and he insisted that I fix the chapter to get this right. So I have.

VINILA ICE CREAM

This is the only dessert Jamie likes. He does like one other sweet thing— chocolate milk. But the world of cupcakes and Ho-Hos and Ding Dongs and banana splits is simply alien to him. His "birthday cakes," growing up, were pizzas. (We did serve cake to the other kids.)

CAMAFLAUGE RETAINER

Jamie knows this story is in the book, but he wanted to list it here any-way, just because.

PENNSYLVANIA COUNTIES

All sixty-seven of them, in alphabetical order, sometimes annotated with the names of their county seats (Bellefonte for Centre County, for exam-ple). For the sake of variety, Jamie sometimes lists them not in alphabeti-cal order but by the year of their founding. Yes, he does this all by memory.

HANNING WITH NEW FRIENDS IN STATE COLLEGE

I am puzzled by "hanning." Jamie almost never misspells the name of even the most exotic creatures in animal hangman. But yes, he does like hanging with new friends!

OFFICIAL STUFF LIKE OFFICIAL PUDDING

This is a curious feature of contemporary capitalism that never fails to amuse Jamie: the designation of products or corporations as the Official

Thing of a sports franchise or league. It began at a Mets game in 2010, when Jamie and I were surprised to learn that Cozy Shack is the official pudding of the New York Mets. *Official pudding?* The official beer and the official hot dog, that makes sense. But pudding?

We soon learned that the sports world is full to bursting with all manner of official products, from the official pizza and TV of the National Football League (Papa John's, Samsung) to the official salty snack of the Pittsburgh Pirates and the official training restaurant (say what?) of the Mets (Utz, Subway). If you hang with us for long enough in State College you will also learn that the Philadelphia Eagles have an official coffee (Dunkin' Donuts) and the Pittsburgh Penguins have an official ketchup (Heinz, of course). And as this book goes to press, Jamie reminds me that I have to acknowledge that Casillero del Diablo is the official wine of the New Jersey Devils. It is a strange world we live in, is it not?

FUNNY NAME IN EVERY STATE

Lover, Pennsylvania. Romney, Virginia. Horseheads, New York. Jamie reads highway signs on all our road trips, and never fails to call out town names he finds silly. We have not yet found a funny name in every state, because Jamie has been to only—only!—thirty-nine of the fifty. But we are getting there. Ketchum, Idaho, and Smackover, Arkansas, someday you will be ours.

SUTDY ABOUT THE COMPOSERS

Jamie has those composers locked down. He knows how to spell "study," too—he just gets a little careless sometimes. Perhaps relatedly, he sometimes skips small words when he reads aloud. He does not sweat the small stuff.

SUCBA DIVING IN SAINT JOHN'S

He did not actually scuba dive in St. John in the US Virgin Islands in 2014. What he *did* do—and it took as much courage as going off the diving board—was agree to wear a mask and fins for swimming. He was leery of the deep water and afraid to go down into it to see all the fish.

But with Janet's help, he managed to get an eyeful of hundreds of beautiful tropical fish, and now he's totally up for doing that again. Perhaps next time he will try the snorkel. . . .

Update: In March 2016, he tried the snorkel! It was difficult for him, and sometimes he would put the entire mouthpiece behind his teeth, which induced gagging. But when he got his teeth clamped in the right spot and closed his lips over the mouthpiece, he was able to snorkel and see tropical fish *and* a couple of sea turtles *and* a couple of manta rays. (Neither of us had ever seen manta rays except in aquariums.) He was thrilled. And as I held his hand and paddled around the coral reefs of Saltpond Bay on the southeast end of St. John, I kept thinking, *He is a brave and very good young man,* and *je suis très, très fier.*

"BEATLES"
So central to Jamie's love of the world they get quotation marks!

THE SIMPSONS
Jamie is not really a big *Simpsons* fan. In the past, his favorite TV shows have been things like *SpongeBob SquarePants* (which he now considers "annoying," as he informed me as we went to press), *iCarly* (he owns the DVDs of the first three seasons), *Big Time Rush,* and *Monk* (he asked me if he could have my mother's DVDs of the first four seasons after she died). But like millions of his nondisabled peers, Jamie knows that sometimes, a quote from *The Simpsons* is the perfect response to the world. *Mmmmm . . . donuts. What can't they do?*

ZOMBIES
Not the band, the creatures. It all started with Jamie's meditations on the Inferi in *Harry Potter.* Now *Night of the Living Dead* is among Jamie's favorite movies, and he's especially tickled that it was filmed near George Romero's native city, Pittsburgh.

THE FIRST DVD OF BIG TIME RUSH
Apparently this is the better of the two *BTR* DVDs Jamie owns.

LOST OLD DEBIT CARD IN NORTH CAROLINA

You know, you absent-mindedly leave just one debit card in one ATM in Durham and your kid never lets you forget it. From 2006.

HOW LONG SUBMARGED IN THE POOL

Inspired, as I mention in the chapter on Jamie's athletic accomplishments, by Percy Jackson.

THE HUB CORAL

In Penn State's HUB-Robeson student center, there is an aquarium, a gift from the Class of 1999. In it is a small coral reef populated by tangs, sea stars, giant cucumbers, snails, blue-legged hermits, and about forty species of coral. When we moved here, Jamie would visit the tank on weekends, and he could look at it for hours or until his father's patience wore out, whichever came first. (It really is a beautiful thing.)

ATLAS OF THE WORLD

Which Jamie takes with him every time he travels, and in which he finds hours of edification and material for lists and lists.

SOCCER IN THE LIVING ROOM

Another weekend amusement from when we first moved to State College. We didn't use a real soccer ball—we played with something much lighter and less likely to do damage. I had to defend the entrance to the kitchen, and Jamie had to defend a piece of furniture whose legs constituted the goalposts—goalposts that were just barely wider than the diameter of the ball. Jamie won every single game we played.

□   □   □

And now for three things Jamie didn't write down but told me:

ARCHITECTURAL DIGEST

Jamie often visits Schlow Library in downtown State College, where he peruses the magazines—including this one, to which he has had a subscription since fall 2014. He is very enthusiastic about it, asking me every month whether his new issue has arrived yet. I do not know what drew him to lavish depictions of rich people's houses; it could be that he finds lavish depictions of rich people's houses worthy objects of his attention, or it could be that he associates the magazine with his brother the architect, who was given a gift subscription by fond Lyon grandparents who wanted to encourage teenage Nick and apparently believed that *Architectural Digest* had something to do with architecture. Either way, Jamie is delighted whenever a new issue arrives, and he keeps his issues in his basement lair.

MAGIC CARDS

Oh, goodness, the Magic cards. I estimate that there are over two thousand of these things in the house, most of them in shoeboxes in the basement lair. I have asked Jamie more than once if he wants to learn to play the game, but he is not interested—he just likes the cards. All his many many many many cards.

SHARKS

They endured.

Acknowledgments

□ □ □ □ □

This book is dedicated to all the people who have cared for or worked with Jamie, but I'd like also to single out the people who have been indelible influences on his life. Some of his teachers and paraprofessionals are mentioned by name in the book, as well they should be, for their great work; but I wanted to try—with Jamie's help—to give a shout-out to everyone Jamie remembers especially fondly.

His earliest aides and helpers appear in *Life as We Know It*: Rita Huddle and Sara Jane Annin, his first early-intervention supervisors; Ofra Tandoor, the physical therapist who got him to the point at which he could try to walk; Nancy Yeagle, the occupational therapist who got him to the point at which he could try to write; and Anne Osterling, the speech therapist who got him to the point at which he could begin to chatter. Doctors Donald Davidson and Kenneth Weiss were his first pediatricians; in State College, Craig Collison and Jeffrey Pro have been his primary-care physicians.

His teachers, from kindergarten through eighth grade: Ms. Warner, Ms. Walker, Ms. Borgeson, and Ms. Williams in Champaign; Mr. Hockenberry, Ms. Wolf, Ms. Peachy, Mr. Tranell, Ms. Owens, Ms. Pelligrini, Ms. Westerhaus, Ms. Lee, Ms. Hetrick, Ms. Kump, and Mme. Eid in State College. His paraprofessionals: Ms. Avellone, Ms. Hiser, and Ms. McCabe in Champaign; Ms. Poorman, Ms. Pontano, Ms. Moyer, Mr. Burruss, Ms. Kaufmann, and Ms. Walker in State College. At LifeLink PSU, Marla Yukelson was consistently supportive; at Penn State, Marianne Karwacki hired Jamie into his first two paying jobs; Sandy Cecco of United Cerebral Palsy-Central Pennsylvania works with him twice a week at the animal shelter and on independent-living skills more generally; and at the Arc, Terry and Alex have been his job coaches and Lisa Schencker his caseworker. Thanks also to Luke Ebeling for shepherding us through the maze of Pennsylvania bureaucracy.

And his many companions, chiefly Denise O'Brien and Liz Minster in Champaign, who were far more than babysitters; they were guides and mentors. In State College, chiefly Vita McHale, Erin Greech, Clairen Percival, Jenna Groff, Anthony Alberici-Bainbridge, and the amazing Lindsay Northup-Moore, who not only gave that moving speech at his graduation from LifeLink PSU but stayed with him at our house for *nine days* in the summer of 2012, while Janet was teaching in Ireland and I was attending a conference in Australia. Jamie's LifeLink PSU mentors included Peggy Reals, Stephanie Berdya, Brin Kendal, and Sara Licata, whose names still bring a smile to his face. And then there were all the companions Jamie remembers only by first name: Julene (his first), Heidi, Wendy, Amanda, Josh, David, Sibi, and Laura.

All of these people treated Jamie with care, friendship, and respect. All of them treated him like a fully-fledged member of the human family. All of them helped Janet and me lead our lives as college professors—indeed, as college professors whose schedules sometimes take one of them to Dublin while the other heads off to Canberra.

And then there is Jamie's extended family. From day one—literally, from the day I dashed home from the hospital to call everyone with the news that Jamie was born (this used to be one of Jamie's favorite stories, but he has long since outgrown it)—his grandparents and aunts (seven) and uncles (three) and cousins (four, all younger than he) have been a source of love and constant delight for him. Special thanks are surely due to the relatives who have hosted him when we have traveled for business: Bud Lyon, Sarah Higgins, and the twins, Trevor and Dash (and special thanks to Trevor for his own Adventures with Jamie); to Barbara Lyon and Steve Maggs (who have also vacationed with us many times); to my parents, Maurice Bérubé and the late Anne Clarke Bérubé (who also watched Jamie and Nick while Janet and I took three-day mini-vacations on Cape Hatteras in the mid-'90s); to Kay Lyon, Janet's mother, and

Janet's dear departed father, Brad, for taking Jamie for more overnights than we can count; and to my sister Katherine Bérubé Boyer. But everyone else—Cynthia Lyon and Collin Tilton; Jeannie Bérubé, Clair Bérubé, Johnny Bérubé, and Marie and Christopher Boyer; Todd Lyon and Hayward Gatling—is just as important in Jamie's world and have helped to make Jamie's world as rich and as enjoyable as it is. There is nothing Jamie enjoys so much as a large family gathering with all the people he loves, and with good reason. Bud and Barbara deserve another round of thanks for being willing (and able!) to sing Beatles songs to Jamie over and over and over again. . . .

Oddly enough, since 2002, Jamie has attended eight conventions of the Modern Language Association (MLA) in venues ranging from Vancouver to Philadelphia to Austin, Texas. MLA executive director Rosemary Feal has always welcomed him warmly, and Jamie knows it and is grateful; he genuinely enjoys going and greeting everyone he knows and many people he doesn't. One year he decided to get acquainted with Simon Gikandi, from Princeton by way of Uganda, who was sitting by himself at a party (Jamie opened by asking where Professor Gikandi was from, and he loved the answer). Within five minutes of Jamie's arrival, that table became The Table Everyone Sat At. At the 2016 MLA convention Jamie decided that, as an employee of Penn State Press, it was his job to go to the book exhibit and work the Penn State Press booth, asking passersby what their field was and what kind of books they liked, and then handing them copies of the Penn State Press brochure. So thanks also to Kendra Boileau, editor in chief of the press, and of course to Tony Sanfilippo, who hired Jamie in 2014.

Our closest family friends are practically family. Here at Penn State, Susan Squier, Gowen Roper, Hester Blum, and Jonathan Eburne have been not only great friends but great souls; Amanda Anderson, once our neighbor on Willis Avenue in Champaign (and our English Department colleague at Illinois), remains one of Jamie's favorite people; and Gail Corbin and her family have been boon companions for decades. All our family friends have offered Jamie a place in their homes (whenever he should need one) and a place in their hearts, and Jamie thinks of them with great affection. As do we.

Christopher Robinson and Phyllis Eisenson Anderson read most of this book in manuscript; Conal Ho read the chapter on Nick—as did Nick, passing around the pages to Rachel and to his friend Arthur Shufran. Joanna Green at Beacon Press is an eagle-eyed and sympathetic editor, and I thank her for making this book so much better than I could have managed on my own. I am of course deeply grateful that she and Helene Atwan supported this book so strongly and enthusiastically. And a special thanks to J. M. Coetzee, who graciously gave me permission to borrow hundreds of his words—that brilliant passage from *Elizabeth Costello* that closes the discussion of Jamie's relationship to his animal companions. I have solemnly promised Mr. Coetzee that I will return these words when I am done with them.

Everyone who knows our family knows that Janet Lyon is an extraordinary woman. Scholar, nurse, dancer, teacher, singer, writer, ridiculously talented and resourceful mother, gorgeous, generous, and delightfully witty wife, and—not least—a merciless editor. You should know this too, because without her, nothing in this book or in my life makes sense.

Notes

□ □ □ □ □

[11] **about whom she has written movingly in *Raising Henry*** Rachel Adams, *Raising Henry: A Memoir of Motherhood, Disability, and Discovery* (New Haven, CT: Yale University Press, 2013).

[17] **Jean Bethke Elshtain, reviewing the book for a Christian journal** Elshtain, "Idiots, Imbeciles, Cretins," *Books and Culture: A Christian Review* 4, no. 1 (January/February 1998), http://www.booksandculture.com/articles/1998/janfeb/8b1018.html.

[17] **Here's the relevant passage** Michael Bérubé, *Life as We Know It: A Father, A Family, and an Exceptional Child* (New York: Pantheon, 1996), 89–90.

[18] **such openness is the very essence of parenting** Michael Sandel, *The Case Against Perfection: Ethics in the Age of Genetic Engineering* (Cambridge, MA: Harvard University Press, 2004), 45.

[28] **the extraordinary account of her nearly fatal stroke** Jill Bolte Taylor, *My Stroke of Insight: A Brain Scientist's Personal Journey* (New York: Viking, 2008).

[28] **"deserving of love, opportunity, and acceptance just as they are"** Timothy Shriver, *Fully Alive: Discovering What Matters Most* (New York: Farrar, Straus and Giroux, 2014), 23.

[53] **the 2006 Hastings Center report** Erik Parens, ed., *Surgically Shaping Children: Technology, Ethics and the Pursuit of Normality* (Baltimore: Johns Hopkins University Press, 2006).

[62] **"parents have a definitional license to be paternalistic"** Andrew Solomon, *Far from the Tree: Parents, Children, and the Search for Identity* (New York: Scribner, 2012), 111. Harlan Lane is a professor of psychology at Northeastern University and an advocate for the Deaf community.

[63] **"Eat Too Many Doughnuts and Take a Nap"** D. J. Bannerman, J. B. Sheldon, J. A. Sherman, and A. E. Harchik, "Balancing the Right to Habilitation with the Right to Personal Liberties: The Rights of People with Developmental Disabilities to Eat Too Many Doughnuts and Take a Nap," *Journal of Applied Behavior Analysis* 23, no. 1 (Spring 1990): 79–89.

[63] **Jamie's Supplemental Security Income** In December 2014, Congress passed, and President Obama signed into law, the Achieving a Better Life Experience (ABLE) Act, which allows people with disabilities to own up to $100,000 in assets. The plan is to be administered by the states, very much like 529 plans for college savings. (Indeed, since the ABLE Act amends Section 529 of the IRS code, ABLE accounts will be another variety of 529s.) Until we can open an ABLE account in Pennsylvania, however, Jamie will maintain his special-needs trust.

[64] **"shards of wood and glass"** Courtney Jolley, "Dynamic Duo," *Potential* (Kennedy Krieger Institute) (Fall 2005), http://www.kennedykrieger.org/potential-online/potential-fall-2005/dynamic-duo.

[65] **"Could the Dems really have done that bad of a job vetting this family?"** For the antics of Malkin and Limbaugh, and the response of Senator McConnell, see Paul Krugman, "Sliming Graeme Frost," *New York Times*, October 12, 2007, http://www.nytimes.com/2007/10/12/opinion/12krugman.html.

[65] **"kicking the crutches out from under Tiny Tim"** Bérubé, *Life as We Know It*, 51.

[68] **"The liberal media attacked Sarah Palin"** Andy Barr and Mike Allen, "Barone: Media Wanted Palin Abortion," *Politico*, November 11, 2008, http://www.politico.com/story/2008/11/barone-media-wanted-palin-abortion-015527.

[68] **"baby boomers' vast sense of entitlement"** George F. Will, "Jon Will, 40 Years and Going with Down Syndrome," *Washington Post*, May 2, 2012, https://www.washingtonpost.com/opinions/jon-will-40-years-and-going-with-down-syndrome/2012/05/02/gIQAdGiNxT_story.html.

[69] **"It would be unfair to single out "** Tucker Carlson, "Eugenics, American Style," *Weekly Standard*, December 1, 1996, http://www.weeklystandard.com/article/9150. For *Slate*'s reframing of the essay, see http://www.slate.com/articles/news_and_politics/politics/2012/02/rick_santorum_prenatal_testing_and_abortion_tucker_carlson_s_classic_essay_on_prenatal_testing_and_the_abortion_of_down_syndrome_babies_.html.

[80] **a searingly honest chronicler of her own battles with brain tumors and seizure disorders** Alison Piepmeier's blog, http://alisonpiepmeier.blogspot.com/, is titled *Every Little Thing*. It is, I think, among the most important blogs I have ever read, and I have read many thousands.

[82] **"The guest post here on Friday"** Lisa Belkin, "Should Down Syndrome Be Cured?," *New York Times*, January 11, 2010, http://parenting.blogs. nytimes .com/2010/01/11/should-down-syndrome-be-cured/.

[83–84] **"As you know, I have many years"** Parker Donham, "A 'Cure' for Down Syndrome?—Reader Feedback #6," *Contrarian*, November 27, 2009, http:// contrarian.ca/2009/11/27/a-cure-for-down-syndrome-%E2%80%94-reader -feedback-6/.

[84] **"the Enlightenment prejudice against prejudice"** Hans-Georg Gadamer, *Truth and Method* (London: Continuum International, 1975).

[87] **its pity-laden anti-polio campaigns** See, for example, Joseph P. Shapiro, *No Pity: People with Disabilities Forging a New Civil Rights Movement* (New York: Times Books, 1993), and Rosemarie Garland-Thompson, "The Politics of Staring: Visual Rhetorics of Disability in Popular Photography," in *Disability Studies: Enabling the Humanities* (New York: Modern Language Association, 2002), ed. Sharon L. Snyder, Brenda Jo Brueggemann, and Rosemarie Garland-Thomson, 56–75.

[88] **essays on the overlap between disability activism and gay/lesbian activism** Robert McRuer, *Crip Theory: Cultural Signs of Queerness and Disability* (New York: New York University Press, 2006).

[89] **as the Autism Self-Advocacy Network points out** "2014 Joint Letter to the Sponsors of Autism Speaks," January 6, 2014, http://autisticadvocacy.org/2014 /01/2013-joint-letter-to-the-sponsors-of-autism-speaks/.

[89–90] **"Are babies who are born"** The comment is signed "Denarthurdent" and was posted on the same day as Belkin's essay. *New York Times,* January 11, 2010, http://parenting.blogs.nytimes.com/2010/01/11/should-down-syndrome -be-cured/?_r=0#permid=14.

[90] **"A Drug for Down Syndrome"** Dan Hurley, *New York Times*, July 31, 2011. http://www.nytimes.com/2011/07/31/magazine/a-fathers-search-for-a-drug -for-down-syndrome.html.

[91] **building brain power** Dan Hurley, *Diabetes Rising: How a Rare Disease Became a Modern Pandemic, and What to Do About It* (New York: Kaplan, 2011), and *Smarter: The New Science of Building Brain Power* (New York: Plume, 2013).

[92] **"Can a Pill Make People with Down Syndrome Smarter?"** Ilena Silverman, *The 6th Floor* (blog), *New York Times*, July 17, 2012, http://6thfloor.blogs .nytimes.com/2012/07/17/can-a-pill-make-people-with-down-syndrome -smarter/.

[98] **"the eventually predictable alternation"** Roslyn Sulcas, "A Seascape Dotted by Chaotic Bursts," *New York Times*, November 30, 2007, http://www .nytimes.com/2007/11/30/arts/dance/30papp.html.

[101] **"A domesticated dog"** Alasdair MacIntyre, *Dependent Rational Animals: Why Human Beings Need the Virtues* (Peru, IL: Open Court, 1999), 44.

[103] **"Sultan [a chimpanzee] is alone in his pen"** J. M. Coetzee, *Elizabeth Costello* (New York: Penguin, 2003), 72–74.

[113] **"blown out of proportion"** Chuck Brittain, "Boy Says Coach Paid Him $25 to Injure Player," *Pittsburgh Tribune*, July 16, 2005, http://triblive.com/x /pittsburghtrib/news/regional/fayette/s_354047.html.

[118] **"Obama is allowed"** Editorial, *Washington Times*, March 22, 2009, http:// www.washingtontimes.com/news/2009/mar/22/in-defense-of-humor -and-president-obama/.

[118–119] **"All over Soldier Field"** Shriver, *Fully Alive*, 98.

[132] **"that glow has to last"** Lawrence Downes, "Special Olympics and the Burden of Happiness," *New York Times*, July 31, 2015, http://www.nytimes .com/2015/08/ 01/opinion/special-olympics-and-the-burden-of-happiness.html.

[137] **"retarded children [in] classrooms"** Roger Kimball, "What's Wrong with Equality?," *New Criterion* (October 1994), http://www.newcriterion.com/articles .cfm/What-s-wrong-with-equality--8149. Of one such child, Henry wrote, "If she is not 'stupid,'"—as her guardian insisted—"then what does mentally retarded mean?" This, I submit, is an exceptionally stupid question. William A. Henry III, *In Defense of Elitism* (New York: Anchor, 1994), 130.

[139] **"the ideal scheme"** Bérubé, *Life as We Know It*, 218.

[151] **Lindsay's speech, and half of Jamie's, can be seen on YouTube** Lindsay's is at https://www.youtube.com/watch?v=YddIad1CaKg, and Jamie's is at https:// www.youtube.com/watch?v=09aL-_n9cZI.

[163] **an account of Jamie's search for work** Michael Bérubé, "For Hire: Dedicated Young Man with Down Syndrome," *Al Jazeera America*, May 25, 2014, http://projects.aljazeera.com/2014/portrait-of-down-syndrome/.

[165] **1100 CE constituted the good old days** Henri-Jacques Stiker, *A History of Disability*, trans. William Sayers (Ann Arbor: University of Michigan Press, 1999).

[166] **That's not just because courts** In the late 1990s and early 2000s, a series of particularly absurd cases demonstrated the lengths to which the Supreme

Court was willing to go to find against plaintiffs—not on the grounds that they were actually incapable of performing their jobs, but on the grounds that they were "not disabled enough" to sue, even though they were too disabled to perform specific jobs. In *Sutton v. United Air* (1999), the Court held that severely nearsighted sisters could not become airline pilots, not because of their nearsightedness but because their nearsightedness was "easily correctable." The same logic extended to a truck driver: in *Albertsons v. Kirkingburg*, the Court found against the truck driver, Hallie Kirkingburg, and for his employer, because his vision did not meet Department of Transportation standards. Again, the Court did not rule against Kirkingburg because of his eyesight; indeed, Kirkingburg was fired *after* he had obtained the necessary Department of Transportation waiver that would permit him to keep driving. Rather, the Court found against him because he had, by the majority's logic, no standing to sue under the ADA as a person with an "easily correctable" disability. Finally, in 2002, in *Toyota v. Williams*, the Court found for Toyota and against Ella Williams not because Williams's carpal tunnel syndrome prevented her from working on an assembly line, but because the ADA defines disability as a physical impairment that "substantially limits one or more . . . major life activities," and Ms. Williams was capable of brushing her teeth. It would have been perfectly reasonable for the Court to decide that Toyota had in fact tried to offer Williams "reasonable accommodation" (they had offered her various other tasks) and that anything more would constitute "undue hardship" for an employer under the law. But no, the Court was primarily concerned with limiting the number of potential plaintiffs under the law, and so Ms. Williams was deemed non-disabled insofar as she was capable of taking care of her daily dental hygiene. Leaving aside the question of whether brushing one's teeth was a major life activity for most humans over the course of human history, surely the Court should have asked whether it is possible for people to earn a living by brushing their teeth. But that would involve reading the ADA as some kind of employment law.

[167] **"There are exceptions "** Michelle Diamant, "Obama Signs Law Limiting Sheltered Workshop Eligibility," *Disability Scoop*, July 22, 2014, https://www.disabilityscoop.com/2014/07/22/obama-law-limiting-sheltered/19538/.

[167] **Within three years** Halle Stockton, "Vermont Closed Workshops For People with Disabilities; What Happened Next?," *PublicSource*, September 28, 2014, http://publicsource.org/investigations/vermont-closed-workshops-for-people-with-disabilities-what-happened-next#.VrPTf7IrJD8.

[171] **the first major works in disability studies** Lennard J. Davis, *Enforcing Normalcy: Disability, Deafness, and the Body* (New York: Verso, 1995); Rosemarie

Garland-Thompson, *Freakery: Cultural Spectacles of the Extraordinary Body* (New York: New York University Press, 1996); David T. Mitchell and Sharon L. Snyder, *The Body and Physical Difference: Discourses of Disability* (Ann Arbor: University of Michigan Press, 1997); and Simi Linton, *Claiming Disability: Knowledge and Identity* (New York: New York University Press, 1998).

[172] **"the philosopher's nightmare"** Licia Carlson, *The Faces of Intellectual Disability: Philosophical Reflections* (Bloomington: Indiana University Press, 2009), 4.

[173] **"Progress in genetics"** Jonathan Glover, *Choosing Children: Genes, Disability, and Design* (Oxford, UK: Oxford University Press, 2006).

[173] **"argument against 'designer babies'"** Michael Sandel, *The Case Against Perfection: Ethics in the Age of Genetic Engineering* (Cambridge, MA: Harvard University Press, 2004).

[173] **"it is common to say"** Glover, *Choosing Children*, 36.

[180] **James Watson** "James Watson's Legacy," *Biopolitical Times* (blog of the Center for Genetics and Society), October 22, 2007, http://www.biopolitical times.org/article.php?id=3723. Watson's quote on Down syndrome is from a 1997 article in the UK *Telegraph*: Victoria Macdonald, "Abort Babies with Gay Genes, Says Nobel Winner," February 16, 1997, https://web.archive.org /web/20071022153711/http://telegraph.co.uk/htmlContent.jhtml?html= /archive/1997/02/16/nabort16.html. In 2007, Michael Gerson, speechwriter for President George W. Bush, wrote about these remarks here: "The Eugenics Temptation," *Washington Post*, October 24, 2007, http://www.washingtonpost .com/wp-dyn/content/article/2007/10/23/AR2007102301803.html.

[180] **"I am against society imposing rules"** quoted in Glover, *Choosing Children*, 73.

[180] **"genetic tourism"** Ibid., 77.

[180] **"the film's genetics counselor"** See my discussion of *Gattaca*, race, and disability: "Disability, Democracy, and the New Genetics," in *The Disability Studies Reader*, 4th ed. (New York: Routledge, 2013), ed. Lennard J. Davis, 101–4.

[181] **"sometimes disabilities arouse"** Glover, *Choosing Children*, 75–76.

[182] **"banish disease from the human frame"** Mary Shelley, *Frankenstein, or The Modern Prometheus*, 1818 text, ed. Marilyn Butler (Oxford, UK: Oxford University Press, 1994), 24.

[183–184] **"To me, disability is not neutral"** Tom Shakespeare, reply to Michael Bérubé, "Humans, Disabilities, and the Humanities?," *On the Human*, a project of the National Humanities Center, January 29, 2011, http://national humanitiescenter.org/on-the-human/2011/01/humans-disabilities-humanities /comment-page-1/#comment-4573.

[185] **"legislatures are trying to outlaw abortion when the fetus has Down syndrome"** See Rachel Adams, "My Son with Down Syndrome Is Not a Mascot for Abortion Restrictions," *Washington Post*, February 19, 2016, https://www .washingtonpost.com/opinions/my-son-has-down-syndrome-is-not-a-mascot -for-abortion-restrictions/2016/02/19/cecd3c78-d119-11e5-88cd-753e80cd29ad _story.html.

[185] **"If I had this baby at 44"** Rayna Rapp, *Testing Women, Testing the Fetus: The Social Impact of Amniocentesis in America* (New York: Routledge, 1999), 146.

[186] **"Affected individuals typically"** "Klinefelter Syndrome," *Genetics Home Reference*, http://ghr.nlm.nih.gov/condition/klinefelter-syndrome, accessed February 1, 2016.

[187] **"I remain unpersuaded"** Bérubé, "Disability, Democracy, and the New Genetics," 104–5.

[187] **"In both the deontological and utilitarian traditions"** Michael Bérubé, michaelberube.com, blog post, "Liberals in Their Own Words," April 6, 2005, http://www.michaelberube.com/index.php/weblog/liberals_in_their_own _words/.

[188] **the remarkable writing of Emily Rapp** Emily Rapp, *The Still Point of the Turning World: A Memoir* (New York: Penguin, 2013).

[188–189] **"I love my son"** Emily Rapp, "Rick Santorum, Meet My Son," *Slate*, February 27, 2012, http://www.slate.com/articles/double_x/doublex/2012/02 /rick_santorum_and_prenatal_testing_i_would_have_saved_my_son_from _his_suffering_.html.

[190] **who dies in his sleep at the age of seventeen** Marianne Leone, *Jesse: A Mother's Story* (New York: Simon and Schuster, 2010).

[196] **"It is scarcely the same thing"** Henry, *In Defense of Elitism*, 14.

[197] **"MIT and Quaker Oats"** *New York Times*, "Settlement Reached in Suit Over Radioactive Oatmeal Experiment," January 1, 1998, http://www.nytimes. com/1998/01/01/us/settlement-reached-in-suit-over-radioactive-oatmeal -experiment.html.

[197] **the killing of Ethan Saylor** David M. Perry, "Justice for Down Syndrome Man Who Died in Movie Theater," CNN.com, August 29, 2013, http://www.cnn.com/2013/08/29/opinion/perry-down-syndrome-death/.

[198] **"participatory parity"** Nancy Fraser, *Justice Interruptus: Critical Reflections on the "Postsocialist" Condition* (New York: Routledge, 1997).

[199] **what her life with Sesha has taught her about life** Eva Feder Kittay, *Love's Labor: Essays on Women, Equality, and Dependency* (New York: Routledge, 1999).

[200] **I discuss Singer and McMahan briefly** Michael Bérubé and Jennifer Ruth, *The Humanities, Higher Education, and Academic Freedom: Three Necessary Arguments* (New York: Palgrave Macmillan, 2015), 42–47.

[200] **"If it happens that one of you is an alien"** Peter Singer, "Speciesism and Moral Status," in *Cognitive Disability and its Challenge to Moral Philosophy* (Malden, MA: Wiley-Blackwell, 2010), ed. Eva Feder Kittay and Licia Carlson, 336.

[201] **correlation between cognitive capacity and moral standing** The discussion of killing squirrels does not appear in the essay McMahan eventually submitted for publication in Kittay and Carlson, *Cognitive Disability and Its Challenge to Moral Philosophy*, "Cognitive Disability and Cognitive Enhancement." But he has made the argument elsewhere: "While it may be almost as seriously wrong to inflict great pain on a squirrel as it is to inflict a comparable degree of pain on a person, it would clearly be a mistake to suppose that to kill a squirrel is as seriously wrong as it is to kill an innocent person." McMahan, "Animals," in *Blackwell Companion to Applied Ethics* (Oxford, UK: Blackwell, 2002), ed. R. G. Frey and Christopher Wellman, http://jeffersonmcmahan.com/wp-content/uploads/2012/11/Animals1.pdf.

[205] **none of us can be our own author** Stanley Hauerwas, "Timeful Friends: Living with the Handicapped," in *Critical Reflections on Stanley Hauerwas' Theology of Disability: Disabling Society, Enabling Theology* (New York: Routledge, 2004), ed. John Swinton, 16.